THE
DYNAMIC FORCE
OF LIBERTY
IN MODERN EUROPE

Six Problems in Historical Interpretation

THOMAS C. MENDENHALL

BASIL D. HENNING

ARCHIBALD S. FOORD

Department of History, Yale University

Henry Holt and Company · New York

PREFACE

The second volume of Select Problems in Historical Interpretation had as its central theme the historical origins and growth of liberalism, nationalism, and socialism in Europe and the issues which they have forced on modern man. Since its publication many teachers have requested a smaller selection of Problems, for use in courses where limitations of time prevent the use of a larger volume.

To the authors the presence of a connecting theme was one virtue of the Select Problems. Any abridgment threatened both to damage irreparably this original unity and to lack any alternative unity of its own. We believe, however, that the following six Problems preserve its essential continuity. Five are taken bodily from the earlier book with only minor changes; the sixth, on nationalism, represents a combination of three other Problems. The basic feature of the original effort—the origins and transformations of liberalism, nationalism, and socialism—still provides the substance of this volume. The historical development of nationalism has admittedly been telescoped into one Problem, but its arrangement in three Parts lends itself to separate treatment, if desired, of the eighteenth-, nineteenth-, and twentieth-century aspects of the movement.

The presence of two Problems on socialism and communism in such a condensed volume should hardly require any justification in America at the mid-point of the twentieth century. The crying need for Americans to understand the historical origins of these ideas, their appeal, and their limitations obviously represents the first step in combating their spread. Of even greater, more positive importance is a wider understanding of the growth and significance of liberal ideas in the Western tradition. These too were revolutionary in their original implications, and, if they are to continue to operate as living forces in our society, they also must be realistically appraised. If the term *liberal* is suspect in certain quarters in America today, it is because some have appropriated the term who have no claim to it, and out of ignorance of the true nature of the liberal tradition, their opponents have allowed the spurious claim. In keeping with the Problem approach we have thought it best for the student to arrive, through study and discussion, at his own understanding of the central position of liberalism rather than to be given any ready-made formula.

The six Problems in this volume, concerned with the dynamic role played by liberty in the history of modern Europe, serve to complement the theme of the first condensed volume of Select Problems, which treats of the early history of the liberal tradition in the seventeenth century and its classic encounters with the rival doctrine of the strong state. In a sense this theme is carried down into the present volume, for both nationalism and communism have helped to perpetuate this struggle in the contemporary world.

The systematic study of historical documents by undergraduates has long been possible either through "Readings in European History" or through organized problems in the sources. But the following Problems differ in purpose and method both from volumes of supplementary readings and from the earlier attempts to arrange these materials in problem form.

The purpose of these Problems is, first of all, to make the student aware of the complexity of history. Every survey course in European history must impart a knowledge of events, of what happened in the long European past. And no student can pretend to understand European history without a grasp of its narrative. But in addition a comprehension of the interdependence of the many forces operating in society is essential; if the student learns only the narrative of events, his knowledge of history will be painfully superficial. It is believed that the study of these Problems, combined with the use of a textbook and the interpretation derived from lectures, will allow the student to obtain a fuller understanding of the complicated pattern of European civilization. Only a genuine awareness of the sweep and the complexity of this civilization will enable the undergraduate to partake of the philosophical insight, of the serenity which comes with the broad perspective and the deep comprehension, and of the intellectual and moral inspiration which are the richest rewards of historical study.

The Problems are designed to demonstrate the principles of historical reasoning in such a way that the undergraduate may test them for himself. The student has been testing the scientific method in the laboratory work accompanying courses in the natural sciences, but too often the historian has acted as if his techniques were a trade secret and has preferred to guard loyally his fellow guildsman's book from student attack. Often the undergraduate critic has had only common sense or principles drawn from another discipline with which to challenge the dogmatism of the textbook and the prejudices of the pedagogue. This is particularly to be regretted since the historian by his training is especially qualified to teach the student to seek and to find, to evaluate, and to interpret man-made evidence. These lessons are what the Problems are designed to teach, and it is here that they differ most from collections of supplementary readings whose principal and laudable purpose is to enliven and enrich a text.

Each Problem has been divided into two or three Parts, each Part representing one assignment, though the instructor will find quickly that this division is sufficiently flexible to permit a different emphasis if desired. Each Problem is preceded by an introduction which sets the scene by indicating the reason for studying this specific subject and furnishing the necessary background. Included in each Problem are questions for study, designed to guide the student in handling and evaluating the very disparate material which he is called upon to study.

In teaching these Problems at Yale University, the authors have found that college students enjoy working at the stuff of history for themselves, that these readings in original materials, if properly organized, can be made the central, rather than a supplementary, part of a course, and that the techniques of the historian need not be taught at the extreme levels of either unimportant details or unsolvable enigmas but can contribute much to the intellectual powers of every undergraduate.

The authors again thank their colleagues at Yale for assistance cheerfully given with the Problems, and, in the selections for this book, Professor William O. Shanahan of the University of Notre Dame for his sensible advice.

For permission to reprint translations and documents either verbatim or in adapted form the authors acknowledge their obligations to the following publishers: George Allen & Unwin, Ltd.; American Council on Foreign Affairs; *American Historical Review;* Appleton-Century-Crofts, Inc.; Ernest Benn, Ltd.; Chapman & Hall, Ltd.; Columbia University Press; Constable and Co., Ltd.; Peter Davies, Ltd.; The Devin-Adair Co.; Doubleday & Co., Inc.; E. P. Dutton & Co., Inc.; Foreign Affairs; Ginn and Company; William Heinemann, Ltd.; Henry Holt & Co., Inc.; Hutchinson & Co.; Johns Hopkins Press; Longmans, Green & Co., Inc.; Oxford University Press; W. Paxton & Co., Ltd.; Pioneer Publishers; The Royal Institute of International Affairs; Charles Scribner's & Sons; Stanford University Press; University Press, Cambridge; The Viking Press; and H. W. Wilson Co. In the notes at the back of this volume specific credits have been given for all materials reprinted.

T.C.M.
B.D.H.
A.S.F.

Yale University
November 29, 1951

CONTENTS

NOTES

(Unless otherwise specified, translations were made by the authors.)

NOTES TO PROBLEM I

The quotation on the title page is taken from Cecil A. Moore, ed., *English Poetry of the Eighteenth Century* (N. Y., 1935), p. 48. Reprinted by permission of Henry Holt & Company, Inc., publishers.

[1] Sir Isaac Newton, *The Mathematical Principles of Natural Philosophy*, tr. Andrew Motte (N. Y., 1848), pp. lxvii–lxviii, 384–85.

[2] John Locke, *An Essay Concerning Human Understanding* (London, 1690), pp. 1–3, 37–38, 52–53, 323, 325, 327, 348–52.

[3] John Locke, *Two Treatises on Civil Government* (London, 1690), pp. 219–25, 230–32, 241–46, 249–51, 265–69, 273, 281–82, 305–06, 316–17, 319–20, 345–47, 350, 423–24, 441–43.

[4] N. L. Torrey, *Voltaire and the Enlightenment* (N. Y., 1931), pp. 22–24, 29, 33–36, 38–39. Reprinted by permission of Appleton-Century-Crofts, Inc.

[5] *The Complete Works of M. de Montesquieu*, trans. by Thomas Nugent (London, 1777), I, 1–2, 4, 198–99, 202–03, 205.

[6] Adam Smith, *An Inquiry into the Nature and Causes of the Wealth of Nations* (London, 1786), Book I, Chapter 10; Book II, Chapters 3 and 4; Book IV, Introduction and Chapters 1, 2, and 9.

[7] *Outlines of an Historical View of the Progress of the Human Mind: Being a Posthumous Work of the Late M. de Condorcet* (Philadelphia, 1796), pp. 289–93.

[8] This version of the Declaration of Independence is that issued by the United States Department of State.

NOTES TO PROBLEM II

The quotation on the title page is taken from *1066 and All That* by W. C. Sellar and R. J. Yeatman, published by E. P. Dutton & Co., Inc., New York, publisher and copyright holder, 1931, pp. 92–94.

[1] The material to the second ellipsis is taken from the 1st edition of Malthus' *Essay on the Principle of Population* (London, 1798), pp. 1–17; from the second ellipsis to the end of the selection the material is taken from the 6th edition (London, 1826), I, 12–17.

[2] J. Bowring, ed., *The Works of Jeremy Bentham* (Edinburgh, 1843), I, 1–4.

[3] *Ibid.*, III, 33, 35.

[4] Hansard, *Parliamentary Debates*, 2d S., I, 179–82.

[5] *Report from His Majesty's Commissioners for Inquiring into the Administration and Practical Operation of the Poor Laws, Ordered by the House of Commons to be Printed 21 February 1834*, pp. 1, 3, 127, 128, 146, 167, 176–77, 186, 190, 202, 205.

[6] *The Struggle*, No. 1, pp. 1–2.

[7] *The League*, Vol. 1, No. 1, p. 1.

[8] *An Address to the Farmers and Labourers of the North of Devon* (Barnstaple, 1843), pp. 1–2, 9–11.

[9] *The Free Trade Speeches of the Right Hon. Charles Pelham Villiers, M.P.* (London, 1884), pp. 371–73, 378–81.

[10] Hansard, *Parliamentary Debates*, 1st S., XXXVII, 559–60; XXXVIII, 362–63, 367–68.

[11] Hansard, *Parliamentary Debates*, 3d S., XIX, 228, 233–34, 244–45, 246.

[12] *Ibid.*, LXXXIX, 1080, 1084–86; XC, 792–94.

[13] *Speeches of the Earl of Shaftesbury* (London, 1868), pp. 362–64, 370–71.

[14] John Stuart Mill, *Autobiography* (London, 1873), pp. 230–34.

NOTES TO PROBLEM III

The quotation on the title page is from Granville Bantock, *National Airs of the Allies* (London, 1940), p. 7. Reprinted by permission of W. Paxton and Company, Ltd.

[1] Alexander Gray, *The Development of Economic Doctrine* (London, 1931), p. 297, quoted with the permission of Longmans, Green and Company, Inc.

[2] Karl Marx and Friedrich Engels, *Manifesto of the Communist Party* (Chicago, 1888), pp. 1–23, 24–39, 41–47, 62–64.

[3] Karl Marx, *The Class Struggles in France (1848–50)* (N. Y., 1934), pp. 12–16, 18, 19–21, 23–24, 25–28.

[4] Peter Kropotkin, *Anarchism: Its Philosophy and Ideal* (London, 1897), pp. 19–21.

[5] Emma Goldman, *Syndicalism, the Modern Menace to Capitalism* (N. Y., 1913), pp. 3, 4–5, 6–7, 8, 9–13, 14.

[6] G. Bernard Shaw, ed., *Fabian Essays in Socialism* (London, 1889), pp. 33–35, 58–61; R. C. K. Ensor, *Modern Socialism* (N. Y., 1904), pp. 359–62, reprinted by permission of Charles Scribner's Sons.

[7] Eduard Bernstein, *Die Voraussetzungen des Sozialismus und die Aufgaben der Sozialdemokratie* (Stuttgart, 1899), pp. v, vii–viii. Translation in Eduard Bernstein, *Evolutionary Socialism: A Criticism and Affirmation* (London, 1909), pp. ix, xiv–xvi.

[8] Alexandre Millerand, *Le Socialisme Réformiste Français* (Paris, 1903), pp. 12–17. Translation in R. C. K. Ensor, *Modern Socialism*, pp. 61–63, reprinted by permission of Charles Scribner's Sons.

NOTES TO PROBLEM IV

The quotation on the title page is taken from the report, *Nationalism,* made by the Royal Institute of International Affairs (Oxford, 1939), p. viii, reprinted by permission of Royal Institute of International Affairs and the publishers, Oxford University Press.

[1] H. I. Woolf, ed., *Voltaire's Philosophical Dictionary* (London, 1923), pp. 131–32. Quoted by permission of George Allen and Unwin, Ltd.

[2] The quotation in the introduction is from *Nationalism,* a report by the Royal Institute of International Affairs (Oxford, 1939), p. 27. The translation of the *Social Contract* is by G. D. H. Cole and is found in J. J. Rousseau, *The Social Contract and Discourses* (New York, 1913), pp. 13, 14–16, 18–19, 22. Published by E. P. Dutton and Company, Inc., New York.

[3] The Herder selections are located as follows: the first paragraph is a translation by Professor C. J. H. Hayes in an article, "Contributions of Herder to the Doctrine of Nationalism," *American Historical Review,* XXXII (1927), 723 from Herder's *Sammtliche Werke* (Berlin, 1877–1913), XIII, 37–38; the next paragraph is from *Sammtliche Werke,* XIV, 83 ff.; the next paragraph is another translation of Professor Hayes (in the article mentioned above) from *Sammtliche Werke,* XIV, 84; the next paragraph is translated by Professor Hayes in his *Essays on Nationalism* (New York, 1926), pp. 53–54, copyright, 1926, by The Macmillan Company and used with their permission; the final selections are from *Sammtliche Werke,* XIII, 339, and I, 366 ff. The Hayes translations from the *American Historical Review* are reprinted by the permission of the editor.

[4] Richard Price, *Discourse on the Love of our Country* (London, 1789), pp. 2–10, 11–15, 19–20.

[5] The translation is by Thomas Paine, *The Rights of Man* (London, 1791), pp. 116–19.

[6] *Ibid.,* pp. 153–55.

[7] *Moniteur,* XII, 188.

[8] *Moniteur,* XIX, 401–02.

[9] The *Levée en Masse* is from F. M. Anderson, *The Constitutions and Other Select Documents Illustrative of the History of France, 1789–1907,* 2d ed. (Minneapolis, 1908), pp. 184–85, reprinted by permission of the H. W. Wilson Company; Law of Suspects, *Ibid.,* pp. 186–87; the letter of young conscript is from H. F. Stewart and P. Desjardins, *French Patriotism in the Nineteenth Century (1814–1833)* (Cambridge, 1925), pp. 21–23. Reprinted by permission of University Press, Cambridge.

[10] Decree for proclaiming the liberty and sovereignty of all peoples is from Anderson, *Constitutions,* 130–32, reprinted by permission of the H. W. Wilson Company; the Carnot report is from H. Carnot, *Mémoires sur Carnot* (Paris, 1861), I, 296–301.

[11] Wilhelm v. Humboldt, *Gesammelte Schriften* (Berlin, 1903–06), XI, 96–100.

[12] Translated by Thomas Riggs, Jr., from the original in E. M. Arndt, *Gedichte* (Berlin, 1870), pp. 233–35.

[13] The first selection is from N. v. Gneisenau, *Denkschriften zum Volksaufstand von 1808 und 1811* (Berlin, 1936), pp. 12, 13; the second from W. Mommsen, *Die deutsche Einheitsbewegung* (Berlin, 1930), pp. 110–11.

[14] The Rotteck selection is translated from Federico Federici, *Der deutsche Liberalismus* (Zurich, 1946), pp. 191–93; the Pfizer, from his *Briefwechsel zweier Deutscher und Ziel und Aufgabe des deutschen Liberalismus* (Leipzig, 1911), pp. 340–43.

[15] *Die deutsche Verfassung vom 28 März 1849.* Abschnitt VI. Translation reprinted from Columbia University, *Introduction to Contemporary Civilization in the West,* copyright, 1946, by Columbia University Press, II, 336–43, reprinted by permission of the Columbia University Press.

[16] The *Prachtbericht* of 1856 is translated from O. v. Bismarck, *Die gesammelten Werke* (Berlin, 1924–35), II, 142; the speech to the Budget Commission, from H. Kohl, ed., *Die politischen Reden des Fürsten Bismarck* (Stuttgart, 1892–1905), II, 30; the letter to Goltz, from H. Rothfels, ed., *Otto von Bismarck: Deutsche Staat* (Munich, 1925), pp. 130–31.

[17] H. v. Moltke, *Gesammelte Schriften und Denkwardigkeiten* (Berlin, 1891), III, 426–27.

[18] H. v. Treitschke, *Briefe* (Leipzig, 1912–20), II, 74–75, 144; *Historische und politische Aufsatze* (Leipzig, 1897), IV, 91; and A. Rapp, *Grossdeutsch-Kleindeutsch,* pp. 239–40.

[19] H. v. Treitschke, *Zehn Jahre deutscher Kampfe* (Berlin, 1874), pp. 289–92.

[20] *Enciclopedia Italiana* (Milan, 1932), XIV, 847–51.

[21] A. Hitler, *Mein Kampf* (N. Y., 1939), pp. 3, 44, 56, 83–84, 99, 103, 105, 11–12, 116–17; G. W. Prange, ed., *Hitler's Words* (Washington, D. C., 1934), pp. 20–21, 80–81. Reprinted by permission of the American Council on Foreign Affairs.

[22] G. Rotrand, *Franco Means Business* (N. Y., n. d.), pp. 56–62, reprinted by permission of the Devin-Adair Company, Publishers.

NOTES TO PROBLEM V

The quotation on the title page is from *A Modern Symposium* by G. Lowes Dickinson, p. 41, copyright, 1905, by Doubleday and Company, Inc.

[1] V. I. Lenin, *State and Revolution* (N. Y., 1932), pp. 30–31, 71–72, 73, 82–85.

[2] Leon Trotsky, *The Permanent Revolution* (N. Y., 1931), pp. xxxii–xxxvi, reprinted by permission of Pioneer Publishers, 116 University Place, New York 3, N. Y.

[3] Frank Alfred Golder, *Documents of Russian History* (N. Y., 1927), pp. 623–25, reprinted by permission of Appleton-Century-Crofts, Inc., copyright, 1927, by The Century Company; James Bunyan and H. H. Fisher, *The Bolshevik Revolution, 1917–1918* (Stanford University, Cal., 1924), pp. 280, 297–98, 314, 323, reprinted by permission of Stanford University Press; James Bunyan, *Intervention, Civil War, and Communism in Russia, April–December 1918* (Balti-

more, 1936) , pp. 397–99, reprinted by permission of the Johns Hopkins Press.

4 Karl Radek, "The Bases of Soviet Foreign Policy," *Foreign Affairs* (N. Y., January, 1934) , XII, 193, 195–96, 198–99, 201, 203–04. 205. Complete text reprinted in *The Foreign Affairs Reader* (N. Y., 1947) , Harper & Brothers for Council on Foreign Relations.

5 Joseph Stalin, *Foundations of Leninism* (N. Y., 1932) , pp. 14–16, 17–20; Leon Trotsky, *The Revolution Betrayed* (Garden City, N. Y., 1937) , pp. 51–52, 255, reprinted by permission of Pioneer Publishers, 116 University Place, New York 3, N. Y.

6 Joseph Stalin, "Deviations on the National Question," January 26, 1934 in his *Marxism and the National Question* (N. Y., 1942) , pp. 208–10.

7 *Report of the Court Proceedings in the Case of the Anti-Soviet 'Bloc of Rights and Trotskyites'* (People's Commissariat of Justice of the USSR, Moscow, 1938) , pp. 777–78.

8 First paragraph from Otto Bauer, *Der Weg zum Sozialismus*, 12th ed. (*Verlag der Wiener Volksbuchhandlung*, Wien, 1921) , pp. 8–9; remainder from Otto Bauer, *Bolschevismus oder Sozialdemokratie?* (*Verlag der Wiener Volksbuchhandlung*, Wien 1920) , pp. 109–115.

9 Leon Blum, *For All Mankind* (N. Y., 1946) , pp. 75, 135–36, 138–39, 143–44, 173–74. 176–77, 179–80, reprinted by permission of The Viking Press, Inc., Publishers.

10 R. H. S. Crossman, " Some Elementary Principles of Socialist Foreign Policy," in G. E. G. Catlin, ed., *New Trends in Socialism* (London, 1935) , pp. 21–23, 24–27, 30, quoted by permission of Peter Davies Limited, Publishers.

11 Radio address of January 3, 1948, by the Rt. Hon. Clement Attlee over the BBC, by courtesy of the British Information Service and reprinted with the permission of Mr. Attlee.

NOTES TO PROBLEM VI

The quotation on the title page is taken from *Essays in Liberalism: Being the Lectures and Papers which were delivered at the Liberal Summer School at Oxford, 1922* (London, 1922) , p. 147.

1 Felix Salomon, *Deutsche Partei Programme* (Leipzig and Berlin, 1907–20) , II, 36.

2 Friedrich Naumann, *Demokratie und Kaisertum*, 4th ed. (Berlin, 1905) , pp. 16–31.

3 Theodor Wolff, *Through Two Decades*, trans. by E. W. Dickes (London, 1936) , pp. 300–02, 304–06, reprinted by permission of William Heinemann, Limited.

4 David Thomson, *Democracy in France: The Third Republic* (London, 1946) , pp. 250–52, reprinted by permission of the Royal Institute of International Affairs and the publishers, Oxford University Press.

5 Emile Chartier, *Éléments d'une doctrine radicale* (Paris, 1933) , pp. 23–28.

6 Thomson, *op. cit.*, pp. 253–57, reprinted by permission of the Royal Institute of International Affairs and the publishers, Oxford University Press.

7 Jacques Maritain, *Les Droits de l'homme et la loi naturelle* (N. Y., 1942) , pp. 7–10, 111–14, reprinted by permission of Charles Scribner's Sons.

8 "The Radical Programme" (London, 1885) , pp. 14–16. C. W. Boyd, ed., *Mr. Chamberlain's Speeches* (London, 1914) , pp. 166–67, 169–70, 194, 195. Reprinted by permission of Constable and Company, Ltd.

9 E. P. Cheyney, *Readings in English History* (Boston, 1922) , pp. 774–75, reprinted by permission of Ginn & Company.

10 W. L. Blease, *A Short History of English Liberalism* (London, 1913) , pp. 328–35, reprinted by permission of Ernest Benn, Limited.

11 Hubert Phillips, *The Liberal Outlook* (London, 1929) , pp. 57, 189–90. Reprinted by permission of Chapman & Hall.

12 Sir Henry Slesser, *A History of the Liberal Party* (London, 1944) , pp. 163–65, reprinted by permission of Hutchinson and Company, Limited.

I

Liberalism and the Enlightenment

THE spacious firmament on high,
With all the blue ethereal sky,
And spangled heav'ns, a shining frame,
Their great original proclaim:
Th' unwearied sun, from day to day,
Does his Creator's pow'r display,
And publishes to ev'ry land
The work of an Almighty Hand.

Soon as the ev'ning shades prevail,
The moon takes up the wondrous tale,
And nightly to the list'ning earth
Repeats the story of her birth:
Whilst all the stars that round her burn,
And all the planets, in their turn,
Confirm the tidings as they roll,
And spread the truth from pole to pole.

What though, in solemn silence, all
Move round the dark terrestrial ball?
What though nor real voice nor sound
Amid the radiant orbs be found?
In Reason's ear, they all rejoice,
And utter forth a glorious voice,
Forever singing, as they shine,
"The hand that made us is divine."

JOSEPH ADDISON, 1672-1719

CONTENTS

[1]

QUESTIONS FOR STUDY

PART I

1. What was Newton's purpose in adducing scientific principles? What does it reveal about his attitude toward natural phenomena?

2. Analyze Newton's scientific method. What was its significance for man's approach to God and nature?

3. Why did Locke make his inquiry into human understanding?

4. According to Locke, what is the source of ideas? What leads man to prefer one thought or action to another?

5. According to Locke, how can man advance and improve his knowledge? Along what lines?

6. What is the relationship between reason and revelation? Is there a connection between Newton's approach to scientific knowledge and Locke's approach to all human knowledge?

7. How does Locke define political power? Did it exist in the state of nature?

8. What is the basis of the inviolability of property?

9. What is the importance of Locke's concept of property for his political thought?

10. How do political societies come into existence? What protection do subjects have against an unjust or tyrannical government?

PART II

11. What is Voltaire's view of human nature?

12. Against what aspects of contemporary society does Voltaire inveigh? In what does he find hope for the future?

13. According to Montesquieu, what are the origins and purposes of laws? What connection is there between the thought of Montesquieu and that of Newton?

14. What virtues does Montesquieu declare must be included in a constitution? How much is he indebted to Locke?

15. Why does Adam Smith oppose economic regulation by the state? Under what circumstances may economic regulation be justified?

16. How does Smith reconcile economic individualism with social utility?

17. "Locke would have denied the validity of Condorcet's conclusions, yet his conclusions are based upon Locke's thought." Explain.

18. For what specific ideas were the founding fathers of the United States indebted to the Enlightenment?

19. Assuming that the documents in this problem are representative of eighteenth-century liberalism, formulate a credo to which an eighteenth-century liberal could have subscribed.

INTRODUCTION TO THE PROBLEM

The seventeenth century was rich in the production of new knowledge and novel ideas. That "Age of Genius," while not renouncing its heritage from Renaissance and Reformation, broke loose from the tyranny of formal theology and the classics to make startling developments in many fields. In particular outstanding advances came in mathematics, natural science, philosophy, and political theory; and to a very large extent these developments determined the direction of Western thought for the next two hundred years.

The great thinkers of the eighteenth century adapted and publicized the ideas of their predecessors. Treatises written for scholars in neo-classical Latin they translated into the European vernaculars and popularized for the reading public. Ideas born of seventeenth-century intellectual and political strife they extended and applied to the conditions of their own time. Supremely confident of the correctness of their knowledge, the eighteenth-century *philosophes,* as they called themselves, looked upon their age as the one which had, for the first time, discerned the pure light of truth after centuries of black ignorance. Hence, they termed the ideological development of their time "The Enlightenment," a label which symbolized their accomplishment.

The Enlightenment was a general European phenomenon. The leading contributions to its body of ideas were made by the thinkers of England and France, but significant contributions were also made by men from the other western European nations. Germany was as proud of her *Aufklaerung* as France of her *Éclaircissement.* The Enlightenment was thus cosmopolitan in character and universal in range of thought. But in its universality, it possessed a unity and direction derived from a single underlying principle—the principle expressed in Alexander Pope's famous line, "The proper study of mankind is man." The eighteenth-century *philosophe* was not a theologian nor yet a natural scientist, though God and nature bulked large in his thinking. He was, to use the term anachronistically, a social scientist. Whatever line of inquiry he pursued, his chief concern was to relate his knowledge to the life of mankind. And there was no phase of man's life which failed to interest him. "Enlightened" thought was thus primarily directed to studies of society, law, government, and economics. In these fields the *philosophe* was certain that he found the most significant truths discoverable to mankind.

His confidence in his "enlightenment"—the incontestable truth of his knowledge—tended to make the *philosophe* a reformer and a doctrinaire. Since life as he saw it about him did not conform to his ideas, he felt impelled to formulate doctrines for the regeneration of society. These doctrines took many forms; often they conflicted. For upon the basis of the same ideas could be erected antithetical doctrines. It was possible, for example, for *philosophes* to differ widely upon the ideal form of government. Yet all shared a common fund of ideas which, they were sure, pointed the way to needful changes in the organization of human society.

Now, this common fund of ideas, as applied to man as a social and political animal, provided the basic material of what is known as liberalism. This body of thought—liberalism as developed in the Enlightenment—became a historic force of outstanding importance. Possessed of a powerful appeal and carrying a conviction of certainty, it exercised a strong influence upon the course of events not only in Europe but wherever European civilization penetrated.

The purpose of this Problem is to examine some of the basic elements in eighteenth-century liberalism. Part I includes selections from some of the seventeenth-century writings upon which was based the liberalism of the Enlightenment.

The selections in Part II, taken from the works of outstanding *philosophes*, illustrate the development of liberal ideas. The student's problem is, from a survey of these materials, to acquire a comprehension of the content and meaning of liberal thought at the outset of its career as a dynamic force in Western civilization.

Part I.   THE BACKGROUND OF THE ENLIGHTENMENT

The great thinkers of the seventeenth century were, for the most part, great synthesizers. Many could lay good claim to originality, but the chief significance of their work was that it drew together and systematized a mass of ideas that had already begun to take shape. Their great syntheses were the foundation upon which was built the structure of "enlightened" thought, and to the eighteenth century they left not only a coherent and organized body of knowledge but also a new approach and method for the acquisition of knowledge. The materials in this Part are therefore selected from seventeenth-century writings which constitute an important element in the background of the Enlightenment.

A.   THE SCIENTIFIC PRINCIPLES OF SIR ISAAC NEWTON

Sir Isaac Newton (1642–1727) was the monumental synthesizer of a long line of scientific discoveries extending back for nearly two centuries. He showed little promise as a student at Cambridge, but within four years after his graduation, the brilliance of his scientific thought secured him a Cambridge professorship at the age of twenty-seven. His reputation as a scientist later led to his appointment as Warden and Master of the Mint, which positions he held from 1695 until his death. During this period he supervised the recoinage of England's debased currency. Newton's scientific fame rests upon *The Mathematical Principles of Natural Philosophy* (1687), in which he explained his theory of gravitation and applied it to the workings of the universe. The educated world, amazed and convinced, accorded him homage such as few men receive in their lifetime, and his *Principles,* translated from his original Latin and popularized in most of the languages of western Europe, became a foundation stone of all succeeding thought. Following are selections from the *Principles* which illustrate two of the basic ingredients of Newtonian thought: his purpose and his method of reasoning. (1)

[Newton's Purpose: "The Author's Preface"]

Since the ancients . . . made great account of the science of mechanics in the investigation of natural things; and the moderns, laying aside substantial forms and occult qualities, have endeavored to subject the phenomena of nature to the laws of mathematics, I have in this treatise cultivated mathematics so far as it regards philosophy. . . .

Our design not respecting arts, but philosophy, and our subject not manual but natural powers, we consider chiefly those things which relate to gravity, levity, elastic force, the resistance of fluids, and the like forces, whether attractive or impulsive; and therefore we offer this work as the mathematical principles of philosophy; for all the difficulty of philosophy seems to consist in this—from the phenomena of motions to investigate the forces of nature, and then from these forces to demonstrate the other phenomena; and to this end the general propositions in the first and second book are directed. In the third book we give an example of this in the explication of the system of the world; for by the propositions mathematically demonstrated in the former books, we in the third derive from the celestial phenomena the forces of gravity with which bodies tend to the sun and the several planets. Then from these forces, by other propositions which are also mathematical, we deduce the motions of the planets, the comets, the moon, and the sea. I wish we could derive the rest of the phenomena of nature by the same kind of reasoning from mechanical principles; for I am induced by many reasons to suspect that they may all depend upon certain forces by which the particles of bodies, by some causes hitherto unknown, are either mutually impelled towards each other, and cohere in regular figures, or are repelled and recede from each other; which forces being unknown, philosophers have hitherto attempted the search of nature in vain; but I hope the principles here laid down will afford some light either to this or some truer method of philosophy.

In the publication of this work the most acute and universally learned Mr. Edmund Halley . . when he had obtained of me my demonstrations of the figure of the celestial orbits, he continually pressed me to communicate the same to the Royal Society, who afterwards, by their kind encouragement and entreaties, engaged me to think of publishing them. But after I had begun to consider the inequalities of the lunar motions, and had entered upon some other things relating to the laws and measures of gravity and other forces; . . . I deferred that publication till I had made a search into those matters,,and could put forth the whole together.

[Newton's Method: His "Rules of Reasoning in Philosophy"]

RULE I

We are to admit no more causes of natural things than such as are both true and sufficient to explain their appearances. To this purpose the philosophers say that nature does nothing in vain, and more is in vain when less will serve; for nature is pleased with simplicity, and affects not the pomp of superfluous causes.

RULE II

Therefore to the same natural effects we must, as far as possible, assign the same causes. As to respiration in a man and in a beast; the descent of stones in Europe and in America; the light of our culinary fire and of the sun; the reflection of light in the earth, and in the planets.

RULE III

The qualities of bodies, which admit neither intension nor remission of degrees, and which are found to belong to all bodies within the reach of our experiments, are to be esteemed the universal qualities of all bodies whatsoever.

For since the qualities of bodies are only known to us by experiments, we are to hold for universal all such as universally agree with experiments; and such as are not liable to diminution can never be quite taken away. We are certainly not to relinquish the evidence of experiments for the sake of dreams and vain fictions of our own devising; nor are we to recede from the analogy of nature, which uses to be simple, and always consonant to itself. We no other way know the extension of bodies than by our senses, nor do these reach it in all bodies; but because we perceive extension in all that are sensible, therefore we ascribe it universally to all others also. That abundance of bodies are hard, we learn by experience; and because the hardness of the whole arises from the hardness of the parts, we therefore justly infer the hardness of the undivided particles not only of the bodies we feel but of all others. That all bodies are impenetrable, we gather not from reason, but from sensation. The bodies which we handle we find impenetrable, and thence conclude impenetrability to be an universal property of all bodies whatsoever. That all bodies are movable, and endowed with certain powers (which

we call the *vires inertiæ*) of persevering in their motion, or in their rest, we only infer from the like properties observed in the bodies which we have seen. The extension, hardness, impenetrability, mobility, and *vis inertiæ* of the whole, result from the extension, hardness, impenetrability, mobility, and *vires inertiæ* of the parts; and thence we conclude the least particles of all bodies to be also all extended, and hard, and impenetrable, and movable, and endowed with their proper *vires inertiæ*. And this is the foundation of all philosophy. Moreover, that the divided but contiguous particles of bodies may be separated from one another is matter of observation; and, in the particles that remain undivided, our minds are able to distinguish yet lesser parts, as is mathematically demonstrated. But whether the parts so distinguished, and not yet divided, may, by the powers of nature, be actually divided and separated from one another, we cannot certainly determine. Yet, had we the proof of but one experiment that any undivided particle, in breaking a hard and solid body, suffered a division, we might by virtue of this rule conclude that the undivided as well as the divided particles may be divided and actually separated to infinity.

Lastly, if it universally appears, by experiments and astronomical observations, that all bodies about the earth gravitate towards the earth, and that in proportion to the quantity of matter which they severally contain; that the moon likewise, according to the quantity of its matter, gravitates towards the earth; that, on the other hand, our sea gravitates towards the moon; and all the planets mutually one towards another; and the comets in like manner towards the sun; we must, in consequence of this rule, universally allow that all bodies whatsoever are endowed with a principle of mutual gravitation. For the argument from the appearances concludes with more force for the universal gravitation of all bodies than for their impenetrability; of which, among these in the celestial regions, we have no experiments, nor any manner of observation. Not that I affirm gravity to be essential to bodies; by their *vis insita* I mean nothing but their *vis inertiæ*. This is immutable. Their gravity is diminished as they recede from the earth.

RULE IV

In experimental philosophy we are to look upon propositions collected by general induction from phenomena as accurately or very nearly true, notwithstanding any contrary hypotheses that may be imagined, till such time as other phenomena occur, by which they may either be made more accurate, or liable to exceptions.

This rule we must follow, that the argument of induction may not be evaded by hypotheses.

B. ## THE THEORY OF KNOWLEDGE OF JOHN LOCKE

John Locke (1632–1704) was the son of a Puritan soldier in the English civil war. Educated at Oxford, he became a physician by profession, but for fifteen years he served as secretary to the Earl of Shaftesbury, a stormy petrel in politics and founder of the Whig party. Locke's connection with Shaftesbury twice forced him into exile, whence he returned the second time after his friend William of Orange had secured the English throne in 1688. Locke's broad experience and philosophical turn of mind focussed his attention for some years on the problem of human knowledge, which had first piqued his interest at Oxford. The eventual result of this interest was *An Essay Concerning Human Understanding* (1690) —"the first attempt in modern times to arrive at a comprehensive theory of knowledge"—which had a profound effect upon the thinking of his successors. Selections from the *Essay* follow. (2)

Introduction

1. Since it is the *understanding* that sets man above the rest of sensible beings, and gives him all the advantage and dominion which he has over them, it is certainly a subject, even for its nobleness, worth our labor to enquire into. The understanding, like the eye, whilst it makes us see and perceive all other things, takes no notice of itself; and it requires art and pains to set it at a distance, and make it its own object. But whatever be the difficulties that lie in the way of this enquiry; whatever it be that keeps us so much in the dark to ourselves; sure I am that all the light we can let in upon our own minds, all the acquaintance we can make with our own understandings, will not only be very pleasant, but bring us great advantage in directing our thoughts in the search of other things. . . .

5. For though the comprehension of our understandings comes exceeding short of the vast extent of things, yet we shall have cause enough to magnify the bountiful Author of our being for that portion and degree of knowledge he has bestowed on us, so far above all the rest of the inhabitants of this our mansion. Men have reason to be well satisfied with what God hath thought fit for them, since he has given them, as St. Peter says . . . "whatsoever is necessary for the conveniences of life, and information of virtue"; and has put within the reach of their discovery the comfortable provision for this life, and the way that leads to a better. How short soever their knowledge may come of an universal or perfect comprehension of whatsoever is, it yet secures their great concernments that they have light enough to lead them to the knowledge of their Maker, and the sight of their own duties. Men may find matter sufficient to busy their heads and employ their hands with variety, delight, and satisfaction, if they will not boldly quarrel with their own constitution, and throw away the blessings their hands are filled with, because they are not big enough to grasp everything. . . . It will

be no excuse to an idle and untoward servant, who would not attend his business by candlelight, to plead that he had not broad sunshine. The candle that is set up in us shines bright enough for all our purposes. The discoveries we can make with this ought to satisfy us; and we shall then use our understandings right, when we entertain all objects in that way and proportion that they are suited to our faculties, and upon those grounds they are capable of being proposed to us; and not peremptorily or intemperately require demonstration, and demand certainty, where probability only is to be had, and which is sufficient to govern all our concernments. If we will disbelieve everything because we cannot certainly know all things, we shall do much-what as wisely as he who would not use his legs, but sit still and perish, because he had no wings to fly. . . .

6. When we know our own strength, we shall the better know what to undertake with hopes of success: and when we have well surveyed the *powers* of our own minds, and made some estimate what we may expect from them, we shall not be inclined either to sit still, and not set our thoughts on work at all, in despair of knowing anything; nor on the other side question everything, and disclaim all knowledge, because some things are not to be understood. . . . Our business here is not to know all things, but those which concern our conduct. If we can find out those measures whereby a rational creature, put in that state which man is in in this world, may and ought to govern his opinions, and actions depending thereon, we need not be troubled that some other things escape our knowledge. . . .

Of Ideas in General and Their Original

1. Every man being conscious to himself that he thinks, and that which his mind is applied about whilst thinking being the ideas that are there, it is past doubt that men have in their minds several ideas, such as are those expressed by the words, "whiteness, hardness, sweetness,

thinking, motion, man, elephant, army, drunkenness," and others. It is in the first place then to be enquired, How he comes by them? I know it is a received doctrine, that men have native ideas and original characters stamped upon their minds in their very first being. This opinion I have at large examined already; and, I suppose, what I have said in the foregoing book will be much more easily admitted, when I have shown whence the understanding may get all the ideas it has, and by what ways and degrees they may come into the mind; for which I shall appeal to every one's own observation and experience.

2. Let us then suppose the mind to be, as we say, white paper [*tabula rasa*], void of all characters, without any ideas; how comes it to be furnished? Whence comes it by that vast store, which the busy and boundless fancy of man has painted on it with an almost endless variety? Whence has it all the materials of reason and knowledge? To this I answer, in one word, from EXPERIENCE; in that all our knowledge is founded, and from that it ultimately derives itself. Our observation, employed either about external sensible objects, or about the internal operations of our minds, perceived and reflected on by ourselves, is that which supplies our understandings with all the materials of thinking. These two are the fountains of knowledge, from whence all the ideas we have, or can naturally have, do spring.

3. First, our senses, conversant about particular sensible objects, do convey into the mind several distinct perceptions of things, according to those various ways wherein those objects do affect them; and thus we come by those *ideas* we have of yellow, white, heat, cold, soft, hard, bitter, sweet, and all those which we call sensible qualities; which when I say the senses convey into the mind, I mean, they from external objects convey into the mind what produces there those perceptions. This great source of most of the ideas we have, depending wholly upon our senses, and derived by them to the understanding, I call, SENSATION.

4. Secondly, the other fountain, from which experience furnisheth the understanding with ideas, is the perception of the operations of our own minds within us, as it is employed about the ideas it has got; which operations, when the soul comes to reflect on and consider, do furnish the understanding with another set of ideas which could not be had from things without: and such are perception, thinking, doubting, believing, reasoning, knowing, willing, and all the different actings of our own minds; which we being conscious of, and observing in ourselves, do from these receive into our understanding as distinct ideas, as we do from bodies affecting our senses. This source of ideas every man has wholly in him-

self: and though it be not sense, as having nothing to do with external objects, yet it is very like it, and might properly enough be called internal sense. But as I call the other sensation, so I call this REFLECTION, the ideas it affords being such only as the mind gets by reflecting on its own operations within itself. By reflection, then, . . . I would be understood to mean that notice which the mind takes of its own operations, and the manner of them, by reason whereof there come to be ideas of these operations in the understanding. These two, I say, viz., external material things as the objects of sensation, and the operations of our own minds within as the objects of reflection, are, to me, the only originals from whence all our ideas take their beginnings. The term *operations* here, I use in a large sense, as comprehending not barely the actions of the mind about its ideas, but some sort of passions arising sometimes from them, such as is the satisfaction or uneasiness arising from any thought. . . .

Of Simple Ideas of Both Sensation and Reflection

1. There be other simple ideas which convey themselves into the mind by all the ways of sensation and reflection, viz., *pleasure* or *delight,* and its opposite, *pain* or *uneasiness; power; existence; unity.*

2. Delight or uneasiness, one or other of them, join themselves to almost all our ideas both of sensation and reflection; and there is scarce any affection of our senses from without, any retired thought of our mind within, which is not able to produce in us pleasure or pain. By pleasure and pain, I would be understood to signify whatsoever delights or molests us; whether it arises from the thoughts of our minds, or anything operating on our bodies. For whether we call it satisfaction, delight, pleasure, happiness, &c., on the one side, or uneasiness, trouble, pain, torment, anguish, misery, &c., on the other, they are still but different degrees of the same thing, and belong to the ideas of pleasure and pain, delight or uneasiness, which are the names I shall most commonly use for those two sorts of ideas.

3. The infinite wise Author of our being, to excite us to these actions of thinking and motion that we are capable of, has been pleased to join to several thoughts and several sensations a perception of delight. If this were wholly separated from all our outward sensations and inward thoughts, we should have no reason to prefer one thought or action to another, negligence to attention, or motion to rest. And so we should neither stir our bodies, nor employ our minds, but let our thoughts (if I may so call it) run adrift, without any direction or design; and suffer the ideas of our minds, like unregarded shad-

ows, to make their appearances there as it happened, without attending to them. In which state man, however furnished with the faculties of understanding and will, would be a very idle, unactive creature, and pass his time only in a lazy, lethargic dream.

4. Pain has the same efficacy and use to set us on work that pleasure has, we being as ready to employ our faculties to avoid that, as to pursue this: only this is worth our consideration, that pain is often produced by the same objects and ideas that produce pleasure in us. Thus heat, that is very agreeable to us in one degree, by a little greater increase of it proves no ordinary torment; and the most pleasant of all sensible objects, light itself, if there be too much of it, if increased beyond a due proportion to our eyes, causes a very painful sensation. Which is wisely and favorably so ordered by nature, that when any object does by the vehemency of its operation disorder the instruments of sensation, whose structures cannot but be very nice and delicate, we might by the pain be warned to withdraw before the organ be quite put out of order, and so be unfitted for its proper functions for the future. . . .

Of the Improvement of Our Knowledge

1. It having been the common received opinion amongst men of letters, that *maxims* were the foundation of all knowledge; and that the sciences were each of them built upon certain *praecognita,* the beaten road of the schools has been, to lay down in the beginning one or more general propositions, as foundations whereon to build the knowledge that was to be had of that subject. These doctrines thus laid down for foundations of any science were called *principles,* as the beginnings from which we must set out. . . .

2. One thing which might probably give an occasion to this way of proceeding in other sciences was, as I suppose, the good success it seemed to have in mathematics, wherein men being observed to attain a great certainty of knowledge, these sciences came by pre-eminence to be called . . . learning, or things learned, as having, of all others, the greatest certainty, clearness, and evidence in them.

3. But if anyone will consider, he will (I guess) find that the great advancement and certainty of real knowledge which men arrived to in these sciences, was not owing to the influence of these principles, nor derived from any peculiar advantage they received from two or three general maxims laid down in the beginning; but from the clear, distinct, complete ideas their thoughts were employed about, and the relation of equality and excess so clear between some of them, that they had an intuitive knowledge, and

by that, a way to discover it in others, and this without the help of those maxims.

7. We must therefore, if we will proceed as reason advises, adapt our methods of enquiry to the nature of the ideas we examine, and the truth we search after. General and certain truths are only founded in the habitudes and relations of abstract ideas. A sagacious and methodical application of our thoughts, for the finding out these relations, is the only way to discover all that can be put, with truth and certainty concerning them, into general propositions. By what steps we are to proceed in these, is to be learned in the schools of the mathematicians, who, from very plain and easy beginnings, by gentle degrees, and a continued chain of reasonings, proceed to the discovery and demonstration of truths that appear at first sight beyond human capacity. The art of finding proofs, and the admirable methods they have invented for the singling out and laying in order those intermediate ideas that demonstratively show the equality or inequality of unapplicable quantities, is that which has carried them so far, and produced such wonderful and unexpected discoveries. . . .

11. From whence it is obvious to conclude, that since our faculties are not fitted to penetrate into the internal fabric and real essences of bodies; but yet plainly discovered to us the being of a God, and the knowledge of ourselves, enough to lead us into a full and clear discovery of our duty and great concernment; it will become us, as rational creatures, to employ those faculties we have about what they are most adapted to, and follow the direction of nature, where it seems to point us out the way. For it is rational to conclude that our proper employment lies in those enquiries, and in that sort of knowledge which is most suited to our natural capacities, and carries in it our greatest interest, *i.e.,* the condition of our eternal estate. Hence I think I may conclude, that morality is the proper science and business of mankind in general.

Of Faith and Reason, and Their Distinct Provinces

2. I find every sect, as far as reason will help them, make use of it gladly; and, where it fails them, they cry out, It is matter of faith, and above reason.

Reason therefore here, as contradistinguished to faith, I take to be the discovery of the certainty or probability of such propositions or truths, which the mind arrives at by deductions made from such ideas which it has got by the use of its natural faculties, viz., by sensation or reflection.

Faith, on the other side, is the assent to any proposition, not thus made out by the deductions of reason, but upon the credit of the proposer, as coming from God in some extraordinary way of communication. This way of discovering truths to men we call *revelation*.

3. First, then, I say, that no man inspired by God can, by any revelation, communicate to others any new simple ideas which they had not before from sensation or reflection. For whatsoever impressions he himself may have from the immediate hand of God, this revelation, if it be of new simple ideas, cannot be conveyed to another, either by words or any other signs. . . . For our simple ideas, then, which are the foundation and sole matter of all our notions and knowledge, we must depend wholly on our reason, I mean, our natural faculties, and can by no means receive them, or any of them, from traditional revelation.

4. Secondly, I say, that the same truths may be discovered and conveyed down from revelation, which are discoverable to us by reason and by those ideas we naturally may have. So God might, by revelation, discover the truth of any proposition in Euclid. In all things of this kind there is little need or use of revelation, God having furnished us with natural and surer means to arrive at the knowledge of them. For the knowledge we have that this revelation came at first from God, can never be so sure as the knowledge we have from the clear and distinct perception of the agreement or disagreement of our own ideas. . . .

5. Since no evidence of our faculties by which we receive such revelations can exceed, if equal, the certainty of our intuitive knowledge, we can never receive for a truth anything that is directly contrary to our clear and distinct knowledge: *e.g.*, the ideas of one body and one place do so clearly agree, and the mind has so evident a perception of their agreement, that we can never assent to a proposition that affirms the same body to be in two distant places at once, however it should pretend to the authority of a divine revelation: since the evidence, first, that we deceive not ourselves in ascribing it to God, secondly, that we understand it right, can never be so great as the evidence of our own intuitive knowledge, whereby we discern it impossible for the same body to be in two places at once. And therefore no proposition can be received for divine revelation, or obtain the assent due to all such, if it be contradictory to our clear intuitive knowledge, because this would be to subvert the principles and foundations of all knowledge, evidence, and assent whatsoever.

7. But, thirdly, there being many things wherein we have very imperfect notions, or none at all; and other things, of whose past, present, or future existence, by the natural use of our faculties, we can have no knowledge at all: these,

as being beyond the discovery of our natural faculties and above reason, are, when revealed, the proper matter of faith. . . . Revelation, where God has been pleased to give it, must carry it against the probable conjectures of reason. But yet it still belongs to reason to judge of the truth of its being a revelation, and of the signification of the words wherein it is delivered.

10. Thus far the dominion of faith reaches, and that without any violence or hindrance to reason; which is not injured or disturbed, but assisted and improved, by new discoveries of truth, coming from the eternal Fountain of all knowledge. Whatever God hath revealed is certainly true; no doubt can be made of it. This is the proper object of faith: but whether it be a divine revelation or no, reason must judge; which can never permit the mind to reject a greater evidence to embrace what is less evident, nor allow it to entertain probability in opposition to knowledge and certainty. There can be no evidence that any traditional revelation is of divine original, in the words we receive it, and in the sense we understand it, so clear and so certain as that of the principles of reason. And therefore nothing that is contrary to, and inconsistent with, the clear and self-evident dictates of reason, has a right to be urged or assented to, as a matter of faith, wherein reason hath nothing to do. . . .

Of Enthusiasm

4. Reason is natural revelation, whereby the eternal Father of light, and Fountain of all knowledge, communicates to mankind that portion of truth which he has laid within the reach of their natural faculties. Revelation is natural reason enlarged by a new set of discoveries communicated by God immediately, which reason vouches the truth of, by the testimony and proofs it gives that they come from God. So that he that takes away reason to make way for revelation, puts out the light of both; and does much-what the same as if he would persuade a man to put out his eyes, the better to receive the remote light of an invisible star by a telescope. . . .

13. Light, true light in the mind, is or can be nothing else but the evidence of the truth of any proposition; and if it be not a self-evident proposition, all the light it has, or can have, is from the clearness and validity of those proofs upon which it is received. To talk of any other light in the understanding, is to put ourselves in the dark, or in the power of the prince of darkness, and by our own consent, to give ourselves up to delusion, to believe a lie. For if strength of persuasion be the light which must guide us, I ask, how shall any one distinguish between the delusions of Satan, and the inspirations of the Holy Ghost?

14. He therefore that will not give himself up to all the extravagances of delusion and error, must bring this guide of his light within to the trial. God, when he makes the prophet, does not unmake the man. He leaves all his faculties in their natural state, to enable him to judge of his inspirations, whether they be of divine original or no. When he illuminates the mind with supernatural light, he does not extinguish that which is natural. If he would have us assent to the truth of any proposition, he either evidences that truth by the usual methods of natural reason, or else makes it known to be a truth which he would have us assent to by his authority, and convinces us that it is from him, by some marks which reason cannot be mistaken in. Reason must be our last judge and guide in everything.

C. THE POLITICAL THEORY OF JOHN LOCKE

Locke's close connection with politics also directed his thoughts into the realm of political theory. After the Glorious Revolution of 1688 he wrote *Two Treatises on Civil Government* as an elaborate philosophical defense of the revolutionary settlement. Having replied in the *First Treatise* to the supporters of divine right, Locke proceeded in the *Second Treatise* to deal with "the true original extent and end of civil government," wherein he synthesized much of the political speculation of the previous century into a systematic theory which became the basis for much of the eighteenth-century's liberal doctrine. Portions of the *Second Treatise* follow. (3)

Chapter I

Political power . . . I take to be a right of making laws, with penalties of death, and consequently all less penalties for the regulating and preserving of property, and of employing the force of the community in the execution of such laws, and in the defense of the commonwealth from foreign injury, and all this only for public good.

Chapter II: Of the State of Nature

To understand political power aright, and derive it from its original, we must consider what estate all men are naturally in, and that is, a state of perfect freedom to order their actions, and dispose of their possessions and persons as they think fit, within the bounds of the law of nature, without asking leave or depending upon the will of any other man.

A state also of equality, wherein all the power and jurisdiction is reciprocal, no one having more than another, there being nothing more evident than that creatures of the same species and rank, promiscuously born to all the same advantages of nature, and the use of the same faculties, should also be equal one amongst another, without subordination or subjection, unless the Lord and Master of them all should, by any manifest declaration of His will, set one above another, and confer on him, by an evident and clear appointment, an undoubted right to dominion and sovereignty. . . .

But though this be a state of liberty, yet it is not a state of licence; though man in that state have an uncontrollable liberty to dispose of his person or possessions, yet he has not liberty to destroy himself, or so much as any creature in his possession, but where some nobler use than its bare preservation calls for it. The state of nature has a law of nature to govern it, which obliges every one, and reason, which is that law, teaches all mankind who will but consult it, that being all equal and independent, no one ought to harm another in his life, health, liberty or possessions; for men being all the workmanship of one omnipotent and infinitely wise Maker; all the servants of one sovereign Master, sent into the world by His order and about His business; they are His property, whose workmanship they are made to last during His, not one another's pleasure. And, being furnished with like faculties, sharing all in one community of nature, there cannot be supposed any such subordination among us that may authorize us to destroy one another, as if we were made for one another's uses, as the inferior ranks of creatures are for ours. Every one as he is bound to preserve himself, and not to quit his station wilfully, so by the like reason, when his own preservation comes not in competition, ought he as much as he can to preserve the rest of mankind, and not unless it be to do justice on an offender, take away or impair the life, or what tends to the preservation of the life, the liberty, health, limb, or goods of another.

And that all men may be restrained from invading others' rights, and from doing hurt to one another, and the law of nature be observed, which willeth the peace and preservation of all mankind, the execution of the law of nature is in that state put into every man's hands, whereby every one has a right to punish the transgressors of that law to such a degree as may hinder its violation. For the law of nature would, as all other laws that concern men in this world, be in vain if there were nobody that in the state of nature had a power to execute that law, and thereby preserve the innocent and restrain offenders; and if any one in the state of nature may punish another for any evil he has done, every one may do so. For in that state of perfect equality, where naturally there is no superiority or jurisdiction of one over another, what any may do in prosecution of that law, every one must needs have a right to do.

And thus, in the state of nature, one man comes by a power over another, but yet no absolute or arbitrary power to use a criminal, when he has got him in his hands, according to the passionate heats or boundless extravagancy of his own will, but only to retribute to him so far as calm reason and conscience dictate, what is proportionate to his transgression, which is so much as may serve for reparation and restraint. For these two are the only reasons why one man may lawfully do harm to another, which is that we call punishment. In transgressing the law of nature, the offender declares himself to live by another rule than that of reason and common equity, which is that measure God has set to the actions of men for their mutual security, and so he becomes dangerous to mankind; the tie which is to secure them from injury and violence being slighted and broken by him, which being a trespass against the whole species, and the peace and safety of it, provided for by the law of nature, every man upon this score, by the right he hath to preserve mankind in general, may restrain, or where it is necessary destroy things noxious to them, and so may bring such evil on any one who hath transgressed that law, as may make him repent the doing of it, and thereby deter him, and, by his example, others from doing the like mischief. And in this case, and upon this ground, every man hath a right to punish the offender, and be executioner of the law of nature. . . .

To this strange doctrine—viz., that in the state of nature every one has the executive power of the law of nature—I doubt not but it will be objected that it is unreasonable for men to be judges in their own cases, that self-love will make men partial to themselves and their friends; and, on the other side, ill-nature, passion, and revenge will carry them too far in punishing others, and hence nothing but confusion and disorder will follow, and that therefore God hath certainly appointed government to restrain the partiality and violence of men. I easily grant that civil government is the proper remedy for the inconveniences of the state of nature, which must certainly be great where men may be judges in their own case, since it is easy to be imagined that he

who was so unjust as to do his brother an injury will scarce be so just as to condemn himself for it. But I shall desire those who make this objection to remember that absolute monarchs are but men; and if government is to be the remedy of those evils which necessarily follow from men being judges in their own cases, and the state of nature is therefore not to be endured, I desire to know what kind of government that is, and how much better it is than the state of nature, where one man commanding a multitude has the liberty to be judge in his own case, and may do to all his subjects whatever he pleases without the least question or control of those who execute his pleasure? and in whatsoever he doth, whether led by reason, mistake, or passion, must be submitted to? which men in the state of nature are not bound to do one to another. And if he that judges, judges amiss in his own or any other case, he is answerable for it to the rest of mankind. . . .

Chapter IV: Of Slavery

The natural liberty of man is to be free from any superior power on earth, and not to be under the will or legislative authority of man, but to have only the law of nature for his rule. The liberty of man in society is to be under no other legislative power but that established by consent in the commonwealth, nor under the dominion of any will, or restraint of any law, but what that legislative shall enact according to the trust put in it. Freedom, then, is not what Sir Robert Filmer tells us: "A liberty for every one to do what he lists, to live as he pleases, and not to be tied by any laws"; but freedom of men under government is to have a standing rule to live by, common to every one of that society, and made by the legislative power erected in it. A liberty to follow my own will in all things where that rule prescribes not, not to be subject to the inconstant, uncertain, unknown, arbitrary will of another man, as freedom of nature is to be under no other restraint but the law of nature.

This freedom from absolute, arbitrary power is so necessary to, and closely joined with, a man's preservation, that he cannot part with it but by what forfeits his preservation and life together. For a man, not having the power of his own life, cannot by compact or his own consent enslave himself to any one, nor put himself under the absolute arbitrary power of another to take away his life when he pleases. Nobody can give more power than he has himself, and he that cannot take away his own life cannot give another power over it. Indeed, having by his fault forfeited his own life by some act that deserves death, he to whom he has forfeited it may, when he has him in his power, delay to take it, and make use of him to his own service; and he does him no injury by it. For, whenever he finds the hardship of his slavery outweigh the value of his life, it is in his power, by resisting the will of his master, to draw on himself the death he desires.

Chapter V: Of Property

Whether we consider natural reason, which tells us that men, being once born, have a right to their preservation, and consequently to meat and drink and such other things as nature affords for their subsistence, or "revelation," which gives us an account of those grants God made of the world to Adam, and to Noah and his sons, it is very clear that God, as King David says (Psalm CXV. 16), "has given the earth to the children of men," given it to mankind in common. But, this being supposed, it seems to some a very great difficulty how any one should ever come to have a property in anything, I will not content myself to answer, that, if it be difficult to make our "property" upon a supposition that God gave the world to Adam and his posterity in common, it is impossible that any man but one universal monarch should have any "property" upon a supposition that God gave the world to Adam and his heirs in succession, exclusive of all the rest of his posterity; but I shall endeavor to show how men might come to have a property in several parts of that which God gave to mankind in common, and that without any express compact of all the commoners.

God, who hath given the world to men in common, hath also given them reason to make use of it to the best advantage of life and convenience. The earth and all that is therein is given to men for the support and comfort of their being. And though all the fruits it naturally produces, and beasts it feeds, belong to mankind in common, as they are produced by the spontaneous hand of nature, and nobody has originally a private dominion exclusive of the rest of mankind in any of them, as they are thus in their natural state, yet being given for the use of men, there must of necessity be a means to appropriate them some way or other before they can be of any use, or at all beneficial, to any particular men. The fruit or venison which nourishes the wild Indian, who knows no enclosure, and is still a tenant in common, must be his, and so his—*i.e.,* a part of him, that another can no longer have any right to it before it can do him any good for the support of his life.

Though the earth and all inferior creatures be common to all men, yet every man has a "property" in his own "person." This nobody has any right to but himself. The "labor" of his body and the "work" of his hands, we may say, are properly

his. Whatsoever, then, he removes out of the state that nature hath provided and left it in, he hath mixed his labor with it, and joined to it something that is his own, and thereby makes it his property. It being by him removed from the common state nature placed it in, it hath by this labor something annexed to it that excludes the common right of other men. For this "labor" being the unquestionable property of the laborer, no man but he can have a right to what that is once joined to, at least where there is enough, and as good left in common for others. . . .

It will, perhaps, be objected to this, that if gathering the acorns or other fruits of the earth, etc., makes a right to them, then any one may engross as much as he will. To which I answer, Not so. The same law of nature that does by this means give us property, does also bound that property too. "God has given us all things richly." Is the voice of reason confirmed by inspiration? But how far has He given it us—"to enjoy"? As much as any one can make use of to any advantage of life before it spoils, so much he may by his labor fix a property in. Whatever is beyond this is more than his share, and belongs to others. Nothing was made by God for man to spoil or destroy. And thus considering the plenty of natural provisions there was a long time in the world, and the few spenders, and to how small a part of that provision the industry of one man could extend itself and engross it to the prejudice of others, especially keeping within the bounds set by reason of what might serve for his use, there could be then little room for quarrels or contentions about property so established.

But the chief matter of property being now not the fruits of the earth and the beasts that subsist on it, but the earth itself as that which takes in and carries with it all the rest, I think it is plain that property in that too is acquired as the former. As much land as a man tills, plants, improves, cultivates, and can use the product of, so much is his property. He by his labor does, as it were, enclose it from the common. Nor will it invalidate his right to say everybody else has an equal title to it, and therefore he cannot appropriate, he cannot enclose, without the consent of all his fellow-commoners, all mankind. God, when He gave the world in common to all mankind, commanded man also to labor, and the penury of his condition required it of him. God and his reason commanded him to subdue the earth—*i.e.,* improve it for the benefit of life and therein lay out something upon it that was his own, his labor. He that, in obedience to this command of God, subdued, tilled, and sowed any part of it, thereby annexed to it something that was his property, which another had no title to, nor could without injury take from him.

Nor was this appropriation of any parcel of land, by improving it, any prejudice to any other man, since there was still enough and as good left, and more than the yet unprovided could use. . . .

God gave the world to men in common, but since He gave it them for their benefit and the greatest conveniencies of life they were capable to draw from it, it cannot be supposed He meant it should always remain common and uncultivated. He gave it to the use of the industrious and rational (and labor was to be his title to it); not to the fancy or covetousness of the quarrelsome and contentious. He that had as good left for his improvement as was already taken up needed not complain, ought not to meddle with what was already improved by another's labor. . . .

Now of those good things which nature hath provided in common, every one hath a right (as hath been said) to as much as he could use, and had a property in all he could effect with his labor; all that his industry could extend to, to alter from the state nature had put it in, was his. He that gathered a hundred bushels of acorns or apples had thereby a property in them; they were his goods as soon as gathered. He was only to look that he used them before they spoiled, else he took more than his share, and robbed others. And, indeed, it was a foolish thing, as well as dishonest, to hoard up more than he could make use of. If he gave a part to anybody else, so that it perished not uselessly in his possession, these he also made use of. And if he also bartered away plums that would have rotted in a week, for nuts that would last good for his eating a whole year, he did no injury; he wasted not the common stock; destroyed no part of the portion of goods that belonged to others, so long as nothing perished uselessly in his hands. Again, if he would give his nuts for a piece of metal, pleased with its color, or exchange his sheep for shells, or wool for a sparkling pebble or a diamond, and keep those by him all his life, he invaded not the right of others; he might heap up as much of these durable things as he pleased; the exceeding of the bounds of his just property not lying in the largeness of his possession, but the perishing of anything uselessly in it.

And thus came in the use of money; some lasting thing that men might keep without spoiling, and that, by mutual consent, men would take in exchange for the truly useful but perishable supports of life.

And as different degrees of industry were apt to give men possessions in different proportions, so this invention of money gave them the opportunity to continue and enlarge them. . . .

Thus, in the beginning, all the world was America, and more so than that is now; for no such thing as money was anywhere known. Find out something that hath the use and value of money amongst his neighbors, you shall see the same man will begin presently to enlarge his possessions.

But since gold and silver, being little useful to the life of man, in proportion to food, raiment, and carriage, has its value only from the consent of men—whereof labor yet makes in great part the measure—it is plain that the consent of men have agreed to a disproportionate and unequal possession of the earth—I mean out of the bounds of society and compact; for in governments the laws regulate it; they having, by consent, found out and agreed in a way how a man may, rightfully and without injury, possess more than he himself can make use of by receiving gold and silver, which may continue long in a man's possession without decaying for the overplus, and agreeing those metals should have a value. . . .

Chapter VI: Of Paternal Power

Though I have said above "that all men by nature are equal," I cannot be supposed to understand all sorts of "equality." Age or virtue may give men a just precedency. Excellency of parts and merit may place others above the common level. Birth may subject some, and alliance or benefits others, to pay an observance to those to whom nature, gratitude, or other respects, may have made it due; and yet all this consists with the equality which all men are in in respect of jurisdiction or dominion one over another, which was the equality I there spoke of as proper to the business in hand, being that equal right that every man hath to his natural freedom, without being subjected to the will or authority of any other man. . . .

The freedom then of man, and liberty of acting according to his own will, is grounded on his having reason, which is able to instruct him in that law he is to govern himself by, and make him know how far he is left to the freedom of his own will. To turn him loose to an unrestrained liberty, before he has reason to guide him, is not the allowing him the privilege of his nature to be free, but to thrust him out amongst brutes, and abandon him to a state as wretched and as much beneath that of a man as theirs. This is that which puts the authority into the parents' hands to govern the minority of their children. God hath made it their business to employ this care on their offspring, and hath placed in them suitable inclinations of tenderness and concern to temper this power, to apply it as His wisdom designed it, to the children's good as long as they should need to be under it.

Chapter VII: Of Political or Civil Society

Man being born, as has been proved, with a title to perfect freedom and an uncontrolled enjoyment of all the rights and privileges of the law of nature, equally with any other man, or number of men in the world, hath by nature a power not only to preserve his property—that is, his life, liberty, and estate—against the injuries and attempts of other men, but to judge of and punish the breaches of that law in others, as he is persuaded the offense deserves, even with death itself, in crimes where the heinousness of the fact, in his opinion, requires it. But because no political society can be, nor subsist, without having in itself the power to preserve the property, and in order thereunto punish the offenses of all those of that society, there, and there only, is political society where every one of the members hath quitted this natural power, resigned it up into the hands of the community in all cases that exclude him not from appealing for protection to the law established by it. And thus all private judgment of every particular member being excluded, the community comes to be umpire, and by understanding indifferent rules and men authorized by the community for their execution, decides all the differences that may happen between any members of that society concerning any matter of right, and punishes those offenses which any member hath committed against the society with such penalties as the law has established; whereby it is easy to discern who are, and are not, in political society together. Those who are united into one body, and have a common established law and judicature to appeal to, with authority to decide controversies between them and punish offenders, are in civil society one with another; but those who have no such common appeal, I mean on earth, are still in the state of nature, each being where there is no other, judge for himself and executioner; which is, as I have before showed it, the perfect state of nature.

Chapter VIII: Of the Beginning
of Political Societies

Men being, as has been said, by nature all free, equal, and independent, no one can be put out of this estate and subjected to the political power of another without his own consent, which is done by agreeing with other men, to join and unite into a community for their comfortable, safe, and peaceable living, one amongst another, in a secure enjoyment of their properties, and a greater security against any that are not of it. This any number of men may do, because it injures not the freedom of the rest; they are left, as they were, in the liberty of the state of nature. When any number of men have so consented to make one community or government, they are thereby presently incorporated, and make one body politic, wherein the majority have a right to act and conclude the rest.

For, when any number of men have, by the consent of every individual, made a community, they have thereby made that community one body, with a power to act as one body, which is only by the will and determination of the majority. For that which acts [moves] any community, being only the consent of the individuals of it, and it being one body, must move one way, it is necessary the body should move that way whither the greater force carries it, which is the consent of the majority, or else it is impossible it should act or continue one body, one community, which the consent of every individual that united into it agreed that it should; and so every one is bound by that consent to be concluded by the majority. And therefore we see that in assemblies empowered to act by positive laws where no number is set by that positive law which empowers them, the act of the majority passes for the act of the whole, and of course determines as having, by the law of nature and reason, the power of the whole. . . .

Whosoever, therefore, out of a state of nature unite into a community, must be understood to give up all the power necessary to the ends for which they unite into society to the majority of the community, unless they expressly agreed in any number greater than the majority. And this is done by barely agreeing to unite into one political society, which is all the compact that is, or needs be, between the individuals that enter into or make up a commonwealth. And thus, that which begins and actually constitutes any political society is nothing but the consent of any number of freemen capable of majority, to unite and incorporate into such a society. And this is that, and that only, which did or could give beginning to any lawful government in the world.

To this I find two objections made: 1. That there are no instances to be found in story of a company of men, independent and equal one amongst another, that met together, and in this way began and set up a government. 2. It is impossible of right that men should do so, because all men, being born under government, they are to submit to that, and are not at liberty to begin a new one.

To the first there is this to answer: . . . if we may not suppose men ever to have been in the state of nature, because we hear not much of them in such a state, we may as well suppose the armies of Salmanasser or Xerxes were never children, because we hear little of them till they were men and embodied in armies. Government is everywhere antecedent to records. . . .

Chapter IX: Of the Ends of Political Society and Government

If man in the state of nature be so free as has been said, if he be absolute lord of his own person and possessions, equal to the greatest and subject to nobody, why will he part with his freedom, this empire, and subject himself to the dominion and control of any other power? To which it is obvious to answer, that though in the state of nature he hath such a right, yet the enjoyment of it is very uncertain and constantly exposed to the invasion of others; for all being kings as much as he, every man his equal, and the greater part no strict observers of equity and justice, the enjoyment of the property he has in this state is very unsafe, very insecure. This makes him willing to quit this condition which, however free, is full of fears and continual dangers; and it is not without reason that he seeks out and is willing to join in society with others who are already united, or have a mind to unite for the mutual preservation of their lives, liberties, and estates, which I call by the general name—property.

The great and chief end, therefore, of men uniting into commonwealths, and putting themselves under government, is the preservation of their property; to which in the state of nature there are many things wanting.

Firstly, there wants an established, settled, known law, received and allowed by common consent to be the standard of right and wrong, and the common measure to decide all controversies between them. . . .

Secondly, in the state of nature there wants a known and indifferent judge, with authority to determine all differences according to the established law. . . .

Thirdly, in the state of nature there often wants power to back and support the sentence when right, and to give it due execution. . . .

And so, whoever has the legislative or supreme power of any commonwealth, is bound to govern by established standing laws, promulgated and known to the people, and not by extemporary decrees, by indifferent and upright judges, who are to decide controversies by those laws; and to employ the force of the community at home only in the execution of such laws, or abroad to prevent or redress foreign injuries and secure the community from inroads and invasion. And all this to be directed to no other end but the peace, safety, and public good of the people.

Chapter XVIII: Of Tyranny

Wherever law ends, tyranny begins, if the law be transgressed to another's harm; and whosoever in authority exceeds the power given him by the law, and makes use of the force he has under his command to compass that upon the subject which the law allows not, ceases in that to be a magistrate, and acting without authority may be opposed, as any other man who by force invades the right of another. This is acknowledged in subordinate magistrates. He that hath authority to seize my person in the street may be opposed as a thief and a robber if he endeavors to break into my house to execute a writ, notwithstanding that I know he has such a warrant and such a legal authority as will empower him to arrest me abroad. And why this should not hold in the highest, as well as in the most inferior magistrate, I would gladly be informed. Is it reasonable that the eldest brother, because he has the greatest part of his father's estate, should thereby have a right to take away any of his younger brothers' portions? Or that a rich man, who possessed a whole country, should from thence have a right to seize, when he pleased, the cottage and garden of his poor neighbor? The being rightfully possessed of great power and riches, exceedingly beyond the greatest part of the sons of Adam, is so far from being an excuse, much less a reason for rapine and oppression, which the endamaging another without authority is, that it is a great aggravation of it. For exceeding the bounds of authority is no more a right in a great than a petty officer, no more justifiable in a king than a constable. But so much the worse in him as that he has more trust put in him, is supposed, from the advantage of education and counsellors, to have better knowledge and less reason to do it, having already a greater share than the rest of his brethren.

Chapter XIX: Of the Dissolution of Government

There is, therefore, . . . another way whereby governments are dissolved, and that is, when the legislative, or the prince, either of them act contrary to their trust. . . .

Whensoever, therefore, the legislative shall transgress this fundamental rule of society, and either by ambition, fear, folly, or corruption, endeavor to grasp themselves, or put into the hands of any other, an absolute power over the lives, liberties, and estates of the people, by this breach of trust they forfeit the power the people had put into their hands for quite contrary ends, and it devolves to the people, who have a right to resume their original liberty, and by the establishment of a new legislative (such as they shall think fit), provide for their own safety and security, which is the end for which they are in society. What I have said here concerning the legislative in general holds true also concerning the supreme executor, who having a double trust put in him, both to have a part in the legislative and the supreme execution of the law, acts against both, when he goes about to set up his own arbitrary will as the law of the society. He acts also contrary to his trust when he employs the force, treasure, and offices of the society to corrupt the representatives and gain them to his purposes, when he openly pre-engages the electors, and prescribes, to their choice, such whom he has, by solicitation, threats, promises, or otherwise, won to his designs, and employs them to bring in such who have promised beforehand what to vote and what to enact.

Part II.   THE LIBERALISM OF THE ENLIGHTENMENT

The manner in which the *philosophes* exploited the ideas and methodology of their forerunners varied greatly. While all applied their thinking to the needs of society, there was no uniform approach. Some *philosophes* were satirists; others were analysts; still others were system builders, poets, or dreamers. The materials in this Part are representative selections from the writings of some of the most celebrated figures of the Enlightenment, who contributed both method and direction to eighteenth-century liberalism.

A.   THE SATIRE OF VOLTAIRE

The name of François Marie Arouet de Voltaire (1694–1778) has become the very symbol of the French Enlightenment. Of middle-class origin, Voltaire early became a popular poet and playwright, but his biting wit led him to prison and a three-year exile in England. This enforced visit made him a *philosophe,* for in England he became acquainted with the works of Locke and Newton, and thereafter he was a self-constituted apostle of *éclaircissement.* His *Letters on the English* (1733) were the first product of his exile. Shortly thereafter he wrote a popularized French exposition of Newton's *Principles,* and before long his literary labors won him fame throughout Europe. He corresponded with kings, and from 1749 to 1752 he lived at Potsdam as the guest of Frederick the Great. He died at the age af eighty-four from exhaustion after an enthusiastic celebration in his honor at Paris. Following are selections from his writings, illustrative of his biting satire. (4)

[Laws]

Sheep live together in society very agreeably; we consider them very meek in character because we do not see the prodigious quantity of animals that they devour. We may believe that they eat them innocently, and without knowing it, just as when we eat a Sassenage cheese. The republic of sheep is the faithful image of the Golden Age.

A poultry yard is plainly the most perfect monarchy. There is no king comparable to a cock. If he marches proudly in the midst of his people, it is not through vanity. If the enemy approaches, he does not order his subjects to go and be killed for him by virtue of his certain knowledge and plenary powers; he goes himself, lines up his hens behind him and fights to the death. If he is victorious, it is he who sings the *Te Deum.* In civil life, there is no one so gallant, so honest, so unselfish. He possesses all virtues. If he holds in his royal beak a grain of wheat or a worm, he gives it to the first of his subjects to present herself. Solomon in all his harem was not to be compared to a barnyard cock.

If it is true that bees are governed by a queen whose subjects all make love to her, that is a still more perfect government. Ants are considered as forming an excellent democracy. It is superior to all other states because everybody in it is equal and every individual works for the common good. The republic of beavers is better than that of the ants, at least if we may judge of them by their masonry. Monkeys resemble mountebanks rather than civilized people; and they do not appear to be united under any fixed and fundamental laws, like the preceding species.

We resemble monkeys more than any other animal in the gift of imitation, in the levity of our ideas, and in inconstancy, which has never allowed us to have uniform and durable laws. When nature formed our species, and imparted to us a few instincts, self-love for our preservation, benevolence for the preservation of others, love which is common to all species, and the inexplicable gift of combining more ideas than all the animals put together; after having thus endowed us, she said to us: "Do the best you can."

There is no good code of laws in any country.

The reason is evident. . . . Laws were established in nearly all states through the selfish interests of the legislator, to meet the need of the moment, through ignorance and superstition. They were made gradually, by chance, irregularly, just as cities were built. . . . London became worthy of being inhabited only after it was reduced to ashes. From that time on, the streets were broadened and straightened: London was a city for having been burned. If you want to have good laws, burn your own, then, and make new ones. . . . Your common law of Paris is interpreted differently in twenty-four commentaries: just so many proofs, then, that it is ill conceived. It contradicts 140 other common laws, all having legal force in the same nation, and all contradicting each other. . . . The intellect of Europe has made greater progress in the last hundred years than the whole world had made since the days of Brahma, Fohi, Zoroaster, and Thaut of the Egyptians. Why is it that the spirit of legislation has made so little?

[Equality]

All the poor are not unhappy. Most of them are born in poverty, and constant toil keeps them from feeling too keenly their situation. But when they do feel it then there are wars, such as that of the popular party against the senatorial party at Rome, and those of the peasants in Germany, England, and France. All these wars end sooner or later with the subjection of the people, because those in power have money, and money is sole master in a state: I say in a state, because it is not true between nations. The nation which makes the best use of the sword will always subjugate the nation which has more gold and less courage.

Every man is born with a rather violent propensity for domination, wealth, and pleasure, and with a strong taste for idleness; consequently every man would like to have the money and the wives or daughters of other men, to be their master, to subject them to his every caprice, and to do nothing, or at least to do nothing but what is most agreeable. It is easily seen that with these handsome propensities it is as impossible for men to be equal as it is impossible for two preachers or two professors of theology not to be jealous of each other.

The human race such as it is cannot subsist unless there is an infinite number of useful men who possess nothing at all: for certainly a man in easy circumstances will not leave his land to come and plough yours; and if you need a pair of shoes, it will not be the judge of petitions who will make them for you. Equality is therefore at the same time most natural and most chimerical.

[Liberty of the Press]

In general, we have the natural right to use our pens like our tongues, at our own risk and peril. I know of many books which have been boring, but I know of none that has done any real harm. Theologians, or self-styled politicians, cry out: Religion is destroyed, the government is ruined, if you print certain truths or certain paradoxes. Never take it into your head to think until you have asked the permission of some monk or of some bureaucrat. It is contrary to good order for a man to think for himself. Homer, Plato, Cicero, Virgil, Pliny, Horace never published anything without the approbation of the Sorbonne doctors and the Holy Inquisition.

See into what horrible decay the liberty of the press has brought England and Holland. It is true that they embrace the commerce of the entire world, and that England is victorious on land and on sea; but it is only false greatness and false opulence: they are marching with long strides to their ruin. An enlightened people cannot subsist.

One cannot reason more justly, my friends; but let's see, pray, what state has been ruined by a book. The most dangerous, the most pernicious of all books is Spinoza's. Not only as a Jew does he attack the New Testament, but as a scholar he ruins the Old; his system of atheism is a thousand times more consistent and better reasoned than the systems of Strato and Epicurus. It takes the most profound sagacity to reply to the arguments by which he attempts to prove that one substance cannot form another.

Like yourself, I detest his book, which I understand perhaps better than you, and to which you replied very weakly; but have you observed that this book has changed the face of the globe? Is there any preacher who has lost a florin of his pension through the sale of Spinoza's works? Is there any bishop whose income has diminished? On the contrary, their revenue has doubled since his time; all the harm boils down to a small number of peaceful readers who have examined the arguments of Spinoza in their studies and who have written for or against them, works that are very little known. . . .

But if there appears among you some new book containing ideas which somewhat shock your own (supposing that you have ideas), or written by an author belonging to a party opposed to your faction, or, what is worse, to no party, then you cry, "Fire!" and there is nothing but noise, scandal, and universal hubbub in your little corner of the earth. Here is an abominable man who has written that if we had no hands, we could make neither stockings nor shoes; what a blasphemy! Pious women cry out, fur-robed doctors assemble, the alarm spreads from college to college and from house to house; entire bodies are set in movement; and for what? For five or six pages that are forgotten at the end of three months. If you don't like a book, refute it; if you are bored by it, don't read it.

"Ah!" you tell me, "the books of Luther and Calvin have destroyed the Roman religion in half of Europe.". . .

You are very seriously mistaken when you think that you have been ruined by books. . . . If Luther the monk, if John Calvin the canon, if Zwingli the curate, had been content with writing, Rome would yet subjugate all the states that she has lost; but those people and their adherents ran from city to city and from house to house, incited women to riot, and were upheld by princes. The fury which tormented Amata, and whipped her like a top, according to Virgil, was not more turbulent. Learn then that an enthusiastic, factious, ignorant, supple, vehement Capuchin friar, the tool of some ambitious man, by preaching, confessing, administering communion, and caballing can overturn a province much sooner than a hundred authors can enlighten it. It was not the Alcoran which brought success to Mohammed, it was Mohammed who brought success to the Alcoran. . . . You fear books as certain small towns have feared violins. Let people read and let them dance; these two amusements will never do the world any harm.

[*Tolerance*]

My friends, when we have preached tolerance in prose and in verse, in a few pulpits and in all our congregations; when we have made these truly human voices resound from our church organs, then we have rendered a service to nature and have reestablished humanity in its rights;

and there is not today an ex-Jesuit or an ex-Jansenist who dares to say: "I am intolerant." There will always be barbarians and rogues who will foment intolerance; but they will not confess it; and that is a substantial gain. . . .

Let us remember that in all English America, which includes nearly a fourth of the known world, entire liberty of conscience is established; and provided that one believes in a God, every religion is well received, and as a result commerce is flourishing and population is increasing. Let us remember always that the first law of the Russian Empire, greater than the Roman Empire, is the tolerance of all sects. The Turkish and the Persian Empires have always practised the same indulgence. Mohammed II, on taking Constantinople, did not force the Greeks to abandon their religion, though he regarded them as idolaters. Each head of a Greek family was let off for five or six crowns a year. Several prebends [cathedral stipend] and several bishoprics were left for them; and even today the Turkish Sultan makes canons and bishops, without the Pope's ever having made an iman or a mollah. My friends, there are only a few monks, and a few Protestants as stupid and as barbarous as these monks, who are still intolerant.

We have been so infected with this fury that in our travels into far countries we have carried it to China, Tonkin [Indo-China], and Japan. We have brought the plague to these beautiful climes. The most indulgent of men have learned from us to be the most inflexible. We told them at the outset in payment for the kind welcome accorded us: "Know that we are the only people on earth who are right, and that we are destined to be masters everywhere." For that we were driven away forever; it cost rivers of blood: that lesson ought to have reformed us.

B.   MONTESQUIEU'S "SPIRIT OF THE LAWS"

One of the most celebrated works of the eighteenth century was *The Spirit of the Laws* by Charles Louis, Baron de Montesquieu (1689–1755). He was a member of the French legal nobility, who spent his early years as a provincial judge in Bordeaux, but later traveled widely throughout Europe. Adequate leisure and an inquiring mind led him to reflect upon society, which resulted in his writing mild satire upon French customs and, after seventeen years of study, his profound analysis of *The Spirit of the Laws* (1748). His conclusions, drawn from his admiration for the British constitution, were not altogether consonant with the beliefs of his fellow *philosophes,* many of whom were advocates of "enlightened despotism," but his work had a profound influence upon the development of political thought. Selections illustrative of Montesquieu's ideas follow. (5)

Book I: Of Laws in General

Laws, in their most general signification, are the necessary relations arising from the nature of things. In this sense all beings have their laws: the Deity His law, the material world its laws, the intelligences superior to man their laws, the beasts their laws, man his laws. They who assert that a blind fatality produced the various effects we behold in this world talk very absurdly; for can any thing be more unreasonable than to pretend that a blind fatality could be productive of intelligent beings? There is, then, a prime reason; and laws are the relations subsisting between it and different beings, and the relations of these to one another. God is related to the universe, as Creator and Preserver; the laws by which He created all things are those by which He preserves them. He acts according to these rules, because He knows them; He knows them because He made them; and He made them because they are in relation of His wisdom and power.

Since we observe that the world, though formed by the motion of matter, and void of understanding, subsists through so long a succession of ages, its motions must certainly be directed by invariable laws; and could we imagine another world, it must also have constant rules, or it would inevitably perish. Thus the creation, which seems an arbitrary act, supposes laws as invariable as those of the fatality of the atheists. It would be absurd to say that the Creator might govern the world without those rules, since without them it could not subsist. . . .

Man, as a physical being, is like other bodies governed by invariable laws. As an intelligent being, he incessantly transgresses the laws established by God, and changes those of his own instituting. He is left to his private direction, though a limited being, and subject, like all finite intelligences, to ignorance and error: even his imperfect knowledge he loses; and as a sensible creature, he is hurried away by a thousand impetuous passions. Such a being might every instant forget his Creator; God has therefore reminded him of his duty by the laws of religion. Such a being is liable every moment to forget himself; philosophy has provided against this by the laws of morality. Formed to live in society, he might forget his fellow-creatures; legislators have, therefore, by political and civil laws, confined him to his duty. . . .

Besides the law of nations relating to all societies, there is a polity or civil constitution for each particularly considered. No society can subsist without a form of government. "The united strength of individuals," as Gravina [Italian poet and jurist (1664–1718)] well observes, "constitutes what we call the body politic." The general strength may be in the hands of a single person, or of many. Some think that nature having established paternal authority, the most natural government was that of a single person. But the example of paternal authority proves nothing. For if the power of a father relates to a single government, that of brothers after the death of a father, and that of cousins-german after the decease of brothers, refer to a government of many. The political power necessarily comprehends the union

of several families. Better is it to say that the government most conformable to nature is that which best agrees with the humor and disposition of the people in whose favor it is established. The strength of individuals cannot be united without a conjunction of all their wills. "The conjunction of those wills," as Gravina again very justly observes, "is what we call the civil state."

Law in general is human reason, inasmuch as it governs all the inhabitants of the earth: the political and civil laws of each nation ought to be only the particular cases in which human reason is applied. They should be adapted in such a manner to the people for whom they are framed that it should be a great chance if those of one nation suit another. They should be in relation to the nature and principle of each government: whether they form it, as may be said of politic laws; or whether they support it, as in the case of civil institutions. They should be in relation to the climate of each country, to the quality of its soil, to its situation and extent, to the principal occupation of the natives, whether husbandmen, huntsmen, or shepherds: they should have relation to the degree of liberty which the constitution will bear; to the religion of the inhabitants, to their inclinations, riches, numbers, commerce, manners, and customs. In fine, they have relations to each other, as also to their origin, to the intent of the legislator, and to the order of things on which they are established; in all of which different lights they ought to be considered. . . .

Book XI: *Of the Laws Which Establish Political Liberty with Regard to the Constitution*

In every government there are three sorts of power: the legislative; the executive in respect to things dependent on the law of nations; and the executive in regard to matters that depend on the civil law. By virtue of the first, the prince or magistrate enacts temporary or perpetual laws, and amends or abrogates those that have been already enacted. By the second, he makes peace or war, sends or receives embassies, establishes the public security, and provides against invasions. By the third, he punishes criminals, or determines the disputes that arise between individuals. The latter we shall call the judiciary power, and the other simply the executive power of the state.

The political liberty of the subject is a tranquility of mind arising from the opinion each person has of his safety. In order to have this liberty, it is requisite the government be so constituted as one man need not be afraid of another. When the legislative and executive powers are united in the same person, or in the same body of magistrates, there can be no liberty; because apprehensions may arise, lest the same monarch or senate should enact tyrannical laws, to execute them in a tyrannical manner. Again, there is no liberty, if the judiciary power be not separated from the legislative and executive. Were it joined with the legislative, the life and liberty of the subject would be exposed to arbitrary control; for the judge would be then the legislator. Were it joined to the executive power, the judge might behave with violence and oppression. There would be an end of everything, were the same man or the same body, whether of the nobles or of the people, to exercise those three powers, that of enacting laws, that of executing the public resolutions, and of trying the causes of individuals. . . .

As in a country of liberty, every man who is supposed a free agent ought to be his own governor; the legislative power should reside in the whole body of the people. But since this is impossible in large states, and in small ones is subject to many inconveniences, it is fit the people should transact by their representatives what they cannot transact by themselves. The inhabitants of a particular town are much better acquainted with its wants and interests than with those of other places; and are better judges of the capacity of their neighbors than of that of the rest of their countrymen. The members, therefore, of the legislature should not be chosen from the general body of the nation; but it is proper that in every considerable place a representative should be elected by the inhabitants.

The great advantage of representatives is their capacity of discussing public affairs. For this the people collectively are extremely unfit, which is one of the chief inconveniences of a democracy. It is not at all necessary that the representatives who have received a general instruction from their constituents should wait to be directed on each particular affair, as is practiced in the diets of Germany. True it is that by this way of proceeding the speeches of the deputies might with greater propriety be called the voice of the nation; but, on the other hand, this would occasion infinite delays; would give each deputy a power of controlling the assembly; and, on the most urgent and pressing occasions, the wheels of government might be stopped by the caprice of a single person. . . .

All the inhabitants of the several districts ought to have a right of voting at the election of a representative, except such as are in so mean a situation as to be deemed to have no will of their own. . . . The executive power ought to be in the hands of a monarch, because this branch of government, having need of dispatch, is better administered by one than by many: on the other hand, whatever depends on the legislative power is oftentimes better regulated by many than by a single person. But if there were no monarch, and the executive power should be committed to a certain number of persons selected from the legislative body, there would be an end then of liberty; by reason the two powers would be united, as the same persons would sometimes possess, and would be always able to possess, a share in both. . . .

C. ADAM SMITH'S "WEALTH OF NATIONS"

Adam Smith (1723–1790) was a Scot, who, having studied at Oxford and traveled on the Continent, returned to his native land to become a professor at Glasgow University. Though he occupied successively the chairs of logic and moral philosophy, he turned his mind for a time to contemporary economic problems, perhaps as a result of his contact with the French physiocrats abroad, and in 1776 he published *An Inquiry into the Nature and Causes of the Wealth of Nations.* The book won for Smith an immediate and enduring fame and established him as one of the outstanding thinkers of his time. As representative of the economic thought of the Enlightenment, portions of the *Wealth of Nations* follow. (6)

The property which every man has in his own labor, as it is the original foundation of all other property, so it is the most sacred and inviolable. The patrimony of a poor man lies in the strength and dexterity of his hands; and to hinder him from employing this strength and dexterity in what manner he thinks proper without injury to his neighbor is a plain violation of this most sacred property. It is a manifest encroachment upon the just liberty both of the workman and of those who might be disposed to employ him. As it hinders the one from working at what he thinks proper, so it hinders the other from employing whom they think proper. To judge whether he is fit to be employed may surely be trusted to the discretion of the employers whose interest it so much concerns. The affected anxiety of the law giver lest they should employ an improper person is evidently as impertinent as it is oppressive.

The institution of long apprenticeships can give no security that insufficient workmanship shall not frequently be exposed to public sale.

When this is done it is generally the effect of fraud, and not of inability; and the longest apprenticeship can give no security against fraud. Quite different regulations are necessary to prevent this abuse. The sterling mark upon plate, and the stamps upon linen and woolen cloth, give the purchaser much greater security than any statute of apprenticeship. He generally looks at these, but never thinks it worth while to inquire whether the workman had served a seven years' apprenticeship. . . .

People of the same trade seldom meet together, even for merriment and diversion, but the conversation ends in a conspiracy against the public or in some contrivance to raise prices. It is impossible indeed to prevent such meetings by any law which either could be executed or would be consistent with liberty and justice. But though the law cannot hinder people of the same trade from sometimes assembling together, it ought to do nothing to facilitate such assemblies, much less to render them necessary.

The pretense that corporations are necessary for the better government of the trade is without any foundation. The real and effectual discipline which is exercised over a workman is not that of his corporation, but that of his customers. It is the fear of losing their employment which restrains his frauds and corrects his negligence. An exclusive corporation necessarily weakens the force of this discipline. A particular set of workmen must then be employed, let them behave well or ill. . . .

Though anciently it was usual to rate wages, first by general laws extending over the whole kingdom, and afterwards by particular orders of the justices of peace in every particular county, both these practices have now gone entirely into disuse. "By the experience of above four hundred years," says Doctor Burn, "it seems time to lay aside all endeavors to bring under strict regulations, what in its own nature seems incapable of minute limitation; for if all persons in the same kind of work were to receive equal wages, there would be no emulation, and no room left for industry or ingenuity."

Particular acts of Parliament, however, still attempt sometimes to regulate wages in particular trades and in particular places. Thus the 8th [Act] of George III prohibits under heavy penalties all master tailors in London, and five miles round it, from giving, and their workmen from accepting, more than two shillings and seven pence halfpenny a day, except in the case of a general mourning. Whenever the legislature attempts to regulate the differences between masters and their workmen, its counselors are always the masters. When the regulation, therefore, is in favor of the workmen, it is always just and equitable; but it is sometimes otherwise when in favor of the masters. Thus the law which obliges the masters in several different trades to pay their workmen in money and not in goods is quite just and equitable. It imposes no real hardships upon the masters. It only obliges them to pay that value in money, which they pretended to pay, but did not always really pay, in goods. This law is in favor of the workmen; but the 8th of George III is in favor of the masters. When masters combine together in order to reduce the wages of their workmen, they commonly enter into a private bond or agreement not to give more than a certain wage under a certain penalty. Were the workmen to enter into a contrary combination of the same kind, not to accept of a certain wage under a certain penalty, the law would punish them very severely; and if it dealt impartially, it would treat the masters in the same manner. But the 8th of George III enforces by law that very regulation which masters sometimes attempt to establish by such combinations. The complaint of the workmen, that it puts the ablest and most industrious upon the same footing with an ordinary workman, seems perfectly well founded.

In ancient times, too, it was usual to attempt to regulate the profits of merchants and other dealers, by rating the price both of provisions and other goods. The assize of bread is, so far as I know, the only remnant of this ancient usage. Where there is an exclusive corporation, it may perhaps be proper to regulate the price of the first necessary of life. But where there is none, the competition will regulate it much better than any assize. . . .

Though the profusion of government must, undoubtedly, have retarded the natural progress of England toward wealth and improvement, it has not been able to stop it. . . . England . . . as it has never been blessed with a very parsimonious government, so parsimony has at no time been the characteristical virtue of its inhabitants. It is the highest impertinence and presumption, therefore, in kings and ministers, to pretend to watch over the economy of private people, and to restrain their expense either by sumptuary laws, or by prohibiting the importation of foreign luxuries. They are themselves always, and without any exception, the greatest spendthrifts in the society. Let them look well after their own expense, and they may safely trust private people with theirs. If their own extravagance does not ruin the state, that of their subjects never will. . . .

In some countries the interest of money has been prohibited by law. But as something can everywhere be made by the use of money, something ought everywhere to be paid for the use of it. This regulation, instead of preventing, has been found from experience to increase the evil of usury, the debtor being obliged to pay, not only for the use of the money, but for the risk which his creditor runs by accepting a compensation for that use. He is obliged, if one may say so, to insure his creditor, from the penalties of usury. . . .

The different progress of opulence in different ages and nations has given occasion to two different systems of political economy with regard to enriching the people. The one may be called a system of commerce, the other that of agriculture. I shall . . . begin with the system of commerce. It is the modern system, and is best understood in our own country and in our own times. . . .

This commercial or "mercantile" system is based on the false but popular notion that wealth consists in money, or in gold and silver. . . . Some of the best English writers upon commerce set out with observing that the wealth of a country consists, not in gold and silver only, but in its lands, houses, and consumable goods of all different kinds. In the course of their reasonings, however, the lands, houses, and consumable goods seem to slip out of their memory, and the strain of their argument frequently supposes that all wealth consists in gold and silver, and that to multiply those metals is the great object of national industry and commerce.

The two principles being established, however, that wealth consisted in gold and silver, and that those metals could be brought into a country which had no mines only by the balance of trade, or by the exporting to a greater value than it imported, it necessarily became the great object of political economy to diminish as much as possible the importation of foreign goods for home consumption, and to increase as much as possible the exportation of the produce of domestic industry. Its two great engines for enriching the country, therefore, were restraints upon importation, and encouragements to exportation. . . .

By restraining, either by high duties, or by absolute prohibitions, the importation of such goods from foreign countries as can be produced at home, the monopoly of the home market is more or less secured to the domestic industry employed in producing them. . . .

That this monopoly of the home market frequently gives great encouragement to that particular species of industry which enjoys it, and frequently turns toward that employment a greater share of the labor and stock of the society than would otherwise have gone into it, cannot be doubted. But whether it tends either to increase the general industry of the society, or to give it the most advantageous direction, is not, perhaps, altogether so evident.

The general industry of the society never can exceed what the capital of the society can employ. As the number of workmen that can be kept in employment by any particular person must bear a certain proportion to his capital, so the number of those who can be continually employed by all the members of a great society must bear a certain proportion to the whole capital of that society, and never can exceed that proportion. No regulation of commerce can increase the quantity of industry in any given society beyond what its capital can maintain. It can only divert a part of it into a direction into which it might not otherwise have gone; and it is by no means certain that this artificial direction is likely to be more advantageous to the society than that into which it would have gone of its own accord.

Every individual is continually exerting himself to find out the most advantageous employment for whatever capital he can command. It is his own advantage, indeed, and not that of the society, which he has in view. But the study of his own advantage, naturally, or rather necessarily, leads him to prefer that employment which is most advantageous to the society.

First, every individual endeavors to employ his capital as near home as he can, and consequently as much as he can in the support of domestic industry; provided always that he can thereby obtain the ordinary, or not a great deal less than the ordinary profits of stock. . . .

Secondly, every individual who employs his capital in the support of domestic industry, necessarily endeavors so to direct that industry that its produce may be of the greatest possible value.

The produce of industry is what it adds to the subject or materials upon which it is employed. In proportion as the value of this produce is great or small, so will likewise be the profits of the employer. But it is only for the sake of profit that any man employs a capital in the support of industry, and he will always, therefore, endeavor to employ it in the support of that industry of which the produce is likely to be of the greatest, or to exchange for the greatest quantity either of money or of other goods.

But the annual revenue of every society is always precisely equal to the exchangeable value of the whole annual produce of its industry, or rather is precisely the same thing with that exchangeable value. As every individual, therefore, endeavors as much as he can both to employ his capital in the support of domestic industry, and so to direct that industry that its produce may be of the greatest value; every individual necessarily labors to render the annual revenue of the society as great as he can. He generally, indeed, neither intends to promote the public interest, nor knows how much he is promoting it. By preferring the support of domestic to that of foreign industry, he intends only his own security; and by directing that industry in such a manner that its produce may be of the greatest value, he intends only his own gain, and he is in this, as in many other cases, led by an invisible hand to promote an end which was no part of his intention. Nor is it always the worse for the society that it was no part of it. By pursuing his own interest he frequently promotes that of the society more effectually than when he really intends to promote it. I have never known much good done by those who affected to trade for the public good. It is an affectation, indeed, not very common among merchants, and very few words need be employed in dissuading them from it.

What is the species of domestic industry which his capital can employ, and of which the produce is likely to be of the greatest value, every individual, it is evident, can, in his local situation, judge much better than any statesman or lawgiver can do for him. The statesman who should attempt to direct private people in what manner they ought to employ their capitals would not only load himself with a most unnecessary attention, but assume an authority which could safely be trusted, not only to no single person, but to no council or senate whatever, and which would nowhere be so dangerous as in the hands of a man who had folly and presumption enough to fancy himself fit to exercise it.

To give the monopoly of the home market to the produce of domestic industry, in any particular art or manufacture, is in some measure to direct private people in what manner they ought to employ their capitals, and must, in almost all cases, be either a useless or a hurtful regulation. If the produce of domestic can be brought there as cheap as that of foreign industry, the regulation is evidently useless. If it cannot, it must generally be hurtful. It is the maxim of every prudent master of a family never to make at home what it will cost him more to make than to buy. The tailor does not attempt to make his own shoes, but buys them of the shoemaker. The shoemaker does not attempt to make his own clothes, but employs a tailor. The farmer attempts to make neither the one nor the other, but employs those different artificers. All of them find it to their interest to employ their whole industry in a way in which they have some advantage over their neighbors, and to purchase with a part of its produce, or what is the same thing, with the price of a part of it, whatever else they have occasion for.

What is prudence in the conduct of every private family can scarce be folly in that of a great kingdom. If a foreign country can supply us with a commodity cheaper than we ourselves can make

it, better buy it of them with some part of the produce of our own industry employed in a way in which we have some advantage. The general industry of the country, being always in proportion to the capital which employs it, will not thereby be diminished, no more than that of the above-mentioned artificers; but only left to find out the way in which it can be employed with the greatest advantage. It is certainly not employed to the greatest advantage when it is thus directed toward an object which it can buy cheaper than it can make. The value of its annual produce is certainly more or less diminished when it is thus turned away from producing commodities evidently of more value than the commodity which it is directed to produce. According to the supposition, that commodity could be purchased from foreign countries cheaper than it can be made at home. It could, therefore, have been purchased with a part only of the commodities, or, what is the same thing, with a part only of the price of the commodities, which the industry employed by an equal capital would have produced at home, had it been left to follow its natural course. The industry of the country, therefore, is thus turned away from a more to a less advantageous employment, and the exchangeable value of its annual produce, instead of being increased, according to the intention of the lawgiver, must necessarily be diminished by every such regulation.

By means of such regulations, indeed, a particular manufacture may sometimes be acquired sooner than it could have been otherwise, and after a certain time may be made at home as cheap or cheaper than in the foreign country. But though the industry of the society may be thus carried with advantage into a particular channel sooner than it could have been otherwise, it will by no means follow that the sum total, either of its industry, or of its revenue, can ever be augmented by any such regulation. The industry of the society can augment only in proportion as its capital augments, and its capital can augment only in proportion to what can be gradually saved out of its revenue. But the immediate effect of every such regulation is to diminish its revenue, and what diminishes its revenue is certainly not very likely to augment its capital faster than it would have augmented of its own accord had both capital and industry been left to find out their natural employments.

Though for want of such regulations the society should never acquire the proposed manufacture, it would not, upon that account, necessarily be the poorer in any one period of its duration. In every period of its duration its whole capital and industry might still have been employed, though upon different objects, in the manner that was most advantageous at the time. In every period its revenue might have been the greatest which its capital could afford, and both capital and revenue might have been augmented with the greatest possible rapidity.

The natural advantages which one country has over another in producing particular commodities are sometimes so great that it is acknowledged by all the world to be in vain to struggle with them. By means of glasses, hotbeds, and hot walls, very good grapes can be raised in Scotland, and very good wine too can be made of them at about thirty times the expense for which at least equally good can be brought from foreign countries. Would it be a reasonable law to prohibit the importation of all foreign wines merely to encourage the making of claret and burgundy in Scotland? But if there would be a manifest absurdity in turning toward any employment thirty times more of the capital and industry of the country than would be necessary to purchase from foreign countries an equal quantity of the commodities wanted, there must be an absurdity, though not altogether so glaring, yet exactly of the same kind, in turning toward any such employment a thirtieth, or even a three-hundredth part more of either. Whether the advantages which one country has over another be natural or acquired is in this respect of no consequence. As long as the one country has those advantages, and the other wants them, it will always be more advantageous for the latter rather to buy of the former than to make. It is an acquired advantage only, which one artificer has over his neighbor, who exercises another trade; and yet they both find it more advantageous to buy of one another than to make what does not belong to their particular trades. . . .

There seem, however, to be two cases in which it will generally be advantageous to lay some burden upon foreign for the encouragement of domestic industry.

The first is, when some particular sort of industry is necessary for the defense of the country. The defense of Great Britain, for example, depends very much upon the number of its sailors and shipping. The Act of Navigation, therefore, very properly endeavors to give the sailors and shipping of Great Britain the monopoly of the trade of their own country, in some cases by absolute prohibitions and in others by heavy burdens upon the shipping of foreign countries. . . .

The second case, in which it will generally be advantageous to lay some burden upon foreign for the encouragement of domestic industry is, when some tax is imposed at home upon the produce of the latter. In this case, it seems reasonable that an equal tax should be imposed upon the like produce of the former. This would not give the monopoly of the home market to domestic industry, nor turn toward a particular employment a greater share of the stock and labor of the country than what would naturally go to it. It would only hinder any part of what would naturally go to it from being turned away by the tax into a less natural direction, and would leave the competition between foreign and domestic industry, after the tax, as nearly as possible upon the same footing as before it. In Great Britain, when any such tax is laid upon the products of domestic industry, it is usual at the same time, in order to stop the clamorous complaints of our merchants and manufacturers that they will be undersold at home, to lay a much heavier duty upon the importation of all foreign goods of the same kind. . . .

The case in which it may sometimes be a matter of deliberation how far it is proper to continue the free importation of certain foreign goods is, when some foreign nation restrains by high duties or prohibitions the importation of some of our manufactures into their country. Revenge in this case naturally dictates retaliation, and that we should impose the like duties and prohibitions upon the importation of some or all of their manufactures into ours. Nations, accordingly, seldom fail to retaliate in this manner. . . .

There may be good policy in retaliations of this kind, when there is a probability that they will secure the repeal of the high duties or prohibitions complained of. The recovery of a great foreign market will generally more than compensate the transitory inconvenience of paying dearer during a short time for some sorts of goods. To judge whether such retaliations are likely to produce such an effect does not, perhaps, belong so much to the science of a legislator, whose deliberations ought to be governed by general principles which are always the same, as to the skill of that insidious and crafty animal, vulgarly called a statesman or politician, whose councils are directed by the momentary fluctuations of affairs. When there is no probability that any such repeal can be procured, it seems a bad method of compensating the injury done to certain classes of our people to do another injury ourselves, not only to those classes, but to almost all the other classes of them. . . .

Every system which endeavors, either by extraordinary encouragements to draw toward a particular species of industry a greater share of the capital of the society than what would naturally go to it, or, by extraordinary restraint, force from a particular species of industry some share of the capital which would otherwise be employed in it, is in reality subversive of the great purpose which it means to promote. It retards, instead of accelerating, the progress of the society toward real wealth and greatness; and diminishes, instead of increasing, the real value of the annual produce of its land and labor.

All systems either of preference or restraint, therefore, being thus completely taken away, the obvious and simple system of natural liberty establishes itself of its own accord. Every man, as long as he does not violate the laws of justice, is left perfectly free to pursue his own interest his own way, and to bring both his industry and cap-

ital into competition with those of any other man, or order of men. The sovereign is completely discharged from a duty, in the attempting to perform which he must always be exposed to innumerable delusions, and for the proper performance of which no human wisdom or knowledge could ever be sufficient; the duty of superintending the industry of private people, and of directing it toward the employments most suitable to the interest of the society.

D. CONDORCET'S "PROGRESS OF THE HUMAN MIND"

The conviction of certainty which characterized the *philosophes* was matched only by their optimism. Their works radiated confidence in the future, and perhaps the finest example of their hopes is to be found in *An Outline of the Progress of the Human Mind* by Marie Jean Antoine Nicolas Caritat, Marquis de Condorcet (1743–94). Condorcet was one of the few *philosophes* who lived on into the French Revolution, and the work, of which a selection is printed below, was finished as he lay in prison under sentence of death in 1794. (7)

All the causes which contribute to the improvement of the human species, all the means we have enumerated that insure its progress, must, from their very nature, exercise an influence always active, and acquire an extent forever increasing. The proofs of this have been exhibited, and from their development in the work itself they will derive additional force: accordingly we may already conclude, that the perfectibility of man is indefinite. Meanwhile we have hitherto considered him as possessing only the same natural faculties, as endowed with the same organization. How much greater would be the certainty, how much wider the compass of our hopes, could we prove that these natural faculties themselves, that this very organization, are also susceptible of melioration? And this is the last question we shall examine.

The organic perfectibility or deterioration of the classes of the vegetable, or species of the animal kingdom, may be regarded as one of the general laws of nature.

This law extends itself to the human race; and it cannot be doubted that the progress of the sanative art [sanitation], that the use of more wholesome food and more comfortable habitations, that a mode of life which shall develop the physical powers by exercise, without at the same time impairing them by excess; in fine, that the destruction of the two most active causes of deterioration, penury and wretchedness on the one hand, and enormous wealth on the other, must necessarily tend to prolong the common duration of man's existence, and secure him a more constant health and a more robust constitution. It is manifest that the improvement of the practice of medicine, become more efficacious in consequence

of the progress of reason and the social order, must in the end put a period to transmissible or contagious disorders, as well to those general maladies resulting from climate, aliments, and the nature of certain occupations. Nor would it be difficult to prove that this hope might be extended to almost every other malady, of which it is probable we shall hereafter discover the most remote causes. Would it even be absurd to suppose this quality of melioration in the human species as susceptible of an indefinite advancement; to suppose that a period must one day arrive when death will be nothing more than the effect either of extraordinary accidents, or of the flow and gradual decay of the vital powers; and that the duration of the middle space, of the interval between the birth of man and this decay, will itself have no assignable limit? Certainly man will not become immortal; but may not the distance between the moment in which he draws his first breath and the common term when, in the course of nature, without malady, without accident, he finds it impossible any longer to exist, be necessarily protracted? As we are now speaking of a progress that is capable of being represented with precision, by numerical quantities or by lines, we shall embrace the opportunity of explaining the two meanings that may be affixed to the word *indefinite*.

In reality, this middle term of life, which in proportion as men advance upon the ocean of futurity, we have supposed incessantly to increase, may receive additions either in conformity to a law by which, though approaching continually an illimitable extent, it could never possibly arrive at it; or a law by which, in the immensity of ages, it may acquire a greater extent than any determinate quantity whatever that may be assigned as its limit. In the latter case, this duration of life is indefinite in the strictest sense of the word, since there exist no bounds on this side of which it must necessarily stop. And in the former, it is equally indefinite to us; if we cannot fix the term, it may forever approach, but can never surpass; particularly if, knowing only that it can never stop, we are ignorant in which of the two senses the term indefinite is applicable to it; and this is precisely the state of the knowledge we have as yet acquired relative to the perfectibility of the species.

Thus, in the instance we are considering, we are bound to believe that the mean duration of human life will forever increase, unless its increase be prevented by the physical revolutions of the system: but we cannot tell what is the bound which the duration of human life can never exceed; we cannot even tell, whether there be any circumstance in the laws of nature which has determined and laid down its limit.

But may not our physical faculties, the force, the sagacity, the acuteness of the senses, be numbered among the qualities, the individual improvement of which it will be practicable to transmit? An attention to the different breeds of domestic animals must lead us to adopt the affirmative of this question, and a direct observation of the human species itself will be found to strengthen the opinion.

Lastly, may we not include in the same circle the intellectual and moral faculties? May not our parents, who transmit to us the advantages or defects of their conformation, and from whom we receive our features and shape, as well as our propensities to certain physical affections, transmit to us also that part of organization upon which intellect, strength of understanding, energy of soul or moral sensibility depend? Is it not probable that education, by improving these qualities will at the same time have an influence upon, will modify and improve this organization itself? Analogy, an investigation of the human faculties, and even some facts, appear to authorize these conjectures, and thereby to enlarge the boundary of our hopes.

Such are the questions with which we shall terminate the last division of our work. And how admirably calculated is this view of the human race, emancipated from its chains, released alike from the dominion of chance, as well as from that of the enemies of its progress, and advancing with a firm and ineviate step in the paths of truth, to console the philosopher lamenting the errors, the flagrant acts of injustice, the crimes with which the earth is still polluted? It is the contemplation of this prospect that rewards him for all his efforts to assist the progress of reason and the establishment of liberty. He dares to regard these efforts as a part of the eternal chain of the destiny of mankind; and in this persuasion he finds the true delight of virtue, the pleasure of having performed a durable service, which no vicissitude will ever destroy in a fatal operation calculated to restore the reign of prejudice and slavery. This sentiment is the asylum into which he retires, and to which the memory of his persecutors cannot follow him: he unites himself in imagination with man restored to his rights, delivered from oppression, and proceeding with rapid strides in the path of happiness: he forgets his own misfortunes while his thoughts are thus employed; he lives no longer to adversity, calumny and malice, but becomes the associate of these wiser and more fortunate beings whose enviable condition he so earnestly contributed to produce.

E.   The Enlightenment Translated into Political Action

While the *philosophes* in Europe outlined and dreamed of social ideals, the thirteen British colonies in North America proclaimed their program of action in the Declaration of Independence, July 4, 1776. An examination of its opening lines, which follow, will show how much the new United States owed to the Enlightenment. (8)

When in the course of human events, it becomes necessary for one people to dissolve the political bands which have connected them with another, and to assume among the powers of the earth, the separate and equal station to which the laws of nature and of nature's God entitle them, a decent respect to the opinions of mankind requires that they should declare the causes which impel them to the separation.—We hold these truths to be self-evident, that all men are created equal, that they are endowed by their Creator with certain unalienable rights, that among these are life, liberty, and the pursuit of happiness—That to secure these rights, governments are instituted among men, deriving their just powers from the consent of the governed, —That whenever any form of government becomes destructive of these ends, it is the right of the people to alter or to abolish it, and to institute new government, laying its foundation on such principles and organizing its powers in such form, as to them shall seem most likely to effect their safety and happiness. Prudence, indeed, will dictate that governments long established should not be changed for light and transient causes; and accordingly all experience hath shewn, that mankind are more disposed to suffer, while evils are sufferable, than to right themselves by abolishing the forms to which they are accustomed. But when a long train of abuses and usurpations, pursuing invariably the same object evinces a design to reduce them under absolute despotism, it is their right, it is their duty, to throw off such government, and to provide new guards for their future security.—Such has been the patient sufferance of these colonies; and such is now the necessity which constrains them to alter their former systems of government. The history of the present king of Great Britain is a history of repeated injuries and usurpations, all having in direct object the establishment of an absolute tyranny over these states. To prove this, let facts be submitted to a candid world.

II

Liberal Reform in England

DURING these wars many very remarkable discoveries and inventions were made. Most memorable among these was the discovery (made by all the rich men in England at once) that women and children could work for 25 hours a day in factories without many of them dying or becoming excessively deformed. This was known as the Industrial Revelation and completely changed the faces of the north of England. . . . The new situation created by the Industrial Revelation was boldly met by the statesmen of the day with a wave of Acts, such as Tory Acts, Factory Acts, Satisfactory Acts and Unsatisfactory Acts. The most soothing of these enacted that children under 5 years of age who worked all day in factories should have meals (at night). This was a good thing, as it enabled them to work much faster.

1066 and All That

CONTENTS

QUESTIONS FOR STUDY

PART I

1. What was Malthus's method of argument? How did it differ from that of some earlier liberals?

2. What were the fundamental postulates in Malthus's thesis? Were they valid?

3. What argument does Malthus erect on his postulates?

4. What are the checks to population in Malthus's thesis?

5. What was the natural effect of the Malthusian "iron law of population" upon the development of liberal ideas?

6. Define Bentham's "principle of utility." Upon what fundamental assumption is it based?

7. How did Bentham define the "community"?

8. How did Bentham believe that the "principle of utility" should be applied to legislation in theory? How in practice?

9. How could a conflict arise between the application of the "principle of utility" in theory and in practice? Did Bentham observe the possibility of such a conflict?

10. Upon what principles did the merchants of London base their petition? Did they admit any exception to their principles?

PART II

11. How did the Poor Law Commission carry out its investigation?

12. What were the principles and recommendations set forth by the Poor Law Commission? What did they hope to achieve?

13. What evidence is there that the "new" Poor Law was "distinctively representative of both the content and method of philosophic radicalism"?

14. What did *The Struggle* lead its readers to believe would be the result of Corn Law repeal?

15. How did the National Anti-Corn Law League organize its campaign?

16. What were the arguments in favor of the Corn Laws? How were they met by Charles Villiers?

17. Why did Peel propose factory legislation in 1818? What were the arguments, then and subsequently, brought up in favor of factory legislation?

18. Why was there such strong opposition to the Factory Acts? Summarize the arguments of this opposition.

19. How did Lord Shaftesbury evaluate the achievements of factory legislation? What hope did he see for the future?

20. How did John Stuart Mill view liberal principles in 1873? How close was his thinking to that of Bentham?

The Age of Revolution, between 1775 and 1815, saw the liberal credo of the eighteenth century transformed from ideal to reality, a process which always exacts a price. "The "self-evident" truths of the *philosophes* provided the basis for the new regime in France, whose example was enough to found liberal and revolutionary parties throughout the rest of Europe. But the forces thus unleashed proved impossible to control, and the young republic was swept into inflation, civil war, and a fight for survival. In 1799 a temporary equilibrium was finally found in the military dictatorship of Napoleon Bonaparte. His efforts to impose a French imperium over Europe included the substitution of liberty for order and the perpetuation of the revolutionary doctrine of equality as a cloak for an authoritarian, centralized state. Thus the despots as well as the philosophers of the Ancien Regime found themselves vindicated by the French Revolution. And liberalism, while moving from the ivory tower to the ballot box, began to encounter some of the obstacles that blocked a fuller realization of its ideals.

On the Continent the Vienna settlement in 1815 represented a temporary triumph for the forces of conservatism and reaction. The monarchs and ministers had done their best to reproduce a facsimile of pre-1789 Europe, and the Quadruple Alliance was formed to perpetuate their achievement. Liberalism was driven underground, and by such means as the Carlsbad Decrees the Continental princes strove to suppress and eradicate liberal ideas. The full tide of revolutionary liberalism, first checked by popular disillusionment under Napoleon, was now reduced to a few subterranean trickles.

England also underwent a period of reaction. The unrest engendered by the postwar depression drove England's fearful statesmen to suspend *habeas corpus* in 1817 and to impose the Six Acts two years later. But the reaction here differed from that on the Continent. British statesmen feared revolution and strove to prevent it, but they did not intend to wipe out their traditional liberties. Parliament provided an arena of free speech. The English press, though heavily taxed and intermittently prosecuted, was allowed to grow as an instrument for the diffusion of ideas. Thus in England liberalism was not driven underground. The tradition which stemmed from Locke remained alive. Parliament, press, and platform gave room for its continued growth and development.

In the early years of the nineteenth century, therefore, England was of necessity the home of liberalism. She gave moral (and occasionally material) support to liberal movements abroad, and for their exiles she was a place of refuge. But even more important, her thinkers enlarged upon the liberal heritage and adapted it to the problems of their time, while propagandists and legislators endeavored to effect reforms which accorded with the new ideas. The growth of liberalism in England was consequently twofold: on the one hand, the continued development of ideas inherent in eighteenth-century liberalism; and on the other, the practical endeavor to convert liberal ideas into legislation for the governance of society.

In the first place, the growth of English liberalism was greatly influenced by the increasing impact of the Industrial Revolution upon British life. The development of the factory system, and with it the complexities of modern industrialism, created new social problems with which the liberal thinker felt obliged to wrestle. He turned his attention, therefore, chiefly to the immediate and pressing issues arising out of factory economy and urban society. In a word, his primary concerns were economic. His thinking, though conditioned by the works of all his predecessors, followed most closely the lines laid down by Adam Smith. The outstanding additions to liberal thought were made in the field of social and economic theory.

In the second place, the practical endeavor to achieve liberal reforms was greatly aided by the increasing sensitivity of government to popular opinion. Publication of parliamentary debates made legislators conscious of public reaction to their speeches and stirred a widespread interest in the affairs of government. After the Reform Act of 1832 the House of Commons reflected middle-class opinion very closely, and the new franchise became the springboard for a number of reforms. Liberal reformers employed numerous instruments of propaganda to manipulate opinion—petitions, the press, pamphlets, mass meetings. Many liberals found seats in Parliament where they could more directly affect the course of legislation, and many others took civil service posts or appointments to royal commissions where they exercised a profound influence upon the framing and execution of laws. The liberal, in brief, became more than a *philosophe:* he was a practical and cogent instrument for the effectuation of his ideas.

Thus, while reactionary repression temporarily stifled liberal growth on the Continent, England again took the lead in the development of liberalism. The purpose of this Problem is, therefore, to examine the new departure taken by English thinkers in the early years of the nineteenth century and to analyze the progress of English legislation—the most important development in this period of liberal evolution.

Part I.   PHILOSOPHIC RADICALISM

"Philosophic radicals" is the title given to a small group of English thinkers in the late eighteenth and early nineteenth centuries. Their approach was peculiarly English, for it combined a love of "clear and self-evident reasoning," as advocated by the French *philosophes,* with a strong native dislike for abstractions. The weight of their influence, as was later observed by John Stuart Mill, was derived from "the air of strong conviction with which they wrote when scarcely anyone else seemed to have an equally strong faith in as definite a creed; the boldness with which they tilted against the very front of both existing parties," Whig and Tory alike; and "their uncompromising profession of opposition of many of the generally received opinions."

A.   MALTHUS ON POPULATION

Thomas Robert Malthus (1766–1834) was a curate and professor in a college near London who reacted against the exuberant optimism and belief in the perfectibility of mankind which were characteristic of Condorcet and of such English supporters of the French Revolution as Thomas Paine and William Godwin. As an answer to this enthusiasm of the *philosophes* he published his *Essay on Population* in 1798. The sections quoted below illustrate the main reasons advanced by Malthus to contradict their optimism. (1)

The great and unlooked-for discoveries that have taken place of late years in natural philosophy; the increasing diffusion of general knowledge from the extension of the art of printing; the ardent and unshackled spirit of inquiry that prevails throughout the lettered, and even unlettered world; the new and extraordinary lights that have been thrown on political subjects, which dazzle and astonish the understanding; and particularly that tremendous phenomenon in the political horizon, the French Revolution, which, like a blazing comet, seems destined either to inspire with fresh life and vigor, or to scorch up and destroy the thinking inhabitants of the earth, have all concurred to lead able men into the opinion, that we were touching upon a period big with the most important changes, changes that would in some measure be decisive of the future fate of mankind.

It has been said that the great question is now at issue whether man shall henceforth start forwards with accelerated velocity toward illimitable and hitherto unconceived improvement; or be condemned to a perpetual oscillation between happiness and misery and after every effort remain still at an immeasurable distance from the wished-for goal.

Yet, anxiously as every friend of mankind must look forward to the termination of this painful suspense; and, eagerly as the inquiring mind would hail every ray of light that might assist its view into futurity, it is much to be lamented that the writers on each side of this momentous question still keep far aloof from each other. Their

mutual arguments do not meet with a candid examination. The question is not brought to rest on fewer points and even in theory scarcely seems to be approaching to a decision.

The advocate for the present order of things is apt to treat the sect of speculative philosophers either as a set of artful and designing knaves, who preach up ardent benevolence, and draw captivating pictures of a happier state of society, only the better to enable them to destroy the present establishments, and to forward their own deeplaid schemes of ambition, or, as wild and madheaded enthusiasts, whose silly speculations, and absurd paradoxes, are not worthy the attention of any reasonable man.

The advocate for the perfectibility of man, and of society, retorts on the defender of establishments a more than equal contempt. He brands him as the slave of the most miserable, and narrow prejudices; or, as the defender of the abuses of civil society, only because he profits by them. He paints him either as a character who prostitutes his understanding to his interest; or as one whose powers of mind are not of a size to grasp anything great and noble; who cannot see above five yards before him; and who must therefore be utterly unable to take in the views of the enlightened benefactor of mankind.

In this unamicable contest, the cause of truth cannot but suffer. The really good arguments on each side of the question are not allowed to have their proper weight. Each pursues his own theory, little solicitous to correct, or improve it, by an attention to what is advanced by his opponents.

The friend of the present order of things condemns all political speculations in the gross. He will not even condescend to examine the grounds from which the perfectibility of society is inferred. Much less will he give himself the trouble in a fair and candid manner to attempt an exposition of their fallacy.

The speculative philosopher equally offends against the cause of truth. With eyes fixed on a happier state of society, the blessings of which he paints in the most captivating colors, he allows himself to indulge in the most bitter invectives against every present establishment, without applying his talents to consider the best and safest means of removing abuses, and without seeming to be aware of the tremendous obstacles that threaten, even in theory, to oppose the progress of man toward perfections.

It is an acknowledged truth in philosophy that a just theory will always be confirmed by experiment. Yet so much friction, and so many minute circumstances occur in practice, which it is next to impossible for the most enlarged and penetrating mind to foresee, that on few subjects can any theory be pronounced just that has not stood the test of experience. But an untried theory cannot be advanced as probable, much less as just, till all the arguments against it have been maturely weighed and clearly and consistently confuted.

I have read some of the speculations on the perfectibility of man and of society with great pleasure. I have been warmed and delighted with the enchanting picture which they hold forth. I ardently wish for such happy improvements. But I see great and, to my understanding, unconquerable difficulties in the way to them. These difficulties it is my present purpose to state, declaring, at the same time, that so far from exulting in them, as a cause of triumphing over the friends of innovation, nothing would give me greater pleasure than to see them completely removed. . . .

In entering upon the argument I must premise that I put out of the question, at present, all mere conjectures; that is, all suppositions, the probable realization of which cannot be inferred upon any just philosophical grounds. A writer may tell me that he thinks man will ultimately become an ostrich. I cannot properly contradict him. But before he can expect to bring any reasonable person over to his opinion he ought to show that the necks of mankind have been gradually elongating; that the lips have grown harder and more prominent; that the legs and feet are daily altering their shape; and that the hair is beginning to change into stubs of feathers. And till the probability of so wonderful a conversion can be shown, it is surely lost time and lost eloquence to expatiate on the happiness of man in such a state; to describe his powers, both of running and flying; to paint him in a condition where all narrow luxuries would be condemned: where he would be employed, only in collecting the necessaries of life; and where, consequently, each man's share of labor would be light, and his portion of leisure ample.

I think I may fairly make two postulata.

First, That food is necessary to the existence of man.

Secondly, That the passion between the sexes is necessary, and will remain nearly in its present state.

These two laws, ever since we have had any knowledge of mankind, appear to have been fixed laws of our nature; and, as we have not hitherto seen any alteration in them, we have no right to conclude that they will ever cease to be what they are now, without an immediate act of power in that Being who first arranged the system of the universe, and for the advantage of His creatures, still executes, according to fixed laws, all its various operations.

I do not know that any writer has supposed that on this earth man will ultimately be able to live without food. But Mr. Godwin has conjectured that the passion between the sexes may in time be extinguished. As, however, he calls this part of his work a deviation into the land of conjecture, I will not dwell longer upon it at present than to say that the best arguments for the perfectibility of man are drawn from a contemplation of the great progress that he has already made from the savage state and the difficulty of saying where he is to stop. But toward the extinction of the passion between the sexes, no progress whatever has hitherto been made. It appears to exist in as much force at present as it did two thousand or four thousand years ago. There are individual exceptions now as there always have been. But as these exceptions do not appear to increase in number, it would surely be a very unphilosophical mode of arguing, to infer merely from the existence of an exception, that the exception would in time become the rule and the rule the exception.

Assuming, then, my postulata as granted, I say that the power of population is indefinitely greater than the power in the earth to produce subsistence for man.

Population, when unchecked, increases in a geometrical ratio. Subsistence only increases in an arithmetical ratio. A slight acquaintance with numbers will show the immensity of the first power in comparison of the second.

By that law of our nature which makes food necessary to the life of man, the effects of these two unequal powers must be kept equal.

This implies a strong and constantly operating

check on population from the difficulty of subsistence. This difficulty must fall somewhere and must necessarily be severely felt by a large portion of mankind.

Through the animal and vegetable kingdoms, nature has scattered the seeds of life abroad with the most profuse and liberal hand. She has been comparatively sparing in the room and the nourishment necessary to rear them. The germs of existence contained in this spot of earth, with ample food and ample room to expand it, would fill millions of worlds in the course of a few thousand years. Necessity, that imperious, all-pervading law of nature, restrains them within the prescribed bounds. The race of plants and the race of animals shrink under this great restrictive law. And the race of man cannot, by any efforts of reason, escape from it. Among plants and animals its effects are waste of seed, sickness, and premature death. Among mankind, misery and vice. The former, misery, is an absolutely necessary consequence of it. Vice is a highly probable consequence, and we therefore see it abundantly prevail; but it ought not, perhaps, to be called an absolutely necessary consequence. The ordeal of virtue is to resist all temptation to evil.

This natural inequality of the two powers of population and of production in the earth, and that great law of our nature which must constantly keep their effects equal, form the great difficulty that to me appears insurmountable in the way to perfectibility of society. All other arguments are of slight and subordinate consideration in comparison of this. I see no way by which man can escape from the weight of this law which pervades all animated nature. No fancied equality, no agrarian regulations in their utmost extent, could remove the pressure of it even for a single century. And it appears, therefore, to be decisive against the possible existence of a society, all the members of which should live in ease, happiness, and comparative leisure; and feel no anxiety about providing the means of subsistence for themselves and their families.

Consequently, if the premises are just, the argument is conclusive against the perfectibility of the mass of mankind.

I have thus sketched the general outline of the argument; but I will examine it more particularly; and I think it will be found that experience, the true source and foundation of all knowledge, invariably confirms its truth. . . .

The ultimate check to population appears then to be a want of food, arising necessarily from the different ratios according to which population and food increase. But this ultimate check is never the immediate check, except in cases of actual famine.

The immediate check may be stated to consist in all those customs, and all those diseases, which seem to be generated by a scarcity of the means of subsistence; and all those causes, independent of this scarcity, which tend prematurely to weaken and destroy the human frame.

These checks to population, which are constantly operating with more or less force in every society, and keep down the number to the level of the means of subsistence, may be classed under two general heads—the preventive and the positive checks.

The preventive check, as far as it is voluntary, is peculiar to man, and arises from that distinctive superiority in his reasoning faculties which enables him to calculate distant consequences. The checks to the indefinite increase of plants and irrational animals are all either positive, or, if preventive, involuntary. But man cannot look around him and see the distress which frequently presses upon those who have large families; he cannot contemplate his present possessions or earnings, which he now nearly consumes himself, and calculate the amount of each share, when with very little addition they must be divided, perhaps, among seven or eight, without feeling a doubt whether, if he follow the bent of his inclinations, he may be able to support the offspring which he will probably bring into the world. In a state of equality, if such can exist, this would be the simple question. In the present state of society other considerations occur. Will he now lower his rank in life, and be obliged to give up in great measure his former habits? Does any mode of employment present itself by which he may reasonably hope to maintain a family? Will he not at any rate subject himself to greater difficulties and more severe labor than in his single state? Will he not be unable to transmit to his children the same advantages of education and improvement that he had himself possessed? Does he even feel secure that, should he have a large family, his utmost exertions can save them from rags and squalid poverty and their consequent degradation in the community? And may he not be reduced to the grating necessity of forfeiting his independence and of being obliged to the sparing hand of charity for support?

The positive checks to population are extremely various, and include every cause, whether arising from vice or misery, which in any degree contributes to shorten the natural duration of human life. Under this head, therefore, may be enumerated all unwholesome occupations, severe labor and exposure to the seasons, extreme poverty, bad nursing of children, great towns, excesses of all kinds, the whole train of common diseases and epidemics, wars, plague, and famine.

On examining these obstacles to the increase of population which I have classed under the heads of preventive and positive checks, it will appear that they are all resolvable into moral restraint, vice, and misery.

Of the preventive checks, the restraint from marriage which is not followed by irregular gratifications may properly be termed moral restraint.

Promiscuous intercourse, unnatural passions, violations of the marriage bed, and improper arts to conceal the consequences of irregular connections, are preventive checks that clearly come under the head of vice.

Of the positive checks, those which appear to arise unavoidably from the laws of nature may be called exclusively misery; and those which we ob-

viously bring upon ourselves, such as wars, excesses, and many others which it would be in our power to avoid, are of a mixed nature. They are brought upon us by vice, and their consequences are misery. . . .

In every country some of these checks are, with more or less force, in constant operation; yet, notwithstanding their general prevalence, there are few states in which there is not a constant effort in the population to increase beyond the means of subsistence. This constant effort as constantly tends to subject the lower classes of society to distress and to prevent any great permanent melioration of their condition.

B. BENTHAM ON THE PRINCIPLE OF UTILITY

Jeremy Bentham (1748–1832) was the son of a wealthy London solicitor, whose private income made it possible for him to devote his long lifetime to a career of speculation and writing. He produced a prodigious volume of work, and one of his earliest books was *An Introduction to the Principles of Morals and Legislation,* privately printed in 1780 and published in 1789. The principles which Bentham laid down in this work were fundamental to all his thinking and exercised a profound influence upon that of his contemporaries. The following selection is from the first chapter of this work. (2)

I. Nature has placed mankind under the governance of two sovereign masters, *pain* and *pleasure*. It is for them alone to point out what we ought to do, as well as to determine what we shall do. On the one hand the standard of right and wrong, on the other the chain of causes and effects, are fastened to their throne. They govern us in all we do, in all we say, in all we think: every effort we can make to throw off our subjection, will serve but to demonstrate and confirm it. In words a man may pretend to abjure their empire, but in reality he will remain subject to it all the while. The *principle of utility* recognizes this subjection, and assumes it for the foundation of that system, the object of which is to rear the fabric of felicity by the hands of reason and of law. Systems which attempt to question it deal in sounds instead of sense, in caprice instead of reason, in darkness instead of light.

But enough of metaphor and declamation: it is not by such means that moral science is to be improved.

II. The principle of utility is the foundation of the present work: it will be proper therefore at the outset to give an explicit and determinate account of what is meant by it. By the principle of utility is meant that principle which approves or disapproves of every action whatsoever, according to the tendency which it appears to have to augment or diminish the happiness of the party whose interest is in question: or, what is the same thing in other words, to promote or to oppose that happiness. I say of every action whatso-

ever; and therefore not only of every action of a private individual, but of every measure of government.

III. By utility is meant that property in any object whereby it tends to produce benefit, advantage, pleasure, good, or happiness (all this in the present case comes to the same thing), or (what comes again to the same thing) to prevent the happening of mischief, pain, evil, or unhappiness to the party whose interest is considered: if that party be the community in general, then the happiness of the community; if a particular individual, then the happiness of that individual.

IV. The interest of the community is one of the most general expressions that can occur in the phraseology of morals: no wonder that the meaning of it is often lost. When it has a meaning, it is this. The community is a fictitious body, composed of the individual persons who are considered as constituting as it were its members. The interest of the community then is—what? The sum of the interests of the several members who compose it.

V. It is in vain to talk of the interest of the community without understanding what is the interest of the individual. A thing is said to promote the interest, or to be for the interest of an individual, when it tends to add to the sum total of his pleasures; or, what comes to the same thing, to diminish the sum total of his pains.

VI. An action then may be said to be conformable to the principle of utility, or, for shortness sake, to utility (meaning with respect to the community at large) , when the tendency it has to augment the happiness of the community is greater than any it has to diminish it.

VII. A measure of government (which is but a particular kind of action, performed by a particular person or persons) may be said to be conformable to or dictated by the principle of utility, when in like manner the tendency which it has to augment the happiness of the community is greater than any which it has to diminish it.

VIII. When an action, or in particular a measure of government, is supposed by a man to be conformable to the principle of utility, it may be convenient, for the purposes of discourse, to imagine a kind of law or dictate, called a law or dictate of utility; and to speak of the action in question as being conformable to such law or dictate.

IX. A man may be said to be a partisan of the principle of utility, when the approbation or disapprobation he annexes to any action, or to any measure, is determined by and proportioned to the tendency which he conceives it to have to augment or to diminish the happiness of the community; or in other words, to its conformity or unconformity to the laws or dictates of utility.

X. Of an action that is conformable to the principle of utility, one may always say either that it is one that ought to be done, or at least that it is not one that ought not to be done. One may say also that it is right it should be done—at least that it is not wrong it should be done; that it is a right action—at least that it is not a wrong action. When thus interpreted, the words *ought,* and *right* and *wrong,* and others of that stamp have a meaning: when otherwise, they have none.

XI. Has the rectitude of this principle been ever formally contested? It should seem that it

had, by those who have not known what they have been meaning. Is it susceptible of any direct proof? It should seem not; for that which is used to prove everything else cannot itself be proved: a chain of proofs must have their commencement somewhere. To give such proof is as impossible as it is needless.

XII. Not that there is or ever has been that human creature breathing, however stupid or perverse, who has not on many, perhaps on most occasions of his life, deferred to it. By the natural constitution of the human frame, on most occasions of their lives men in general embrace this principle, without thinking of it; if not for the ordering of their own actions, yet for the trying of their own actions, as well as of those of other men. There have been, at the same time, not many perhaps even of the most intelligent, who have been disposed to embrace it purely and without reserve. There are even few who have not taken some occasion or other to quarrel with it, either on account of their not understanding always how to apply it, or on account of some prejudice or other which they were afraid to examine into, or could not bear to part with. For such is the stuff that man is made of: in principle and in practice, in a right track and in a wrong one, the rarest of all human qualities is consistency.

XIII. When a man attempts to combat the principle of utility, it is with reasons drawn, without his being aware of it, from that very principle itself. His arguments, if they prove anything, prove not that the principle is *wrong,* but that according to the applications he supposes to be made of it, it is *misapplied.* Is it possible for a man to move the earth? Yes; but he must first find out another earth to stand upon.

C.   Bentham on Political Economy

Among Bentham's voluminous works was his *Manual of Political Economy,* which, though published only in part before his death, contained an incisive summary of the manner in which Bentham believed that his principle of utility should be applied. Bentham's manner of application, as set forth in this work, was typical of the philosophic radicals as a whole. Following is a selection from the opening chapter of the *Manual.* (3)

Political Economy is at once a science and an art. The value of the science has for its efficient cause and measure its subserviency to the art.

According to the principle of utility in every branch of the art of legislation, the object or end in view should be the production of the maximum of happiness in a given time in the community in question.

In the instance of this branch of the art, the object or end in view should be the production of that maximum of happiness, in so far as this

more general end is promoted by the production of the maximum of wealth and the maximum of population.

The practical questions, therefore, are—how far the measures respectively suggested by these two branches of the common end agree?—how far they differ, and which requires the preference?—how far the end in view is best promoted by individuals acting for themselves?—and in what cases these ends may be best promoted by the hands of government? . . .

With the view of causing an increase to take place in the mass of national wealth, or with a view to increase of the means either of subsistence or enjoyment, without some special reason, the general rule is, that nothing ought to be done or attempted by government. The motto, or watchword of government, on these occasions, ought to be—*Be quiet*.

For this quietism there are two main reasons:

1. Generally speaking, any interference for this purpose on the part of government is needless. The wealth of the whole community is composed of the wealth of the several individuals belonging to it taken together. But to increase his particular portion is, generally speaking, among the constant objects of each individual's exertions and care. Generally speaking, there is no one who knows what is for your interest so well as yourself—no one who is disposed with so much ardor and constancy to pursue it.

2. Generally speaking, it is moreover likely to be pernicious, viz., by being unconducive, or even obstructive, with reference to the attainment of the end in view. Each individual, bestowing more time and attention upon the means of preserving and increasing his portion of wealth than is or can be bestowed by government, is likely to take a more effectual course than what, in his instance and on his behalf, would be taken by government.

It is, moreover, universally and constantly pernicious in another way, by the restraint or constraint imposed on the free agency of the individual. Pain is the general concomitant of the sense of such restraint, wherever it is experienced. . . .

With few exceptions, and these not very considerable ones, the attainment of the maximum of enjoyment will be most effectually secured by leaving each individual to pursue his own maximum of enjoyment, in proportion as he is in possession of the means. Inclination in this respect will not be wanting on the part of anyone. Power, the species of power applicable to this case—viz., wealth, pecuniary power—could not be given by the hand of government to one without being taken from another; so that by such interference there would not be any gain of power upon the whole. . . .

We have seen above the grounds on which the general rule in this behalf—*Be quiet*—rests. Whatever measures, therefore, cannot be justified as exceptions to that rule, may be considered as *non agenda* on the part of government. The art, therefore, is reduced within a small compass: security and freedom are all that industry requires. The request which agriculture, manufactures, and commerce present to governments is modest and reasonable as that which Diogenes made to Alexander: "Stand out of my sunshine." We have no need of favor—we require only a secure and open path.

D.   The Petition of the Merchants of London

Thomas Tooke (1774–1858) was a noted economist whose doctrines followed closely those of the philosophic radicals. He was deeply interested in the problems relating to currency and prices and published several volumes on these subjects. In 1820 he was engaged by the merchants of London to draw up a petition to Parliament on their behalf. Its contents illustrate well the correspondence between liberal philosophy and the aims of an economic pressure group. (4)

That foreign commerce is eminently conducive to the wealth and prosperity of a country, by enabling it to import the commodities for the production of which the soil, climate, capital, and industry of other countries are best calculated, and to export in payment those articles for which its own situation is better adapted.

That freedom from restraint is calculated to give the utmost extension to foreign trade, and the best direction to the capital and industry of the country.

That the maxim of buying in the cheapest market and selling in the dearest, which regulates every merchant in his individual dealings is strictly applicable as the best rule for the trade of the whole nation.

That a policy founded on these principles would render the commerce of the world an interchange of mutual advantages, and diffuse an increase of wealth and enjoyments among the inhabitants of each state.

That, unfortunately, a policy the very reverse of this has been, and is, more or less, adopted and acted upon by the government of this and of every other country, each trying to exclude the productions of other countries, with the specious and well-meant design of encouraging its own productions; thus inflicting on the bulk of its subjects, who are consumers, the necessity of submitting to privations in the quantity or quality of commodities; and thus rendering what ought to be the source of mutual benefit and harmony among states, a constantly recurring occasion of jealousy and hostility.

That the prevailing prejudices in favor of the protective or restrictive system may be traced to the erroneous supposition that every importation of foreign commodities occasions a diminution of our own productions to the same extent; whereas it may be clearly shown that, although the particular description of production which could not stand against unrestrained foreign competition would be discouraged; yet, as no importation could be continued for any length of time without a corresponding exportation, direct or indirect, there would be an encouragement, for the purpose of that exportation, of some other production to which our situation might be better suited; thus affording at least an equal, and probably a greater, and certainly a more beneficial employment to our own capital and labor.

That, of the numerous protective and prohibitory duties of our commercial code, it may be proved, that, while all operate as a very heavy tax on the community at large, very few are of any ultimate benefit to the classes in whose favor they were originally instituted, and none to the extent of the loss occasioned by them to other classes.

That, among the other evils of the restrictive or protective system, not the least is that the artificial protection of one branch of industry, or source of protection against foreign competition, is set up as a ground of claim by other branches for similar protection; so that, if the reasoning upon which these restrictive or prohibitory regulations are founded were followed out consistently, it would not stop short of excluding us from all foreign commerce whatsoever; and the same train of argument, which with corresponding prohibitions and protective duties should exclude us from foreign trade, might be brought forward to justify the re-enactment of restrictions upon the interchange of productions (unconnected with public revenue) among the kingdoms composing the union, or among the counties of the same kingdom.

That an investigation of the effects of the restrictive system, at this time, is peculiarly called for, as it may, in the opinion of your petitioners, lead to a strong presumption that the distress which now so generally prevails is considerably aggravated by that system; and that some relief may be obtained by the earliest practicable removal of such of the restraints as may be shown to be the most injurious to the capital and industry of the community, and to be attended with no compensating benefit to the public revenue.

That a declaration against the anticommercial principles of our restrictive system is of the more importance at the present juncture, inasmuch as, in several instances of recent occurrence, the merchants and manufacturers in foreign states have assailed their respective governments with applications for further protective or prohibitory duties and regulations, urging the example and authority of this country against which they are almost exclusively directed, as a sanction for the policy of such measures. And certainly, if the reasoning upon which our restrictions have been defended is worth anything, it will apply in behalf of the regulations of foreign states against us. They insist upon our superiority in capital and machinery, as we do upon their comparative exemption from taxation, and with equal foundation.

That nothing would more tend to counteract the commercial hostility of foreign states than the adoption of a more enlightened and more conciliatory policy on the part of this country.

That although, as a matter of mere diplomacy, it may sometimes answer to hold out the removal of particular prohibitions of high duties, as depending upon corresponding concessions by other states in our favor, it does not follow that we should maintain our restrictions in cases where the desired concession on their part cannot be obtained. Our restrictions would not be the less prejudicial to our own capital and industry, because other governments persisted in preserving impolitic regulations.

That, upon the whole, the most liberal would prove to be the most politic course on such occasions.

That, independent of the direct benefit to be derived by this country on every occasion of such concession or relaxation, a great incidental object would be gained by the recognition of a sound principle or standard to which all subsequent arrangements might be referred, and by the salutary influence which a promulgation of such just views by the legislature, and by the nation at large, could not fail to have on the policy of other states.

That in thus declaring, as your petitioners do, their conviction of the impolicy and injustice of the restrictive system, and in desiring every practicable relaxation of it, they have in view only such parts of it as are not connected, or are only subordinately so, with the public revenue. As long as the necessity for the present amount of revenue subsists, your petitioners cannot expect so important a branch of it as the customs to be given up, nor to be materially diminished, unless some substitute, less objectionable, be suggested. But it is against every restrictive regulation of trade not essential to the revenue—against all duties merely protective from foreign competition—and against the excess of such duties as are partly for the purpose of revenue, and partly for that of protection—that the prayer of the present petition is respectfully submitted to the wisdom of Parliament.

Part II.   THE PROGRESS OF REFORM

Liberal pressure produced some tentative reforms before 1832, though most were carried out by administrative action. After the widening of the franchise in 1832 came an increasing number of legislative reforms, carried out by Parliament under heavy pressure from a public opinion strongly indoctrinated with liberal ideas. The documents in this section, therefore, are illustrative of liberalism in action. Three major objects of liberal legislation have been selected to show the new approach to social problems, the difficulties encountered, and, in conclusion, liberal estimates of their own achievements.

A.   THE "NEW" POOR LAW OF 1834

Since the days of Elizabeth the problem of state care for the pauper had been a continual object of legislation. The Industrial Revolution intensified the problem, and severe economic distress drove the Whig ministry of 1832 to seek some more effective means of relieving the poor. Accordingly a royal commission was appointed in that year to investigate the existing Poor Laws. Prominent on the commission were friends and followers of Jeremy Bentham, and after two years of intensive investigation the commission produced a voluminous report deeply impregnated with philosophic radicalism. The recommendations of the report were then converted entire into the "new" Poor Law of 1834, which remained the basis of all British pauper legislation until after the First World War. The report of the Poor Law Commission was thus the most complete and enduring specimen of philosophic radicalism in action, distinctively representative of both its content and its method. Selections from the report follow. (5)

We, the commissioners appointed by your Majesty to make a diligent and full inquiry into the practical operation of the laws for the relief of the poor in England and Wales, and into the manner in which these laws are administered, and to report our opinion whether any and what alterations, amendments, or improvements may be beneficially made in the said laws, or in the manner of administering them, and how the same may be best carried into effect,—humbly certify to your Majesty in manner following our proceedings in the execution of your Majesty's commission, and the opinions which they have led us to form. . . .

It appears from this narrative, that the magnitude of the evidence has been the great difficulty with which we have had to struggle. But we believe, on the other hand, that that very magnitude gives the principal value to our inquiry. All evidence is necessarily subject to error, from the ignorance, forgetfulness, or misrepresentation of the witnesses, and necessarily tinged by their opinions and prejudices. But in proportion as the number of witnesses is increased, these sources of error have a tendency to compensate one another, and general results are afforded more to be depended upon than the testimony of a few witnesses, however unexceptionable. The evidence contained in our appendix comes from every county and almost every town, and from a very large proportion of even the villages in England. It is derived from many thousand witnesses, of every rank and of every profession and employment, members of the two houses of Parliament, clergymen, country gentlemen, magistrates, farmers, manufacturers, shopkeepers, artisans, and peasants, differing in every conceivable degree in education, habits, and interests, and agreeing only in their practical experience as to the matters in question, in their general description both of the mode in which the laws for the relief of the poor are administered, and of the consequences which have already resulted from that administration, and in their anticipation of certain further consequences from its continuance. The amendment of those laws is, perhaps, the most urgent and the most important measure now remaining for the consideration of Parliament; and we trust that we shall facilitate that amendment by tendering to your Majesty the most extensive, and at the same time the most consistent, body of evidence that was ever brought to bear on a single subject. . . .

The most pressing of the evils which we have described are those connected with the relief of the able-bodied. They are the evils, therefore, for which we shall first propose remedies. . . .

In all extensive communities, circumstances will occur in which an individual, by the failure of his means of subsistence, will be exposed to the danger of perishing. To refuse relief, and at the same time to punish mendicity when it cannot be proved that the offender could have obtained subsistence by labor, is repugnant to the common sentiments of mankind; it is repugnant to them to punish even depredation, apparently committed as the only resource against want.

In all extensive civilized communities, therefore, the occurrence of extreme necessity is prevented by almsgiving, by public institutions supported by endowments or voluntary contributions, or by a provision partly voluntary and partly compulsory, or by a provision entirely compulsory, which may exclude the pretext of mendicancy.

But in no part of Europe except England has it been thought fit that the provision, whether compulsory or voluntary, should be applied to more than the relief of indigence, the state of a person unable to labor, or unable to obtain, in return for his labor, the means of subsistence. It has never been deemed expedient that the provision should extend to the relief of poverty; that is, the state of one, who in order to obtain a mere subsistence, is forced to have recourse to labor.

From the evidence collected under this Commission, we are induced to believe that a compulsory provision for the relief of the indigent can be generally administered on a sound and well-defined principle; and that under the operation of this principle, the assurance that no one need perish from want may be rendered more complete than at present, and the mendicant and vagrant repressed by disarming them of their weapon, the plea of impending starvation.

It may be assumed, that in the administration of relief, the public is warranted in imposing such conditions on the individual relieved as are conducive to the benefit either of the individual himself or of the country at large, at whose expense he is to be relieved.

The first and most essential of all conditions, a principle which we find universally admitted, even by those whose practice is at variance with it, is, that his situation on the whole shall not be made really or apparently so eligible as the situation of the independent laborer of the lowest class. Throughout the evidence it is shown, that in proportion as the condition of any pauper class is elevated above the condition of independent laborers, the condition of the independent class is depressed; their industry is impaired, their employment becomes unsteady, and its remuneration in wages is diminished. Such persons, therefore, are under the strongest inducements to quit the less eligible class of laborers and enter the more eligible class of paupers. The converse is the effect when the pauper class is placed in its proper position, below the condition of the independent laborer. Every penny bestowed that tends to render the condition of the pauper more

eligible than that of the independent laborer is a bounty on indolence and vice. We have found, that as the poor's rates are at present administered, they operate as bounties of this description, to the amount of several millions annually. . . .

In all the instances which we have met with, where parishes have been dispauperized, the effect appears to have been produced by the practical application of the principle which we have set forth as the main principle of a good Poor Law administration, namely, the restoration of the pauper to a position below that of the independent laborer.

The principle adopted in the parish of Cookham, Berks, is thus stated: "As regards the able-bodied laborers who apply for relief, giving them hard work at low wages by the piece, and exacting more work at a lower price than is paid for any other labor in the parish. In short, to adopt the maxim of Mr. Whately, to let the laborer find that the parish is the hardest taskmaster and the worst paymaster he can find, and thus induce him to make his application to the parish his last and not his first resource.". . .

From the above evidence, it appears, that wherever the principle which we have thus stated has been carried into effect either wholly or partially, its introduction has been beneficial to the class for whose benefit Poor Laws exist. We have seen that in every instance in which the able-bodied laborers have been rendered independent of partial relief, or of relief otherwise than in a well-regulated workhouse—

1. Their industry has been restored and improved.
2. Frugal habits have been created or strengthened.
3. The permanent demand for their labor has increased.
4. And the increase has been such, that their wages, so far from being depressed by the increased amount of labor in the market, have in general advanced.
5. The number of improvident and wretched marriages has diminished.
6. Their discontent has been abated, and their moral and social condition in every way improved.

Results so important would, even with a view to the interest of that class exclusively, afford sufficient ground for the general introduction of the principle of administration under which those results have been produced. Considering the extensive benefits to be anticipated from the adoption of measures founded on principles already tried and found beneficial, and warned at every part of the inquiry by the failure of previous legislation, we shall, in the suggestion of specific remedies, endeavor not to depart from the firm ground of actual experience.

We therefore submit, as the general principle of legislation on this subject, in the present condition of the country:

That those modes of administering relief which have been tried wholly or partially, and have produced beneficial effects in some districts, be introduced, with modifications according to local circumstances, and carried into complete execution in all.

The chief specific measures which we recommend for effecting these purposes, are—

First, that except as to medical attendance, and subject to the exception respecting apprenticeship hereinafter stated, all relief whatever to able-bodied persons or to their families, otherwise than in well-regulated workhouses (*i.e.,* places where they may be set to work according to the spirit and intention of the 43d of Elizabeth) shall be declared unlawful, and shall cease, in manner and at periods hereafter specified; and that all relief afforded in respect of children under the age of 16 shall be considered as afforded to their parents. . . .

[Second] we recommend . . . the appointment of a central board to control the administration of the Poor Laws, with such assistant commissioners as may be found requisite; and that the commissioners be empowered and directed to frame and enforce regulations for the government of workhouses, and as to the nature and amount of the relief to be given, and the labor to be exacted in them, and that such regulations shall, as far as may be practicable, be uniform throughout the country. . . .

[Third] to effect these purposes we recommend that the central board be empowered to cause any number of parishes which they may think convenient to be incorporated for the purpose of workhouse management, and for providing new workhouses where necessary, to declare their workhouses to be the common workhouses of the incorporated district, and to assign to those workhouses separate classes of poor, though composed of the poor of distinct parishes, each distinct parish paying to the support of the permanent workhouse establishment, in proportion to the average amount of the expense incurred for the relief of its poor, for the three previous years, and paying separately for the food and clothing of its own paupers. . . .

[Seventh] we recommend, that the central board be empowered to direct the parochial consumption in the workhouse to be supplied by tender and contract, and to provide that the competition be perfectly free. . . .

[Ninth] we . . . recommend, that under regulations to be framed by the central board, parishes be empowered to treat any relief afforded to the able-bodied or to their families, and any expenditure in the workhouses or otherwise incurred on their account, as a loan, and recoverable not only by the means given by the 29th section of the 59 Geo. III. c. 12, but also by attachment of their subsequent wages, in a mode resembling that pointed out in the 30th, 31st, and 32d sections of that Act. . . .

[Twenty-second] we recommend . . . that the vestry of each parish be empowered to order the payment, out of the rates raised for the relief of the poor, of the expenses of the emigration of any persons having settlements within such parish, who may be willing to emigrate; provided, that the expense of each emigration be raised and paid, within a period to be mentioned in the Act. . . .

We have now recommended to your Majesty the measures by which we hope that the enormous evils resulting from the present maladministration of the Poor Laws, may be gradually remedied. It will be observed, that the measures which we have suggested are intended to produce rather negative than positive effects; rather to remove the debasing influences to which a large portion of the laboring population is now subject, than to afford new means of prosperity and virtue. We are perfectly aware, that for the general diffusion of right principles and habits we are to look not so much to any economic arrangements and regulations as to the influence of a moral and religious education; and important evidence on the subject will be found throughout our appendix. But one great advantage of any measure which shall remove or diminish the evils of the present system is, that it will in the same degree remove the obstacles which now impede the progress of instruction, and intercept its results; and will afford a freer scope to the operation of every instrument which may be employed for elevating the intellectual and moral condition of the poorer classes.

We believe, that if the funds now destined to the purposes of education, many of which are applied in a manner unsuited to the present wants of society, were wisely and economically employed, they would be sufficient to give all the assistance which can be prudently afforded by the state. As the subject is not within our Commission, we will not dwell on it further, and we have ventured on these few remarks only for the purpose of recording our conviction, that as soon as a good administration of the Poor Laws shall have rendered further improvement possible, the most important duty of the legislature is to take measures to promote the religious and moral education of the laboring classes.

B.   THE REPEAL OF THE CORN LAWS, 1846

> By the nineteenth century England had long had laws which regulated the importation of grain. After Waterloo these laws were frequently amended in the interests of the great landowners to keep up the price of grain and land rents. The liberal attitude to such legislation was clearly set forth in the petition of the merchants of London in 1820, and, as the century progressed, the assault upon the Corn Laws (as they were called) grew into a crushing frontal onslaught. Finally in 1846 Prime Minister Peel reluctantly carried their repeal, a milestone in the progress of liberal legislation.

1. *An Argument for Repeal, 1842.* Among the many instruments of propaganda against the Corn Laws was a little journal entitled *The Struggle,* founded in 1842 to render aid in "the great struggle between Free Trade and Monopoly." Following is the leading article in its first issue. (6)

What Shall We Gain by Free Trade and the Repeal of the Corn Laws?

1. Beef, bread, butter, cheese, milk, fruit, and all kinds of eatables will be about one third less in price than at present. In addition to the stock grown in this country, we should bring shiploads of wheat, barrel flour, butter, cheese, and cattle of all kinds, from other countries; and there would be an abundance in the land both for man and beast. Would not this be a great blessing to thousands of poor families, who cannot now get a bellyful of meat?

2. We should have a great revival of our foreign trade. If we take their provisions, they will take our cottons, linens, woolens, iron goods, earthenware, etc. Masters being then able to exchange their goods, they would employ more hands, and be compelled to keep up wages in order to extend their trade, and get profit to themselves.

3. With a good foreign trade, the people would get employment, and have money to trade with each other. Instead of everything being at a stand, as at present, shoes, hats, clothes, furniture, bedding, books, and a great number of useful articles, would be wanted, and the home trade would be sure to flourish. The retail shops, which are now without customers, would then have plenty to do.

4. The repeal of the Corn Laws would lessen the amount of poor rates. The food of the workhouse people would cost one third less; and the number of outdoor paupers would be greatly diminished. Cheap food and good trade would deprive the new Poor Law of its horrors; for ablebodied men would then be able to rely upon their own resources.

5. It would give us access to the markets of the whole world. The working man could then sell his labor and buy his food at the best market. At present he is compelled to buy dear and sell cheap, and the landowners get all the benefit of the restriction.

6. Working men would then be better able to stand against the competition of machinery. The iron man's meat and drink—his coal and water— are untaxed; they are as cheap as nature can give them: but the meat and drink of the flesh and blood man are taxed 40 percent. Food, air, and water, the three essential articles of life, should be as plentiful as the God of nature intended them.

7. The British artisan would also stand upon fair terms with the foreigner. The labor of both has to be sold in the same market. Unless he gets his food as cheap as others, he cannot expect to derive the advantages of his superior industry.

8. A free trade in corn would prevent those fluctuations in the currency which are occasioned by vast quantities of gold being taken to pay for corn in cases of emergency. Our corn would then be paid for in manufactured goods, and the gold would be kept at home, to enable our manufacturers to extend their trade.

9. It would destroy land monopoly, and place the manufacturing interest on an equal footing with the agricultural. The landowner would be compelled to serve the people with food as cheap as the foreigner, and also to give a fair market price in return for the goods of his manufacturing neighbor.

10. It would produce real prosperity to farmers. High prices only lead to high rents, and eventually ruin this useful class. Rents and taxes would be reduced; their own living, and the food of their whole establishments, would be very much cheaper; and their sons, instead of remaining on the sod competing against each other, would be induced to embark in trade.

11. The agricultural laborer would then get his belly full of good meat. He would then be able to break up a bit of land for himself, and where they are too numerous, instead of being tied to the land, and remaining to depress wages, they would have a choice of engaging either in agricultural labor or manufacturing employment.

12. The land would be freed from the deteriorating influence of monopoly. Instead of absentees, we should have the owners of the soil, like other capitalists, remaining at home improving

their property. At present they are raised above the necessity of this, by the extravagant rents which the Corn Laws enable them to demand.

13. By thus establishing a beneficial exchange, we should fast recruit our national resources, and hence be better able to bear the heavy burden of our national taxation. It is trade that has sustained the national credit; and it is only by freeing it from its shackles, that this country can continue to pay the expense of government and the national debt.

14. Plenty of work and plenty of food would be the result of a repeal, and these would stamp the forced emigration of the people as a cold-hearted scheme for perpetuating injustice.

15. Free trade is the greatest guarantee for the peace of nations. Retaliation follows restriction; but a mutual and commercial intercourse throughout the world would be the likeliest of all other means for removing or modifying embarrassing and prohibitory tariffs, and putting an end to war and bloodshed.

16. In a word, the opening of our ports for all kinds of foreign food would be like two harvests in the year, feeding the hungry, clothing the naked, removing poverty, driving away disease and premature death. It would give life and energy to the nation, now tottering on the verge of ruin. Thousands of artisans, now walking the streets for want of work, or begging a scanty share at the overseer's office, would then find employment, and regain their standing in society. The poor might milk their own cow and feed their own pig. Relieved from the absorbing care of scampering for every ensuing meal, the parents would have time and means to pay attention to the morals of their children, and provide for the education of their own offspring. Drooping sick clubs, deserted schools, and defunct institutions would again revive, and a loyal attachment to the land of our birth, would succeed to the strong feeling of resentment and disaffection now extensively cherished in the breasts of an impoverished and injured people.

2. *The National Anti-Corn Law League*. This organization was founded in 1839 by the Manchester Chamber of Commerce under the leadership of the liberal industrialist, Richard Cobden (1804–65). In 1843 it commenced publication of a paper called *The League,* which explained its policy in its first number, from which the following selection is taken. (7)

We propose to continue the distribution of publications upon the Corn Laws amongst the possessors of the franchise, until every elector, in every borough and county throughout the kingdom, is supplied with the materials for forming a deliberate, enlightened, and sound opinion on the subject. It shall not be our fault if a single vote, in any district whatever, be given ignorantly; and, when it is made quite apparent how much even the poorest are plundered by the existing laws, the chances will be greatly increased against votes being given corruptly. Even the unprincipled voter may be induced to count the cost; and, balancing the exactions of monopoly against the temptations of the bribe or the threatened injuries of sinister influence, may discover that, in the use of the franchise as in other things, honesty is the best policy. . . .

Publications will also continue to be distributed, and lectures encouraged, as extensively as possible amongst all classes of society, without reference to the division into electoral and nonelectoral. We keep the former class distinctly in view, because its privilege enables it, on the first emergency, to decide the great question at issue. The franchise constitutes its possessors a national jury for the trial of the Corn Laws. We submit to its consideration, specifically, the evidence for its verdict. Our appeal, however, is not to power, but to opinion. We trust for success to the action of opinion upon power; and the elements of opinion are in the universal intelligence of the country. For the practical establishment of free trade principles, the privilege of thought is above the privilege of voting. We ask attention, and seek the cooperation of every rational being. Electors cannot be isolated in darkness when the light of knowledge streams over the land. We seek a universal condemnation of monopoly. Let all voices be raised in its reprobation. The reaction upon privilege will be a substitute for direct political power. The course of elections has often been influenced by the interference of the wealthy or the titled, by local or party objects, and by factious or sordid considerations; and it cannot be inaccessible to the common sense of the country, its manifest interests, and its enlightened determination.

Our efforts will, therefore, be directed to harmonize the results of the next election with the industrial rights; the matured opinions, and the well-being and prospects of the entire community. This can only be achieved through the intelligence, the sympathy, and the voluntary agency of the electors. For efficiently embodying their cooperation, the following means are contemplated, as the principle:

1. Copies will be obtained of the registration lists of all boroughs and counties throughout the kingdom, and the collection lodged at the metropolitan office of the League, as a central place of deposit, to be consulted as occasion may require.

2. An extensive correspondence, by means of the post, and of stamped publications, will be

kept up with electors, in all districts, upon matters connected with the progress and success of our cause.

3. It is intended that every borough in the kingdom shall be visited by deputations of the League, and meetings held, which the electors will be specially invited to attend.

4. Prompt measures will be taken to ascertain the opinions of each elector, in every borough, with the view of obtaining an obvious and decided majority in favor of the total and immediate repeal of the Corn Laws.

5. Every constituency, whose representatives have not hitherto supported Mr. Villiers' motion for the repeal of the Corn Laws, will be invited to memorialize its members to vote for such motion when next brought forward.

6. Whenever a vacancy occurs in the representation of any borough, the electors will be recommended to put a free-trade candidate in nomination; and the League pledges itself to give such candidate every possible support, by deputations, lectures, and the distribution of publications.

7. In the event of any borough being unable to procure a suitable candidate, the League pledges itself to bring forward candidates, so as to afford every elector an opportunity of recording his vote in favor of free trade, until the question be decided.

3. *An Argument against Repeal, 1843.* The agriculturalists fought back with the same weapons. Following is a selection from a pamphlet written in 1843 entitled "An Address to the Farmers and Laborers of the North of Devon; with Observations on the Speeches of the Itinerant Agents of the Corn Law League, . . . Exposing Some of the Mischievous Results to Society . . . Should the Pernicious Schemes of These Monopolizing Agitators Be Carried into Effect." (8)

My friends and fellow countrymen, I have waited some time in the hope that an abler pen would expose to your view, some of the monstrous fallacies, and ridiculous assertions, which are contained in these mischievous publications; when taken in connection with the hackneyed speeches which have been recently delivered by the paid emissaries of the Anti-Corn Law League: I am at a loss, whether most to wonder at the misstatements and deceptive arguments which have been studiously written to deceive the ignorant and the unwary; or, at the monstrous effrontery of orators, who are employed to excite discontent, by working on the passions, and on the poverty of a distressed people. It is therefore with great satisfaction that I reflect on having used my best exertions to procure your signatures in support of the Corn Laws, which secure constant employment and bread to the laboring poor of this district; and although with a view to self-interest, I might prefer to see land more generally used for the depasturing and grazing of cattle as affording in many instances a more secure protection to the landlord against the deterioration of the soil, by the nonapplication of lime and manure, sufficient to protect the land in the growth of corn crops; a larger, a more easily collected, and a more certain return of rent; with a diminished outlay for the employment of laborers; yet, I do rejoice, that the Corn Laws which promote the chief manufacture of the north of Devon are maintained; and as our opponents well know, will continue to be maintained by our present enlightened legislature, as the best means of raising, and protecting, an honest, a numerous, and a hardy race of peasantry; at the same time, that they act as a needful stimulant to the further extension and improvement of our agricultural resources; and afford us the chief means we possess, to exchange our agricultural labor with that of the manufacturing districts. That the abolition of the Corn Laws and the free importation of foreign corn, would, therefore, by lowering the value of our home grown corn, as compared with the value of cotton, and other highly protected goods of our home manufacture, admirably suit the interests of the subscribers to the Anti-Corn Law League, cannot be doubted.

The deceptive circular which has lately been placed in your hands has not the candor to state the immense benefits which the members of the League in common with the whole trading portion of the community derive by the imposition of heavy protecting duties on all imported articles of foreign manufacture. These duties protect the manufacturing and trading interests of England from the effects of foreign competition, and materially help to raise a considerable part of the national revenue, but they are most severely felt by the landed interest who are not only taxed for the benefit of the state, but, for the benefit of the home manufacturers, are by these means, compelled to purchase, relatively, higher priced goods of home manufacture; which are frequently acknowledged to be of much inferior quality to foreign productions of the same nature. The Anti-Corn Law League is supported by certain eccentric, or ambitious individuals, some of whom may be found in every country, always wrong-headed enough to be chosen as leaders on such occasions; by a remnant of the disappointed Whig Party, who imagine a repeal of the Corn Laws would promote their return to power; and by a few landed proprietors in the neighborhood of large manufacturing towns. It comprises the cotton lords; and certain other manufacturers on a large scale for the foreign market; political agitators and speculators of various ranks and degrees; a portion of the public press; much of which has been hired for the occasion; the ignorant, and the unwary, who have been duped into the belief that the repeal of the Corn Laws would promote their benefit; and lastly, the ruined and the dissatisfied of all classes who are unfortunately to be found in every country "ready for any change and ripe for every tumult."

These promoters of this nefarious scheme, regardless of your ruin, would, by the importation of foreign corn, become the monopolists of the home markets. All profits attendant on exchange, and on the home trade, would pass through their hands; and to a great extent would be monopolized by them. If we repeal the Corn Laws in like manner, as we have repealed the cattle and timber duties, a fearful agricultural panic will ensue. Agricultural laborers would have to compete with the slavish serfs of Poland, Germany, and northern Europe, who earn from 4d. to 6d. per day, or they must be discharged by their employers; farming, becoming unremunerative in this district, will be neglected; and these schemers will become our masters in every sense of the word; as we shall have freely surrendered to them the sources of our wealth and independence. In return for this suicidal folly, they will speedily show their true colors, and must necessarily prove themselves the most obdurate taskmasters, after having reduced the value of English labor to the standard of the labor of comparatively untaxed foreign countries, which would be effected through the malignant agency of what would be miscalled free trade. . . .

Protection to native agriculture, or corn laws, exists in every country in Europe: in the United States they give protection to the extent of 25 percent on the importation of foreign food. In this country, the deficiency of bread-corn, sufficient to supply the wants of the entire population has amounted on an average of many years, to less than one-twentieth part. The soil of Great Britain and Ireland, contains about 58,000,000 of acres of land, 8,000,000 of acres (the half of which, may be found in Scotland,) is thought to be barren land, but the remaining portion or 50,000,000 of acres of land, by draining and better management is very improvable. The entire population of the United Kingdom may at this period amount to 27,000,000; let sufficient encouragement be given to our agriculture, and we shall easily add one third to or even double the present quantity of our produce, which will afford us a supply of food to so many millions more of inhabitants than the country at present contains; and will enable us, securely to provide sustenance for the annual increase of 200,000 to the population, for very many years to come; but for the

sake of argument, let us suppose, we may for some years to come, import the quantity of food, anticipated by our political theorists, in accordance with their favorite political doctrines, there is not perhaps a truer axiom than this, that "the population of any country will, at least keep pace with any increased quantity of food to be obtained in that country." Our population therefore instead of increasing at the rate of 200,000 yearly as stated by Mr. Grigg; or at the rate of 400,000 yearly as stated by another Anti-Corn-Law writer (The Rev. Baptist Noel) may annually extend to one, or even 2,000,000 or more! A time must come when these corn-growing districts (wherever situated) will become populous in proportion to the extent and fertility of their territory, or their corn produce will be equally sought for by other overpopulous manufacturing nations. Whenever this shall happen (without the intervention of war) we shall find it more difficult and precarious to procure our accustomed and needful supplies of food from them, and the English nation will be unnaturally extended into an immense famishing population, receiving less and less value in exchange for their labor from foreign parts, and grown out of all proportion to the amount of sustenance which can be derived from their native soil.

It has been asserted by the A.C.L.L. that we can always obtain foreign supplies of corn even from those countries with which we may be at war, and to prove their assertion they state that corn was imported into England from France, during the war, contrary to the command of the Emperor Napoleon. This argument does not form any precedent at the present day, as steam vessels would now easily prevent any intercourse or importation of any kind. Do we not prevent the importation of brandies, of silks, of tobacco, and of numerous other articles, although the duties are high, and consequently the temptation to the smuggler is excessive? How would corn, being one of the most bulky articles of exportation, escape the vigilance of the foreign coast guard? British shipping would not gain much by a free trade in corn, as it would not be exclusively employed to convey the imported amount of grain, which would be principally brought in the foreign trading vessels of the countries, which may produce it. Our shipping has suffered severely in the cause of free trade; by the reciprocity acts of Mr. Huskisson, and by the recent commercial treaties entered into with Russia, which have conceded to that power, the free admission of her vessels into our ports. In times of scarcity, we have lately seen foreign countries refuse to allow their corn to be exported; even Russia has of late years prohibited the exportation of grain from her shores; and in time of need we cannot depend upon that, or upon any other country, for our supplies of food as unfortunately, when the wheat crops have been injured by inclement seasons; and are deficient in one part of Europe (from the circumstance of the wheat crops only growing within certain parallels of latitude) they are also injuriously acted on by the same prevailing causes; and the same deficiency of crop is observed to prevail throughout the whole of the corn-growing districts.

4. *A Rebuttal for Repeal, 1844.* The parliamentary campaign for repeal was led by Charles Villiers (1802–98). The selection below is taken from a speech he made in the Commons in 1844 to answer the arguments of those who defended the Corn Laws. Villiers's arguments were among those which weighed most heavily with Prime Minister Peel, when, amid the potato famine of 1846, he finally yielded to liberal agitation and brought in the bill which repealed the Corn Laws. (9)

The ground on which the defense of the Corn Laws was first rested was certainly not without some plausibility before it was tested by experience; namely, that it was dangerous for this country to be dependent on other countries for its supply of food, and that, consequently, our landowners ought to be protected from foreign competition. . . .

Returns laid before this House during the last twenty years prove that the expectation of being independent of supplies of food from abroad, if ever honestly entertained, has been completely disappointed. Since the Laws were passed we have been largely and constantly dependent on other countries for supplies of corn; this dependence is annually increasing; and during the last five years we have fallen short in our home supply to an amount equal to 17,000,000 quarters. . . .

When the only profit or gain connected with the Laws has been traced to the owners of the land, the proprietors in Parliament have repudiated the charge; they have denied that they had any interest in the Laws, and declared the single object of such Laws to be the interest of the occupier and the laborer, whose existence and well-being, as they assert, depend on their continuance. . . . Everybody is now familiar with the fact that the distress of no other class had been more prominently and more frequently obtruded upon the public than that of the farmers. In fact, it is now a matter of notoriety that they have derived no benefit whatever from the Corn Laws. Duped and deceived by them, many a farmer hampered with debt, now finds himself pledged to a rent higher than he could ever afford to pay,

and openly and bitterly complains that he holds his land under circumstances the most disadvantageous for its proper cultivation. . . .

The same has occurred with regard to all the exemptions that have been procured for the farmer in the payment of taxes; there is not a landlord in the House who does not know that they only contribute to swell the rent given for the land. The members of this House dare not call a single farmer before them and ask him whether what they have done in his behalf, as they say, has been at all to his benefit. It is the evidence of one of the most competent among agriculturists that whatever relief has been procured for the farmer through Parliament has been for the advantage of landowners alone.

The assertion that these Laws are for the benefit of the laborer is equally absurd and unfounded. No one would now be bold enough to say that it is for the advantage of the laborer that the price of food should be kept up; and that high prices ensure high wages. There is a volume in this House, produced by the labors of a Commission of the Crown, that effectually disproves that assertion. In the face of that volume, never again can the advantage of the laborer be made the excuse of the Corn Laws. The evidence taken by the Commission is an authority that cannot be disputed; and it proves that no one could be lower in the scale of civilization than the agricultural laborer. Country gentlemen may now study it by the light of incendiary fires in their own neighborhoods. Scarcely a day passes that the papers are not full of accounts of what are called the crimes of the laboring classes. . . .

Another argument to show the necessity of great caution in any change is drawn from the numerical importance of the agricultural classes in the scale of society. An analysis of the late census recently published gives us information on this matter. It appears from these calculations that the agricultural classes about which so much has been written, and which are said to constitute seven ninths of the whole population of the country, are only 7 percent, and a little more, of our population. With what show of right or justice then, can anyone claim to exclude the whole mass of the people of the country from their natural right to buy their food as abundantly and as cheaply as possible, out of regard to the supposed exclusive interests of such a fraction of the community? . . .

The population of the country is increasing rapidly; the produce of our own soil, it is notorious, is not keeping pace with that increase; and yet we refuse to admit an adequate supply from other countries. Let in food from abroad, and customers enough would be found for it, otherwise it would not come in.

C.

FACTORY LEGISLATION

The achievement of Poor Law reform and free trade are each associated with a single legislative measure. Factory regulation, on the contrary, was achieved piecemeal by a series of acts extending over the entire century. Before the Reform Bill, legislation of very limited scope had been passed in 1802, 1819, 1825, and 1831. Then in 1833 factory inspectors were appointed as the first effective measure for the enforcement of regulations. Further limitations on working hours in 1844 were followed by the "Ten Hours Act" of 1847, which accomplished much of what the agitators had sought. Thereafter numerous acts extended the state's control of industry. The materials in this section, therefore, are not grouped about a single legislative measure but have been selected to portray the main issues taken up by liberals and others in the long-continued struggle to obtain effective factory legislation.

1. *The Debate in 1818.* Following are selections from the parliamentary debates upon the proposals of Sir Robert Peel the elder (1750–1830), which were later incorporated in the Factory Act of 1819. (10)

Sir Robert Peel [*the elder*] rose to make his promised motion on a subject, the importance of which increased more and more on every consideration of it. About fifteen years ago he had brought in a bill for the regulation of apprentices in cotton manufactories. At that time they [the apprentices] were the description of persons most employed in those manufactories. He himself had a thousand of them, and felt the necessity of some regulation with respect to them. Since that time, however, the business had been much extended. Manufactories were established in large towns, and the proprietors availed themselves of all the poor population of those towns. In Manchester alone 20,000 persons were employed in the cotton manufactories, and in the whole of England about three times that number. The business was of a peculiar nature, requiring of necessity that adults and children should work in the same rooms and at the same hours. It was notorious that children of a very tender age were dragged from their beds some hours before day light, and confined in the factories not less than fifteen hours; and it was also notoriously the opinion of the faculty, that no children of eight or nine years of age could bear that degree of hardship with impunity to their health and constitution. It had been urged by the humane, that there might be two sets of young laborers for one set of adults. He was afraid this would produce more harm than good. The better way would be to shorten the time of working for adults as well as for children; and to prevent the introduction of the latter at a very early age.

Those who were employers of the children, seeing them from day to day, were not so sensible of the injury that they sustained from this practice as strangers, who were strongly impressed by it.

In fact, they were prevented from growing to their full size. In consequence, Manchester, which used to furnish numerous recruits for the army, was now wholly unproductive in that respect. . . . The hon. baronet concluded by moving "that leave be given to bring in a bill to amend and extend an act made in the 42nd year of his present Majesty, for the preservation of the health and morals of apprentices and others employed in cotton and other mills, and cotton and other factories."

Lord Lascelles said he felt considerable difficulty on the present subject, which was of the highest importance to the manufacturing districts. It was not all evils that were fit subjects for legislative interference; for instance, he highly applauded the bill of an hon. friend of his, respecting chimney sweepers. But in the present case it should be recollected, that the individuals who were the objects of the hon. gentleman's proposition were free laborers. This excited his jealousy; for, were the principle of interference with free laborers once admitted, it was difficult to say how far it might not be carried. . . .

Mr. Philips: It was not enough to act under the impulse of humane feelings alone. To real charity many things were essential, besides almsgiving, which, when indulged indiscriminately, provoked the very evils it wished to alleviate, and caused nothing but idleness and discontent. In the exchange between wages and labor, interference must have a most pernicious tendency. . . . The tendency of interference would be, first, to increase wages—workmen would do less and receive more; an increase of population would follow on this comparative case, and the increased competition for labor must in the end lower wages; while the temporary increase of price, consequent on a temporary increase of wages, would give the Continental manufactories a start, by enabling them to sell at a lower price than ourselves, and thus by lessening our sale, lessen the demand for labor, while the demand for employment was increasing. . . .

Mr. W. Smith: He concurred generally on the impropriety of interfering with labor on indefinite grounds; but here was something tangible and definite, in regulating the age at which persons might enter the cotton factories, and the number of hours which they should work each day. Into the consideration of what was the proper or the exact number of hours he would not now enter. He would put it generally, ought persons under the age of twelve to be employed from thirteen hours and a half to fifteen hours a day in a cotton factory; and was it not injurious to their health and growth to be so employed? . . . The evidence of physicians and others, who having no personal interest to serve, could not be supposed to have a wrong bias, was in favor of legislative interference. All the members of the faculty . . . would be found to declare, that children of the age alluded to, could not, without injury to their health, work so long in factories as children meant to be protected by the bill now did.

2. *The Debate in 1833.* Leadership in the movement for factory reform was taken in 1832 by Lord Ashley, later Earl of Shaftesbury (1801–85). Following are selections from the debate upon a factory bill which he presented to the House of Commons in 1833. (11)

Sir Samuel Whalley: Nothing called for legislative interference more than this frightful outrage upon humanity. When the House had voted £20,000,000 of money for the emancipation of the slaves, surely it would not hesitate to extend its protection to these poor children, when it had the means of doing so without any expenditure. Laws were passed to protect grouse and pheasants, and hares and other game, and even oysters were not excluded from the protection of the legislature. He said, then, that, even putting humanity out of the question, it would be expedient, if only in a financial point of view, to prevent avarice from making a sacrifice of human life. The eyes of all foreign nations were directed upon the course which the legislature would take upon this question, for the cruelties perpetrated in the English factories had rendered us odious to all Europe. . . .

Mr. Brotherton said, that all persons were agreed that some legislation was necessary. That was making a great progress, for twenty years ago not a single master would allow that legislative interference was necessary. Now, the public, the masters, and the workingmen, all agreed in appealing to Parliament to make regulations for the labor of factories. They had different motives for demanding it. The masters demanded it because they desired to prevent some amongst themselves

from working too long. The adults required interference, as the only means of preventing them from being overworked; and the public required the interference of the legislature to protect the children.

He thought that there should be some restriction, and that the restriction should establish one uniform system. He knew that some mills were now working for fifteen or sixteen hours a day; and he knew that infants of a very tender age were so employed. The hon. member quoted two or three cases, from the evidence of the commissioners. The Ten Hours Bill would, he admitted, be a great change from the present system; and he wished, that the protection could be further extended as to age. He wished it extended till the age of twenty-one. Indeed, unless the labor of the adults was regulated, which was requisite, it was impossible to protect the children. He was anxious to make the Bill effective for its objects. . . .

At the present moment the children were so much part of the machinery, that they must work the whole time the mill worked or starve, otherwise the masters would not employ them. Their labor, then, was not free labor. They must be there at the time, and they must stay the whole time, without ever going out. Would not the members of that House feel it a great hardship to be confined there the whole day? He knew what those hardships were, for he had worked in a factory himself till he had reached his sixteenth year. He had worked twelve and fourteen hours a day, and had undergone all the privations which factory children endured. For these young persons he felt the deepest sympathy; and though he had been raised to the highest honor which man could confer on him—that of sitting in the British House of Commons—he could never forget his former station. He did feel much for the sufferings of these children, and a great disposition to stand by his order; and if he could by his labors ameliorate their condition, he should feel that he had not lived in vain. . . .

Mr. Hyett: He must be permitted to observe . . . that there was a quixotic spirit abroad at the present day, which, singling out a few of the abuses to which human nature always had been liable, and to which it always would be liable . . . rushed on to remedy them with breathless haste, regardless of the dangers it might inflict on those whom it wished to relieve, or on society in general. . . . Were they to go on in this pettifogging manner from day to day, adding fetter to fetter, and trammel to trammel, on the industry and the energy, and the enterprise of the country? Were they, in these days of liberty of thought and liberty of action, to recur to the olden time of chartered guilds and exclusive companies, prescribing, if not the modes, at least the hours of manufacture? There was, indeed, in the present day, a zeal, he might almost say an excessive lust, of legislation; a mania for making little laws for little occasions, when they ought rather to be doing their best to be getting rid of those which were causing the mischief. . . . Let us endeavor to exchange what we manufacture more cheaply than our neighbor for what he produces more cheaply than ourselves. If they attempted that, and succeeded even in but a partial degree, he was disposed to believe that there would be but little need for commissions of enquiry, and factory bills, and truck bills; and if they had attempted it, and succeeded but partially, he believed there would have been but little clamor for parliamentary reform, and there would have been no need of coercion. . . .

Mr. Hume said, that though it was an established principle or rule, that any restriction or regulation of labor or wages was mischievous, yet he thought the case of children was an exception to that rule.

3. *The Debate in 1847.* Following are selections from the debates in 1847, the year in which the Ten Hours Act was finally passed. (12)

Mr. Hume: Every act the House had passed for the last three, four, or five years, had been to free industry, to emancipate capital, and relieve the mercantile interest from restriction: and it would be the height of injustice now, to say to men who were willing to work, "you shall not work except for such time as we permit." One man might like to work for twelve hours; another man for less; another for more, that he might support his mother, or his father. Then why should the law interfere? Parliament had no right to interfere either with labor or capital; and for his part he was prepared to sweep away every restriction that now remained, and to let one general and uniform principle of perfect liberty pervade our legislation.

Having stated these general principles, he asked hon. gentlemen to give him an answer to the following points: Were they desirous that England should maintain her manufacturing superiority? If so, were they disposed to give fair play to capital and industry in this country? Were they aware of what was going on in Belgium and Germany? Was there any restriction to ten hours there? Was there any restriction in the United States? In the factories at Lowell they worked, in summer, twelve hours; and he had read a report drawn up by a committee of the legislature of Massachusetts upon a petition praying for a restriction in the hours of labor. It was a most sensible report: "We cannot interfere," said the committee.

"We admit the evil; we wish we could lessen the hours of labor to all classes; we wish that every man could maintain himself and his family by eight or nine hours of labor per day. But we find it cannot be done. Our manufacturers have competition to meet in neutral markets, and we must leave them to their own exertions.". . .

Sir G. Grey: That principle [of noninterference with labor] I believe a sound one; but why did not Parliament . . . completely enforce the principle of noninterference with labor? Parliament has not done so. It has made this an exceptional case; and I think there are just and sufficient grounds for making it an exceptional case. . . . The only new feature, as it appears to me, which the subject offers on the present occasion, and to which we ought to address our attention, is, what is the present feeling of the public mind with regard to this question; and what is the prospect of that final settlement of the question, which, judging from past professions, I confess, I was inclined to think would have taken place, but which, I regret to say, now appears more hopeless—I mean that settlement of it which would be most satisfactory to all the parties concerned, and which should be effected, not by act of Parliament but by mutual agreement between employer and the persons employed. From all the information I have been able to obtain on that subject, my hopes are disappointed as to the attainment of so desirable a result by means so very desirable and unobjectionable. . . . I say it is an argument in favor of legislation that you cannot get persons to agree by common consent to one general arrangement, so long as there are persons whose interest it is to set that arrangement at nought. Where the object in view is practically right, the interference of the legislature may become advisable. What, then, is the state of this question? I do not think it can be denied that there is a great desire on the part of the great body of the people employed in factories to see this question settled by legislative interference; and, on the other hand, I fear that there is still a formidable and general feeling of opposition on the part of the employers of labor to the settlement of this question otherwise than by the interference of legislation. . . .

Mr. T. M. Gibson: The noble lord the member for Lynn (Lord George Bentinck) had reminded the House, that the abolition of the Corn Laws was an interference with vested interests; and that the right hon. gentleman the member for Dorchester (Sir J. Graham) had not, in those days, when the Corn Laws were repealed, shown or expressed much sensibility as to interference with vested interests. He would take the liberty of stating his views, not of the Corn-Law question, but of the analogy which existed between the question now before the House, and that which the noble lord the member for Lynn had recently introduced. The Corn Laws were a restraint upon the industry and the trade of the country. Those who supported that restraint failed to prove that such a regulation was advantageous to the community, consequently the restraint was removed by the legislature.

In the same way the *onus probandi* rested with those who proposed this restraint upon the labor of the country; it was for them to show that the restraint would be advantageous to the persons upon whom it would be imposed; and more than that, it was for them to show that it would be advantageous to the community at large. It was not for those who opposed this restraint to show the particular evils that would arise from it—nothing of the kind; they were not bound to demonstrate mathematically the exact reduction of wages that would follow the proposed limitation of the hours of labor. ("Hear!") No, they were not. Every restraint, he contended, was *per se* an evil, and until the legislature could point out the advantage to the individuals restrained, and the benefit to the community at large in the regulation proposed, it was not justifiable to pass the proposed restraint into a law.

Now, he denied it had been shown that this restraint upon the free labor of adult women, and young persons between the ages of thirteen and eighteen, would be an advantage to them or an advantage to the community at large; he denied its having been shown that this restraint upon

their labor would not produce a large reduction of wages; he denied it had been shown that the compulsory leisure which was proposed to be given to those parties would be employed in any way more to their moral and physical advantage, than the time which they might spend in the factories. It was proposed to give compulsory leisure to certain parties, and there they stopped; they did not follow them into the way in which that leisure should be employed.

When they dealt with the children in the factories, they did follow them in this respect. Children, they then said, should not be employed in mills more than six hours for each day; but they went further, and said that the other six hours, the remaining part of the day when they were out of the mill, should be employed in schooling and in education. In the present case there was nothing of the kind proposed. They simply contented themselves with excluding a number of adult females—free agents, responsible for their actions to the laws of the country—from certain mills, and from certain earnings they were now in possession of, and there they stopped. The House was not told how their leisure was to be employed; it was not in the slightest degree shown that the whole twenty-four hours would be better employed to the moral and physical advantage of the party for whom they were legislating, than they now were; and he contended the supporters of the bill were bound to show these particulars, before they could expect Parliament to impose the proposed restraint upon the labor of those individuals.

D.   Reformers Review the Progress of Reform

By the third quarter of the nineteenth century many of the great reforms for which liberals had agitated early in the century had been achieved. Yet the results had fallen far short of expectation, and the necessity of factory legislation, running counter to the trend of philosophic radicalism, had called into question many points in the liberal program. There was an inevitable tendency, therefore, to reconsider the liberal tenets which, mingled with other forces, had produced the reform movement.

1. *Lord Shaftesbury Looks Back, 1866.* Though factory reformers had attained their major goal in the Ten Hours Act of 1847, much further legislation was found necessary. This was profoundly disturbing to Lord Shaftesbury, who had led the reform movement for over thirty years, and in 1866 he revealed the nature of his concern in a speech before the Social Science Congress, a selection from which follows. (13)

Public opinion may lead to good laws, or supersede the necessity of them, and so avoid the abundant variety and complication of enactments

which eventually break down, or fall into disuse by their minuteness and extent. Is it not a frightful condition of things that, here in the nineteenth century, we are compelled by disclosures which astonish and shock the inmost conscience, to demand, year by year, of the legislature, protection for tens of thousands of women and children of the tenderest age, against a system of physical and moral suffering and degradation, such as reduces all past "history to an old almanac"? And is it not frightful when we consider that the vast proportion of these intolerable tribulations to which the children are subjected are in all cases permitted, and in many cases inflicted, by the parents themselves? The law has stepped in and rescued many; the law will again step in and rescue many more; but I tremble, I confess, for the efficiency and permanency of any machinery, that is "cabined, cribbed, confined" by the union of money interests, perverted natures, and the mercenary belief that godliness is gain, and therefore gain must be godliness. Turn your thoughts to the numerous females, some 600,000, engaged in the various departments of dress, from the royal milliner to the most abject sempstress. Their sufferings have oftentimes excited the deepest emotion. Restrictions and regulations are demanded. But in this matter who can invent them? And, if invented, who can enforce them? A more considerate spirit, a more enlarged sympathy, and a profounder and more practical appreciation of "do as you would be done by" would stay the cries of these unhappy victims, and leave our legislators but little to do. . . .

I do not say this in a vain hope, or even with a wish to restrict the tendencies of the age and introduce a new science of political economy. I only implore you, in your meditative moments, to reflect how far such things are necessary, and whether by thoughtful and convenient arrangements, while the enjoyments of the consumer will not be stinted, the happiness of the producer may not be very greatly advanced.

2. *John Stuart Mill Revaluates Liberalism, 1873.* John Stuart Mill (1806–73) had been brought up a strict "utilitarian" by his father, an intimate of Jeremy Bentham and a prominent member of the philosophic radicals. All his life Mill had been deeply interested in reform and had written much on the question of freedom in society. In the following selection from his autobiography, written in the last year of his life, Mill revaluates the principles he had learned in his youth. (14)

In those days I had seen little further than the old school of political economists into the possibilities of fundamental improvement in social arrangements. Private property, as now understood, and inheritance, appeared to me, as to them, the *dernier mot* of legislation: and I looked no further than to mitigating the inequalities consequent on these institutions, by getting rid of primogeniture and entails. The notion that it was possible to go further than this in removing the injustice—for injustice it is, whether admitting of a complete remedy or not—involved in the fact that some are born to riches and the vast majority to poverty, I then reckoned chimerical, and only hoped that by universal education, leading to voluntary restraint on population, the portion of the poor might be made more tolerable.

In short, I was a democrat, but not the least of a socialist.

We were now much less democrats than I had been, because so long as education continues to be so wretchedly imperfect, we dreaded the ignorance and especially the selfishness and brutality of the mass: but our ideal of ultimate improvement went far beyond democracy, and would class us decidedly under the general designation of socialists. While we repudiated with the greatest energy that tyranny of society over the individual which most socialistic systems are supposed to involve, we yet looked forward to a time when society will no longer be divided into the idle and the industrious; when the rule that they who do not work shall not eat, will be applied not to paupers only, but impartially to all; when the division of the produce of labor, instead of depending, as in so great a degree it now does, on the accident of birth, will be made by concert on an acknowledged principle of justice; and when it will no longer either be, or be thought to be, impossible for human beings to exert themselves strenuously in procuring benefits which are not to be exclusively their own, but to be shared with the society they belong to.

The social problem of the future we considered to be, how to unite the greatest individual liberty of action, with a common ownership in the raw material of the globe, and an equal participation of all in the benefits of combined labor. We had not the presumption to suppose that we could already foresee by what precise form of institutions these objects could most effectually be attained, or at how near or how distant a period they would become practicable. We saw clearly that to render any such social transformation either possible or desirable, an equivalent change of character must take place both in the uncultivated herd who now compose the laboring masses, and in the immense majority of their employers. Both these classes must learn by practice to labor and combine for generous, or at all events for public and social purposes, and not, as hitherto, solely for narrowly interested ones. But the capacity to do this has always existed in mankind, and is not, nor is ever likely to be, extinct. Education, habit, and the cultivation of the sentiments, will make a common man dig or weave for his country, as readily as fight for his country. True enough, it is only by slow degrees, and a system of culture prolonged through successive generations, that men in general can be brought up to this point. But the hindrance is not in the essential constitution of human nature.

Interest in the common good is at present so weak a motive in the generality, not because it can never be otherwise, but because the mind is not accustomed to dwell on it as it dwells from morning till night on things which tend only to personal advantage. When called into activity, as only self-interest now is, by the daily course of life, and spurred from behind by the love of distinction and the fear of shame, it is capable of producing, even in common men, the most strenuous exertions as well as the most heroic sacrifices. The deep-rooted selfishness, which forms the general character of the existing state of society, is so deeply rooted only because the whole course of existing institutions tends to foster it; and modern institutions in some respects more than ancient, since the occasions on which the individual is called on to do anything for the public without receiving its pay, are far less frequent in modern life than in the smaller commonwealths of antiquity.

These considerations did not make us overlook the folly of premature attempts to dispense with the inducements of private interest in social affairs, while no substitute for them has been or can be provided: but we regarded all existing institutions and social arrangements as being (in a phrase I once heard from Austin) "merely provisional," and we welcomed with the greatest pleasure and interest all socialistic experiments by select individuals (such as the cooperative societies), which, whether they succeeded or failed, could not but operate as a most useful education of those who took part in them, by cultivating their capacity of acting upon motives pointing directly to the defects which render them and others incapable of doing so.

III

Socialism

Rise up, ye victims of privation,
Rise up, all ye who are forlorn;
For there's an end to degradation,
For now a new world's being born.
Right close at hand emancipation
Will loose the chains that held you fast;
The time is near for your salvation,
A better day has dawned at last.
    O comrades, assemble from afar to face the fight;
    The Internationale bids all the world unite.
    O comrades, assemble from afar to face the fight;
    The Internationale bids all the world unite!

Come workers of the world as brothers
To wrest the wealth from land and sea;
Your rights demand, and for all others,
Crush the foes of Liberty.
Too long the rich our lives are taking,
Trampling Freedom to the ground;
O now arise, from sleep awaking,
Land to land our tocsin sound.
    O comrades, assemble from afar to face the fight;
    The Internationale bids all the world unite.
    O comrades, assemble from afar to face the fight;
    The Internationale bids all the world unite!

"THE INTERNATIONALE," 1888

CONTENTS

[55]

QUESTIONS FOR STUDY

PART I

1. What is Marx's philosophy of history?

2. How does it differ from other philosophies of history with which you are familiar?

3. Why, according to Marx, has the bourgeoisie played historically a most revolutionary part?

4. According to Marx, is a socialist society inevitable?

5. What is the Marxist interpretation of the first French Revolution? How far do the facts, as you know them, justify this interpretation?

6. To what extent is Marx indebted to Malthus?

7. What is the importance of Marx's theory of value in his general philosophy?

8. How accurate was Marx's analysis of the existing state of "national-differences and antagonisms"?

9. To what authority does Marx appeal in his arguments? How does this compare with Locke and Condorcet?

PART II

10. What earlier Marxist ideas did Engel abandon or modify in 1895? Why?

11. On what point are anarchists and syndicalists agreed?

12. How do syndicalists and revisionists disagree on *method?* According to the syndicalists what is the danger in the methods proposed by the revisionists?

13. To the logical syndicalist, direction action is not immoral. Why?

14. How does Sidney Webb's approach to the subject of socialism differ from that of Marx?

15. Why might the methods of the Fabian Society appeal to many workers?

16. Why did Bernstein think it was necessary to revise Marx?

17. How do Millerand's ideas differ from those in the *Communist Manifesto?* Explain the difference.

Socialism, or at least certain of the tendencies of socialism, is very old, dating back to St. Thomas More's *Utopia* (1516) or perhaps even to Plato's *Republic* (c. 400 B.C.). That is to say, there have always been those who have denounced the exploitation of the poor and inveighed against the evils of private property. The turn of the nineteenth century, however, was marked by a great increase in socialist thought, an increase indubitably caused by the Industrial Revolution which had, in its early stages, brought into stark contrast the condition of the new industrial rich with that of the new industrial poor. Men such as St. Simon (1760–1825) and Fourier (1772–1837) in France, and Robert Owen (1771–1858) in England, sought in their writings and sometimes in their actions to refashion the world. They have been called "Utopian socialists," for, while their ideas differed greatly, they all believed that the coming of socialism would be accomplished through the efforts of individuals in founding communities whose members would live happily together on socialistic principles. The existence of this body of Utopian socialist doctrine led Karl Marx, the most influential of all socialists, to label his doctrines "communism" to distinguish them from the "socialism" of the Utopians. Marx's followers have also called Marxism "scientific" socialism.

Karl Marx (1813–83) came of a well-to-do German Jewish family, but when he was six years old his father embraced Christianity and Marx was brought up in that faith. He was a brilliant student and was educated at the universities of Bonn, Jena, and Berlin. At this last seat of learning he was introduced to the philosophic method of Hegel, a fact of great importance in shaping his subsequent ideas. Briefly, the Hegelian dialectic conceived that change took place through the struggle of antagonistic elements or ideas and their resolution into a synthesis in which a new and higher idea or concept was formed by virtue of the union of contradictory elements.

After receiving his doctorate Marx entered journalism and in 1843 went to Paris to practice that profession. It was there that he met his lifetime friend and collaborator, Friedrich Engels, a German businessman who also was the highly successful operator of spinning mills in England. It was Engels, himself the author of a book entitled *The Condition of the Working Class in 1844,* who had in his firsthand knowledge of working conditions in the early days of technological change the wherewithal to supply Marx with much of his factual materials. Ousted from France at the request of the Prussian government, Marx went to Brussels and thence in January 1848 to London, where he and Engels composed *The Communist Manifesto*. It is this pamphlet which constitutes Part I of the Problem.

When the revolutions of 1848 broke out, Marx returned to Germany. After their failure, however, he resumed his exile in London, where he spent practically the remainder of his life. Marx wrote voluminously, his most famous work being the monumental *Capital,* of which the first volume appeared in 1867. In Marx's own lifetime his writings had, in the quantitative sense, little circulation, and even today *Capital* is more talked about than read. But a militant and vocal minority made socialism a force to be reckoned with in European politics, and Marx must be regarded as the father of the movement. "The indubitable fact is that all subsequent socialism has been dominated by Marx; and that even when subsequent schools have disowned him, they have owed their existence to a reaction from Marx." (1) The Second Part of this Problem contains examples of several of the more prominent post-Marxist varieties of socialism.

Part I. THE COMMUNIST MANIFESTO

In November 1847 the Communist League held a congress in London. Although the League was then composed exclusively of German workingmen, the meeting had to be held outside Germany to avoid the attention of the German police. This congress asked Marx and Engels to draw up a complete program for the League; *The Communist Manifesto* was the result. It was written in German the following January and went to press shortly before the outbreak of the revolutions of 1848. While it was produced jointly by Marx and Engels, the latter admitted that the principal ideas were developed by Marx. The *Manifesto* has been translated into almost all languages and has run through many editions. The selections which follow are taken from an English translation authorized and edited by Engels. (2)

A specter is haunting Europe—the specter of communism. All the powers of old Europe have entered into a holy alliance to exorcise this specter; Pope and Czar, Metternich and Guizot, French radicals and German police spies.

Where is the party in opposition that has not been decried as communistic by its opponents in power? Where the opposition that has not hurled back the branding reproach of communism against the more advanced opposition parties, as well as against its reactionary adversaries?

Two things result from this fact.

I. Communism is already acknowledged by all European powers to be in itself a power.

II. It is high time that communists should openly, in the face of the whole world, publish their views, their aims, their tendencies, and meet this nursery tale of the specter of communism with a manifesto of the party itself.

To this end the communists of various nationalities have assembled in London, and sketched the following manifesto to be published in the English, French, German, Italian, Flemish, and Danish languages.

I: Bourgeois and Proletarians

The history of all hitherto existing society is the history of class struggles.

Freeman and slave, patrician and plebeian, lord and serf, guild master and journeyman, in a word, oppressor and oppressed, stood in constant opposition to one another, carried on an uninterrupted, now hidden, now open fight, that each time ended, either in the revolutionary reconstitution of society at large, or in the common ruin of the contending classes.

In the earlier epochs of history we find almost everywhere a complicated arrangement of society into various orders, a manifold gradation of social rank. In ancient Rome we have patricians, knights, plebeians, slaves; in the Middle Ages, feudal lords, vassals, guild masters, journeymen, apprentices, serfs; in almost all of these classes, again, subordinate gradations.

The modern bourgeois society that has sprouted from the ruins of feudal society has not done away with class antagonisms. It has but established new classes, new conditions of oppression, new forms of struggle in place of the old ones.

Our epoch, the epoch of the bourgeois, possesses, however, this distinctive feature: it has simplified the class antagonisms. Society as a whole is more and more splitting up into two great hostile camps, into two great classes directly facing each other: Bourgeoisie and Proletariat.

From the serfs of the Middle Ages sprang the chartered burghers of the earliest towns. From these burgesses the first elements of the bourgeoisie were developed.

The discovery of America, the rounding of the Cape, opened up fresh ground for the rising bourgeoisie. The East Indian and Chinese markets, the colonization of America, trade with the colonies, the increase in the means of exchange and in commodities generally, gave to commerce, to navigation, to industry, an impulse never before known, and thereby, to the revolutionary element in the tottering feudal society, a rapid development.

The feudal system of industry, under which industrial production was monopolized by close guilds, now no longer sufficed for the growing wants of the new markets. The manufacturing system took its place. The guild masters were pushed on one side by the manufacturing middle class; division of labor between the different corporate guilds vanished in the face of division of labor in each single workshop.

Meantime the markets kept ever growing, the demand ever rising. Even manufacture no longer sufficed. Thereupon steam and machinery revolutionized industrial production. The place of manufacture was taken by the giant, Modern Industry, the place of the industrial middle class, by industrial millionaires, the leaders of whole industrial armies, the modern bourgeois.

Modern industry has established the world's market, for which the discovery of America paved the way. The market has given an immense development to commerce, to navigation, to communication by land. This development has, in its turn, reacted on the extension of industry; and in proportion as industry, commerce, navigation, and railways extended, in the same proportion the bourgeoisie developed, increased its capital, and pushed into the background every class handed down from the Middle Ages.

We see, therefore, how the modern bourgeoisie is itself the product of a long course of development, of a series of revolutions in the modes of production and of exchange.

Each step in the development of the bourgeoisie was accompanied by a corresponding political advance of that class. An oppressed class under the sway of the feudal nobility, an armed and self-governing association in the medieval commune, here independent urban republic (as in Italy and Germany), there taxable "third estate" of the monarchy (as in France), afterwards, in the period of manufacture proper, serving either the semifeudal or the absolute monarchy as a counterpoise against the nobility, and, in fact, cornerstone of the great monarchies in general, the bourgeoisie has at last, since the establishment of modern industry and of the world's market, conquered for itself, in the modern representative state, exclusive political sway. The executive of the modern state is but a committee for managing the common affairs of the whole bourgeoisie.

The bourgeoisie, historically, has played a most revolutionary part.

The bourgeoisie, wherever it has got the upper hand, has put an end to all feudal, patriarchal, idyllic relations. It has pitilessly torn asunder the motley feudal ties that bound man to his "natural superiors," and has left remaining no other nexus between man and man than naked self-interest, callous "cash payment." It has drowned the most heavenly ecstacies of religious fervor, of chivalrous enthusiasm, of philistine sentimentalism, in the icy water of egotistical calculation. It has resolved personal worth into exchange value, and in place of the numberless indefeasible chartered freedoms, has set up that single, unconscionable freedom—Free Trade. In one word, for exploitation, veiled by religious and political illusions, it has substituted naked, shameless, direct, brutal exploitation.

The bourgeoisie has stripped of its halo every occupation hitherto honored and looked up to with reverent awe. It has converted the physician, the lawyer, the priest, the poet, the man of science, into its paid wage laborers.

The bourgeoisie has torn away from the family its sentimental veil, and has reduced the family relation to a mere money relation.

The bourgeoisie has disclosed how it came to pass that the brutal display of vigor in the Middle Ages, which reactionists so much admire, found its fitting complement in the most slothful indolence. It has been the first to show what man's activity can bring about. It has accomplished wonders far surpassing Egyptian pyramids, Roman aqueducts, and Gothic cathedrals; it has conducted expeditions that put in the shade all former exoduses of nations and crusades.

The bourgeoisie cannot exist without constantly revolutionizing the instruments of production, and thereby the relations of production, and with them the whole relations of society. Conservation of the old modes of production in unaltered forms, was, on the contrary, the first condition of existence for all earlier industrial classes. Constant revolutionizing of production, uninterrupted disturbance of all social conditions, everlasting uncertainty and agitation, distinguish the bourgeois epoch from all earlier ones. All fixed, fast-frozen relations, with their train of ancient and venerable prejudices and opinions, are swept away; all new-formed ones become antiquated before they can ossify. All that is solid melts into air, all that is holy is profaned, and man is at last compelled to face with sober senses his real conditions of life and his relations with his kind.

The need of a constantly expanding market for its products chases the bourgeoisie over the whole surface of the globe. It must nestle everywhere, settle everywhere, establish connections everywhere.

The bourgeoisie has through its exploitation of the world's market given a cosmopolitan character to production and consumption in every country. To the great chagrin of reactionists, it has drawn from under the feet of industry the national ground on which it stood. All old-established national industries have been destroyed or are daily being destroyed. They are dislodged by new industries, whose introduction becomes a life and death question for all civilized nations, by industries that no longer work up indigenous raw material, but raw material drawn from the remotest zones, industries whose products are consumed, not only at home, but in every quarter of the globe. In place of the old wants, satisfied by the productions of the country, we find new wants, requiring for their satisfaction the products of distant lands and climes. In place of the old local and national seclusion and self-sufficiency, we have intercourse in every direction, universal interdependence of nations. And as in material, so also in intellectual production. The intellectual creations of individual nations become common property. National one-sidedness and narrow-mindedness become more and more impossible, and from the numerous national and local literatures, there arises a world literature.

The bourgeoisie, by the rapid improvement of all instruments of production, by the immensely facilitated means of communication, draws all, even the most barbarian, nations into civilization. The cheap prices of its commodities are the heavy artillery with which it batters down all Chinese walls, with which it forces the barbarians' intensely obstinate hatred of foreigners to capitulate. It compels all nations, on pain of extinction, to adopt the bourgeois mode of production; it compels them to introduce what it calls civilization into their midst, *i.e.,* to become bourgeois themselves. In one word, it creates a world after its own image.

The bourgeoisie has subjected the country to the rule of the towns. It has created enormous cities, has greatly increased the urban population as compared with the rural, and has thus rescued a considerable part of the population from the idiocy of rural life. Just as it has made the country dependent on the towns, so it has made barbarian and semibarbarian countries dependent on the civilized ones, nations of peasants on nations of bourgeois, the East on the West.

The bourgeoisie keeps more and more doing away with the scattered state of the population, of the means of production, and of property. It has agglomerated population, centralized means of production, and has concentrated property in a few hands. The necessary consequence of this was political centralization. Independent, or but loosely connected provinces, with separate interests, laws, governments and systems of taxation, became lumped together into one nation, with one government, one code of laws, one national class interest, one frontier, and one customs tariff.

The bourgeoisie, during its rule of scarce one hundred years, has created more massive and more colossal productive forces than have all preceding generations together. Subjection of nature's forces to man, machinery, application of chemistry to industry and agriculture, steam navigation, railways, electric telegraphs, clearing of whole continents for cultivation, canalization of rivers, whole populations conjured out of the ground—what earlier century had even a presentiment that such productive forces slumbered in the lap of social labor?

We see then: the means of production and of exchange on whose foundation the bourgeoisie built itself up, were generated in feudal society. At a certain stage in the development of these means of production and of exchange, the conditions under which feudal society produced and exchanged, the feudal organization of agriculture and manufacturing industry, in one word, the feudal relations of property, became no longer compatible with the already developed productive forces; they became so many fetters. They had to be burst asunder.

Into their place stepped free competition, accompanied by a social and political constitution adapted to it, and by the economical and political sway of the bourgeois class.

A similar movement is going on before our own eyes. Modern bourgeois society with its relations of production, of exchange, and of property, a society that has conjured up such gigantic means of production and of exchange, is like the sorcerer, who is no longer able to control the powers of the nether world whom he has called up by his spells. For many a decade past the history of industry and commerce is but the history of the revolt of modern productive forces against modern conditions of production, against the property relations that are the conditions for the existence of the bourgeoisie and of its rule. It is enough to mention the commercial crises that by their periodical return put on its trial, each time more threateningly, the existence of the bourgeois society. In these crises a great part not only of the existing products, but also of the previously created productive forces, is periodically destroyed. In these crises there breaks out an epidemic that, in all earlier epochs, would have seemed an absurdity—the epidemic of overproduction. Society suddenly finds itself put back into a state of momentary barbarism; it appears as if a famine, a universal war of devastation had cut off the supply of every means of subsistence; industry and commerce seem to be destroyed; and why? because there is too much civilization, too much means of subsistence, too much industry, too much commerce. The productive forces at the disposal of society no longer tend to further the development of the conditions of bourgeois property; on the contrary, they have become too powerful for these conditions, by which they are fettered, and so soon as they overcome these fetters, they bring disorder into the whole of bourgeois society, endanger the existence of bourgeois property. The conditions of bourgeois society are too narrow to comprise the wealth created by them. And how does the bourgeoisie get over these crises? On the one hand by enforced destruction of a mass of productive forces; on the other, by the conquest of new markets, and by the more thorough exploitation of the old ones. That is to say, by paving the way for more extensive and more destructive crises, and by diminishing the means whereby crises are prevented.

The weapons with which the bourgeoisie felled feudalism to the ground are now turned against the bourgeoisie itself.

But not only has the bourgeoisie forged the weapons that bring death to itself; it has also called into existence the men who are to wield those weapons—the modern working class—the proletarians.

In proportion as the bourgeoisie, *i.e.,* capital, is developed, in the same proportion is the proletariat, the modern working class, developed; a class of laborers, who live only so long as they find work, and who find work only so long as their labor increases capital. These laborers, who must sell themselves piecemeal, are a commodity, like every other article of commerce, and are consequently exposed to all the vicissitudes of competition, to all the fluctuations of the market.

Owing to the extensive use of machinery and to division of labor, the work of the proletarians has lost all individual character, and, consequently, all charm for the workman. He becomes an appendage of the machine, and it is only the most simple, most monotonous, and most easily acquired knack, that is required of him. Hence, the cost of production of a workman is restricted almost entirely to the means of subsistence that he requires for his maintenance, and for the propagation of his race. But the price of a commodity, and therefore also of labor, is equal, in the long run, to its cost of production. In proportion, therefore, as the repulsiveness of the work increases, the wage decreases. Nay, more, in proportion as the use of machinery and division of labor increase, in the same proportion the burden of toil also increases, whether by prolongation of the working hours, by increase of the work exacted in a given time, or by increased speed of the machinery, etc. . . .

No sooner is the exploitation of the laborer by the manufacturer so far at an end that he receives his wages in cash, than he is set upon by the other portions of the bourgeoisie, the landlord, the shopkeeper, the pawnbroker, etc.

The lower strata of the middle class—the small tradespeople, shopkeepers, and retired tradesmen generally, the handicraftsmen, and peasants—all these sink gradually into the proletariat, partly because their diminutive capital does not suffice for the scale on which modern industry is carried on, and is swamped in the competition with the large capitalists, partly because their specialized skill is rendered worthless by new methods of production. Thus the proletariat is recruited from all classes of the population.

The proletariat goes through various stages of development. With its birth begins its struggle with the bourgeoisie. At first the contest is carried on by individual laborers, then by the workpeople of a factory, then by the operatives of one trade, in one locality, against the individual bourgeois who directly exploits them. They direct their attacks not against the bourgeois conditions of production, but against the instruments of production themselves; they destroy imported wares that compete with their labor, they smash to pieces machinery, they set factories ablaze, they seek to restore by force the vanished status of the workman of the Middle Ages.

At this stage the laborers still form an incoherent mass scattered over the whole country, and broken up by their mutual competition. If anywhere they unite to form more compact bodies, this is not yet the consequence of their own active union, but of the union of the bourgeoisie, which class, in order to attain its own political ends, is compelled to set the whole proletariat in motion, and is moreover yet, for a time, able to do so. At this stage, therefore, the proletarians do not fight their enemies, but the enemies of their enemies, the remnants of absolute monarchy, and land owners, the nonindustrial bourgeois, the petty bourgeoisie. Thus the whole historical movement is concentrated in the hands of the bourgeoisie; every victory so obtained is a victory for the bourgeoisie.

But with the development of industry the proletariat not only increases in number; it becomes concentrated in greater masses, its strength grows and it feels that strength more. The various interests and conditions of life within the ranks of the proletariat are more and more equalized, in proportion as machinery obliterates all distinctions of labor, and nearly everywhere reduces wages to the same low level. The growing competition among the bourgeois, and the resulting commercial crises, make the wages of the workers ever more fluctuating. The unceasing improvement of machinery, ever more rapidly developing, makes their livelihood more and more precarious; the collisions between individual workman and individual bourgeois take more and more the character of collisions between two classes. Thereupon the workers begin to form combinations (trades' unions) against the bourgeois; they club together in order to keep up the rate of wages; they found permanent associations in order to make provision beforehand for these occasional revolts. Here and there the contest breaks out into riots.

Now and then the workers are victorious, but only for a time. The real fruit of their battles lies not in the immediate result but in the ever expanding union of the workers. This union is furthered by the improved means of communication that are created in modern industry and that place the workers of different localities in contact with one another. It was just this contact that was needed to centralize the numerous local struggles, all of the same character, into one national struggle between classes. But every class struggle is a political struggle. And that union, to attain which the burghers of the Middle Ages, with their miserable highways, required centuries, the modern proletarians, thanks to railways, achieve in a few years.

This organization of the proletarians into a class and consequently into a political party, is continually being upset again by the competition between the workers themselves. But it ever rises up again; stronger, firmer, mightier. It compels legislative recognition of particular interests of the workers, by taking advantage of the divisions among the bourgeoisie itself. Thus the Ten Hours' Bill in England was carried.

Altogether collisions between the classes of the old society further, in many ways, the course of the development of the proletariat. The bourgeoisie finds itself involved in a constant battle. At first with the aristocracy; later on, with those portions of the bourgeoisie itself whose interests have become antagonistic to the progress of industry; at all times with the bourgeoisie of foreign countries. In all these countries it sees itself compelled to appeal to the proletariat, to ask for its help, and thus to drag it into the political arena. The bourgeoisie itself, therefore, supplies the proletariat with weapons for fighting the bourgeoisie.

Further, as we have already seen, entire sections of the ruling classes are, by the advance of industry, precipitated into the proletariat, or are at least threatened in their conditions of existence. These also supply the proletariat with fresh elements of enlightenment and progress.

Finally, in times when the class struggle nears the decisive hour, the process of dissolution going on within the ruling class, in fact within the whole range of old society, assumes such a violent, glaring character, that a small section of the ruling class cuts itself adrift, and joins the revolutionary class; the class that holds the future in its hands. Just as, therefore, at an earlier period, a section of the nobility went over to the bourgeoisie, so now a portion of the bourgeoisie goes over to the proletariat, and in particular, a portion of the bourgeois ideologists, who have raised themselves to the level of comprehending theoretically the historical movement as a whole.

Of all the classes that stand face to face with the bourgeoisie today, the proletariat alone is a really revolutionary class. The other classes decay and finally disappear in the face of modern industry; the proletariat is its special and essential product. . . .

In the conditions of the proletariat, those of old society at large are already virtually swamped. The proletarian is without property; his relation to his wife and children has no longer anything in common with the bourgeois family relations; modern industrial labor, modern subjection to capital, the same in England as in France, in America as in Germany, has stripped him of every trace of national character. Law, morality, religion, are to him so many bourgeois prejudices, behind which lurk in ambush just as many bourgeois interests.

All the preceding classes that got the upper hand sought to fortify their already acquired status by subjecting society at large to their conditions of appropriation. The proletarians cannot become masters of the productive forces of society, except by abolishing their own previous mode of appropriation, and thereby also every other previous mode of appropriation. They have nothing of their own to secure and to fortify; their mission is to destroy all previous securities for, and insurances of, individual property.

All previous historical movements were movements of minorities, or in the interest of minorities. The proletarian movement is the self-conscious, independent movement of the immense majority, in the interest of the immense majority. The proletariat, the lowest stratum of our present society, cannot stir, cannot raise itself up, without the whole superincumbent strata of official society being sprung into the air.

Though not in substance, yet in form, the struggle of the proletariat with the bourgeoisie is at first a national struggle. The proletariat of each country must, of course, first of all settle matters with its own bourgeoisie.

In depicting the most general phases of the development of the proletariat, we traced the more or less veiled civil war, raging within existing society, up to the point where that war breaks out into open revolution, and where the violent overthrow of the bourgeoisie lays the foundation for the sway of the proletariat.

Hitherto every form of society has been based, as we have already seen, on the antagonism of oppressing and oppressed classes. But in order to oppress a class certain conditions must be assured to it under which it can, at least, continue its slavish existence. The serf, in the period of serfdom, raised himself to membership in the commune, just as the petty bourgeois, under the yoke of feudal absolutism, managed to develop into a bourgeois. The modern laborer, on the contrary, instead of rising with the progress of industry, sinks deeper and deeper below the conditions of existence of his own class. He becomes a pauper, and pauperism develops more rapidly than population and wealth. And here it becomes evident that the bourgeoisie is unfit any longer to be the ruling class in society and to impose its conditions of existence upon society as an overriding law. It is unfit to rule because it is incompetent to assure an existence to its slave within his slavery, because it cannot help letting him sink into such a state that it has to feed him instead of being fed by him. Society can no longer live under this bourgeoisie; in other words, its existence is no longer compatible with society.

The essential condition for the existence, and for the sway of the bourgeois class, is the formation and augmentation of capital; the condition for capital is wage-labor. Wage-labor rests exclusively on competition between the laborers. The advance of industry, whose involuntary promoter is the bourgeoisie, replaces the isolation of the laborers, due to competition, by their revolutionary combination, due to association. The development of modern industry, therefore, cuts from under its feet the very foundation on which the bourgeoisie produces and appropriates products. What the bourgeoisie therefore produces, above all, are its own grave diggers. Its fall and the victory of the proletariat are equally inevitable.

II: Proletarians and Communists

In what relation do the communists stand to the proletarians as a whole?

The communists do not form a separate party opposed to other working-class parties.

They have no interests separate and apart from those of the proletariat as a whole.

They do not set up any sectarian principles of their own by which to shape and mold the proletarian movement.

The communists are distinguished from the other working-class parties by this only: 1. In the national struggles of the proletarians of the different countries, they point out and bring to the front the common interests of the entire proletariat, independently of all nationality. 2. In the various stages of development which the struggle of the working class against the bourgeoisie has to pass through, they always and everywhere represent the interests of the movement as a whole.

The communists, therefore, are on the one hand, practically, the most advanced and resolute section of the working-class parties of every country, that section which pushes forward all others; on the other hand, theoretically, they have over the great mass of the proletariat the advantage of clearly understanding the line of march, the conditions, and the ultimate general results of the proletarian movement.

The immediate aim of the communists is the same as that of all the other proletarian parties: formation of the proletariat into a class, overthrow of the bourgeois supremacy, conquest of political power by the proletariat.

The theoretical conclusions of the communists are in no way based on ideas or principles that have been invented, or discovered, by this or that would-be universal reformer.

They merely express, in general terms, actual relations springing from an existing class struggle, from a historical movement going on under our very eyes. The abolition of existing property relations is not at all a distinctive feature of communism.

All property relations in the past have continually been subject to historical change, consequent upon the change in historical conditions.

The French Revolution, for example, abolished feudal property in favor of bourgeois property.

The distinguishing feature of communism is not the abolition of property generally, but the abolition of bourgeois property. But modern bourgeois private property is the final and most complete expression of the system of producing and appropriating products, that is based on class antagonisms, on the exploitation of the many by the few.

In this sense the theory of the communists may be summed up in the single sentence: abolition of private property.

We communists have been reproached with the desire of abolishing the right of personally acquiring property as the fruit of a man's own labor, which property is alleged to be the ground work of all personal freedom, activity, and independence.

Hard-won, self-acquired, self-earned property! Do you mean the property of the petty artisan and of the small peasant, a form of property that preceded the bourgeois form? There is no need to abolish that; the development of industry has to a great extent already destroyed it, and is still destroying it daily.

Or do you mean modern bourgeois private property?

But does wage-labor create any property for the laborer? Not a bit. It creates capital, *i.e.*, that kind of property which exploits wage-labor, and which cannot increase except upon condition of begetting a new supply of wage-labor for fresh exploitation. Property, in its present form, is based on the antagonism of capital and wage-labor. Let us examine both sides of this antagonism.

To be a capitalist, is to have not only a purely personal, but a social *status* in production. Capital is a collective product, and only by the united action of many members, nay, in the last resort, only by the united action of all members of society, can it be set in motion.

Capital is therefore not a personal, it is a social power.

When, therefore, capital is converted into common property, into the property of all members of society, personal property is not thereby transformed into social property. It is only the social character of the property that is changed. It loses its class character.

Let us now take wage-labor.

The average price of wage-labor is the minimum wage, *i.e.*, that quantum of the means of subsistence, which is absolutely requisite to keep the laborer in bare existence as a laborer. What, therefore, the wage-laborer appropriates by means of his labor, merely suffices to prolong and reproduce a bare existence. We by no means intend to abolish this personal appropriation of the products of labor, an appropriation that is made for the maintenance and reproduction of human life, and that leaves no surplus wherewith to command the labor of others. All that we want to do away with, is the miserable character of this appropriation, under which the laborer lives merely to increase capital, and is allowed to live only in so far as the interest of the ruling class requires it.

In bourgeois society living labor is but a means to increase accumulated labor. In communist society accumulated labor is but a means to widen, to enrich, to promote the existence of the laborer.

In bourgeois society, therefore, the past dominates the present; in communist society, the present dominates the past. In bourgeois society capital is independent and has individuality, while the living person is dependent and has no individuality.

And the abolition of this state of things is called by the bourgeois: abolition of individuality and freedom! And rightly so. The abolition of bourgeois individuality, bourgeois independence, and bourgeois freedom is undoubtedly aimed at.

By freedom is meant, under the present bourgeois conditions of production, free trade, free selling and buying.

But if selling and buying disappears, free selling and buying disappears also. This talk about free selling and buying, and all the other "brave words" of our bourgeoisie about freedom in general, have a meaning, if any, only in contrast with restricted selling and buying, with the fettered traders of the Middle Ages, but have no meaning when opposed to the communistic abolition of buying and selling, of the bourgeois conditions of production, and of the bourgeoisie itself.

You are horrified at our intending to do away with private property. But in your existing society private property is already done away with for nine tenths of the population; its existence for the few is solely due to its nonexistence in the hands of those nine tenths. You reproach us, therefore, with intending to do away with a form of property, the necessary condition for whose existence is the nonexistence of any property for the immense majority of society.

In one word, you reproach us with intending to do away with your property. Precisely so: that is just what we intend.

From the moment when labor can no longer be converted into capital, money, or rent, into a social power capable of being monopolized, *i.e.*, from the moment when individual property can no longer be transformed into bourgeois property, into capital, from that moment, you say, individuality vanishes!

You must, therefore, confess that by "individual" you mean no other person than the bourgeois, than the middle-class owner of property. This person must, indeed, be swept out of the way, and made impossible.

Communism deprives no man of the power to appropriate the products of society: all that it does is to deprive him of the power to subjugate the labor of others by means of such appropriation.

It has been objected, that upon the abolition of private property all work will cease, and universal laziness will overtake us.

According to this, bourgeois society ought long ago to have gone to the dogs through sheer idleness; for those of its members who work, acquire nothing, and those who acquire anything, do not work. The whole of this objection is but another expression of tautology, that there can no longer be any wage-labor when there is no longer any capital.

All objections against the communistic mode of producing and appropriating material products, have, in the same way, been urged against the communistic modes of producing and appropriating intellectual products. Just as to the bourgeois the disappearance of class property is the disappearance of production itself, so the disappearance of class culture is to him identical with the disappearance of all culture.

That culture, the loss of which he laments, is, for the enormous majority, a mere training to act as a machine.

But don't wrangle with us so long as you apply to our intended abolition of bourgeois property, the standard of your bourgeois notions of freedom, culture, law, etc. Your very ideas are but the outgrowth of the conditions of your bourgeois production and bourgeois property, just as your jurisprudence is but the will of your class made into a law for all, a will, whose essential character and direction are determined by the economical conditions of existence of your class.

The selfish misconception that induces you to transform into eternal laws of nature and of reason, the social forms springing from your present mode of production and form of property—historical relations that rise and disappear in the progress of production—the misconception you share with every ruling class that has preceded you. What you see clearly in the case of ancient property, what you admit in the case of feudal property, you are of course forbidden to admit in the case of your own bourgeois form of property. . . .

The communists are further reproached with desiring to abolish countries and nationality.

The workingmen have no country. We cannot take from them what they have not got. Since the proletariat must first of all acquire political supremacy, must rise to be the leading class of the nation, must constitute itself *the* nation, it is, so far, itself national, though not in the bourgeois sense of the word.

National differences and antagonisms between peoples are daily more and more vanishing, owing to the development of the bourgeoisie, to freedom of commerce, to the world's market, to uniformity in the mode of production and in the conditions of life corresponding thereto.

The supremacy of the proletariat will cause them to vanish still faster. United action, of the leading civilized countries at least, is one of the first conditions for the emancipation of the proletariat.

In proportion as the exploitation of one individual by another is put an end to, the exploitation of one nation by another will also be put an end to. In proportion as the antagonism between classes within the nation vanishes, the hostility of one nation to another will come to an end.

The charges against communism made from a religious, a philosophical, and, generally, from an ideological standpoint are not deserving of serious examination.

Does it require deep intuition to comprehend that man's ideas, views, and conceptions, in one word, man's consciousness changes with every change in the conditions of his material existence, in his social relations, and in his social life?

What else does the history of ideas prove, than that intellectual production changes its character in proportion as material production is changed? The ruling ideas of each age have ever been the ideas of its ruling class.

When people speak of ideas that revolutionize society they do but express the fact that within the old society the elements of a new one have been created, and that the dissolution of the old ideas keeps even pace with the dissolution of the old conditions of existence.

When the ancient world was in its last throes the ancient religions were overcome by Christianity. When Christian ideas succumbed in the eighteenth century to rationalist ideas, feudal society fought its death battle with the then revolutionary bourgeoisie. The ideas of religious liberty and freedom of conscience merely gave expression to the sway of free competition within the domain of knowledge.

"Undoubtedly," it will be said, "religious, moral, philosophical, and juridical ideas have been modified in the course of historical development. But religion, morality, philosophy, political science, and law, constantly survived this change.

"There are besides, eternal truths, such as Freedom, Justice, etc., that are common to all states of society. But communism abolishes eternal truths, it abolishes all religion and all morality, instead of constituting them on a new basis; it therefore acts in contradiction to all past historical experience."

What does this accusation reduce itself to? The history of all past society has consisted in the development of class antagonisms, antagonisms that assumed different forms at different epochs.

But whatever form they may have taken, one fact is common to all past ages, viz., the exploitation of one part of society by the other. No wonder, then, that the social consciousness of past ages, despite all the multiplicity and variety it displays, moves within certain common forms, or general ideas, which cannot completely vanish except with the total disappearance of class antagonisms.

The communist revolution is the most radical rupture with traditional property relations; no wonder that its development involves the most radical rupture with traditional ideas.

But let us have done with the bourgeois objections to communism.

We have seen above that the first step in the revolution by the working class is to raise the proletariat to the position of the ruling class; to win the battle of democracy.

The proletariat will use its political supremacy to wrest, by degrees, all capital from the bourgeoisie; to centralize all instruments of production in the hands of the state, *i.e.*, of the proletariat organized as the ruling class; and to increase the total of productive forces as rapidly as possible.

Of course, in the beginning this cannot be effected except by means of despotic inroads on the rights of property and on the conditions of bourgeois production; by means of measures, therefore, which appear economically insufficient and untenable, but which, in the course of the movement, outstrip themselves, necessitate further inroads upon the old social order and are unavoidable as a means of entirely revolutionizing the mode of production.

These measures will, of course, be different in different countries.

Nevertheless in the most advanced countries the following will be pretty generally applicable:

1. Abolition of property in land and application of all rents of land to public purposes.

2. A heavy progressive or graduated income tax.

3. Abolition of all right of inheritance.

4. Confiscation of the property of all emigrants and rebels.

5. Centralization of credit in the hands of the state, by means of a national bank with state capital and an exclusive monopoly.

6. Centralization of the means of communication and transport in the hands of the state.

7. Extension of factories and instruments of production owned by the state; the bringing into cultivation of waste lands, and the improvement of the soil generally in accordance with a common plan.

8. Equal liability of all to labor. Establishment of industrial armies, especially for agriculture.

9. Combination of agriculture with manufacturing industries: gradual abolition of the distinction between town and country, by a more equable distribution of the population over the country.

10. Free education for all children in public schools. Abolition of children's factory labor in its present form. Combination of education with industrial production, etc., etc.

When, in the course of development, class distinctions have disappeared and all production has been concentrated in the hands of a vast association of the whole nation, the public power will lose its political character. Political power, properly so called, is merely the organized power of one class for oppressing another. If the proletariat during its contest with the bourgeoisie is compelled, by the force of circumstances, to organize itself as a class, if, by means of a revolution, it makes itself the ruling class, and, as such, sweeps away by force the old conditions of production then it will, along with these conditions, have swept away the conditions for the existence of class antagonisms, and of classes generally, and will thereby have abolished its own supremacy as a class.

In place of the old bourgeois society with its classes and class antagonisms we shall have an association in which the free development of each is the condition for the free development of all. . . .

IV: Position of the Communists in Relation to the Various Existing Opposition Parties

Section II has made clear the relations of the communists to the existing working-class parties, such as the Chartists in England and the Agrarian Reformers in America.

The communists fight for the attainment of the immediate aims, for the enforcement of the momentary interests of the working class; but in the movement of the present, they also represent and take care of the future of that movement. In France the communists ally themselves with the Social-Democrats, against the conservative and radical bourgeoisie, reserving, however, the right to take up a critical position in regard to phrases and illusions traditionally handed down from the great Revolution.

In Switzerland they support the Radicals, without losing sight of the fact that this party consists of antagonistic elements, partly of Democratic Socialists, in the French sense, partly of radical bourgeois.

In Poland they support the party that insists on an agrarian revolution as the prime condition for national emancipation, that party which fomented the insurrection of Cracow in 1846.

In Germany they fight with the bourgeoisie whenever it acts in a revolutionary way against the absolute monarchy, the feudal squirearchy, and the petty bourgeoisie.

But they never cease, for a single instant, to instill into the working class the clearest possible recognition of the hostile antagonism between bourgeoisie and proletariat, in order that the German workers may straightway use, as so many weapons against the bourgeoisie, the social and political conditions that the bourgeoisie must necessarily introduce along with its supremacy, and in order that, after the fall of the reactionary classes in Germany, the fight against the bourgeoisie itself may immediately begin.

The communists turn their attention chiefly to Germany, because that country is on the eve of a bourgeois revolution that is bound to be carried out under more advanced conditions of European civilization, and with a much more developed proletariat, than that of England was in the seventeenth, and of France in the eighteenth century, and because the bourgeois revolution in Germany will be but the prelude to an immediately following proletarian revolution.

In short, the communists everywhere support every revolutionary movement against the existing social and political order of things.

In all these movements they bring to the front, as the leading question in each, the property question, no matter what its degree of development at the time.

Finally, they labor everywhere for the union and agreement of the democratic parties of all countries.

The communists disdain to conceal their views and aims. They openly declare that their ends can be attained only by the forcible overthrow of all existing social conditions. Let the ruling classes tremble at a communistic revolution. The proletarians have nothing to lose but their chains. They have a world to win.

Workingmen of all countries unite!

Part II.

SCHOOLS OF SOCIALIST THOUGHT

The half century which followed the publication of *The Communist Manifesto* produced numerous variants on the original Marxist program as stated in that pamphlet. These variants resulted not only from the natural tendency of a philosophy to proliferate but also from the enormous changes which took place in the economic and political condition of Europe and the world. These variations in socialist thought inspired controversies among socialists, and never since the days when religious arguments were taken seriously have controversies been conducted with more bitterness and malice. Some socialists professed to preach the true faith according to Marx; others sought to reinterpret Marx in the light of changing conditions; others professed to reject Marx entirely and teach a new doctrine; still others rejected these later interpretations and glosses and returned to the true, fundamental, four-square Marxist gospel. Since Marx and Engels produced a vast amount of socialist literature and revised certain of the opinions set forth in *The Communist Manifesto,* there was ample opportunity for exegesis and the higher criticism. Many of these arguments were debated at, or in connection with, meetings of the International. In 1864, under Marx's own influence, the International Workingmen's Association was founded at London. This organization, known as the First International, held several conferences, attended by labor representatives from many countries, but the pressure of internal dissension proved too strong, and it dissolved in 1873. The Second International was founded in 1889 and lasted until the outbreak of World War I in 1914. The documents which follow indicate four important variants on the socialist doctrine as originally stated in *The Communist Manifesto;* the student should attempt to discover their relationship to that doctrine.

A.

MARXISM—LATTER-DAY VERSION

In 1850, Marx wrote four articles for a German newspaper on "The Class Struggles in France" (1848–50). When the articles were republished in book form in 1895, Engels wrote an introduction, selections from which are printed below. The course of events after the revolutions of 1848, including the failure of those revolutions, the fall of the revolutionary French Commune in 1871, and the foundation and development of the German Empire, caused Marx and Engels to modify their original program. Although Engels wrote his introduction more than ten years after Marx's death, the ideas contained therein may be regarded as typical of those held by Marx in his later days. (3)

When the February revolution [1848] broke out, we all of us, as far as our conception of the conditions and the course of revolutionary movements was concerned, were under the spell of previous historical experience, namely that of France. It was, indeed, the latter which had dominated the whole of European history since 1789, and from which now once again the signal had gone forth for general revolutionary change. It was therefore natural and unavoidable that our conceptions of the nature and the path of the "social" revolution proclaimed in Paris in February 1848, of the revolution of the proletariat, were strongly colored by memories of the models of 1789–1830. Moreover, when the Paris upheaval found its echo in the victorious insurrections in Vienna, Milan, and Berlin; when the whole of Europe right up to the Russian frontier was swept into the movement; when in Paris the first great battle for power between the proletariat and the bourgeoisie was joined; when the very victory of their class so shook the bourgeoisie of all countries that they fled back into the arms of the monarchist-feudal reaction which had just been overthrown—for us, under the circumstances of the time, there could be no doubt that the great decisive struggle had broken out, that it would have to be fought out in a single, long and changeful period of revolution, but that it could only end with the final victory of the proletariat.

After the defeats of 1849 we in no way shared the illusions of the vulgar democracy grouped around the would-be provisional governments *in partibus*. This vulgar democracy reckoned on a speedy and finally decisive victory of the "people" over the "usurpers"; we looked to a long struggle, after the removal of the "usurpers," between the antagonistic elements concealed within this "people" itself. Vulgar democracy expected a renewed outbreak from day to day; we declared as early as autumn 1850 that at least the first chapter of the revolutionary period was closed and that nothing further was to be expected until the outbreak of a new world crisis. . . .

But we . . . have been shown to have been wrong by history, which has revealed our point of view of that time to have been an illusion. It has done even more: it has not merely destroyed our error of that time; it has also completely transformed the conditions under which the proletariat has to fight. The mode of struggle of 1848 is today obsolete from every point of view, and this is a point which deserves closer examination on the present occasion.

All revolutions up to the present day have resulted in the displacement of one definite class rule by another; all ruling classes up till now have been only minorities as against the ruled mass of the people. A ruling minority was thus overthrown; another minority seized the helm of state and remodeled the state apparatus in accordance with its own interests. This was on every occasion the minority group able and called to rule by the degree of economic development, and just for that reason, and only for that reason, it happened that the ruled majority either participated in the revolution on the side of the former or else passively acquiesced in it. But if we disregard the concrete content of each occasion, the common form of all these revolutions was that they were minority revolutions. Even where the majority took part, it did so—whether wittingly or not—only in the service of a minority; but because of this, or simply because of the passive, unresisting attitude of the majority, this minority acquired the appearance of being the representative of the whole people.

As a rule, after the first great success, the victorious minority became divided; one half was pleased with what had been gained, the other wanted to go still further, and put forward new demands, which, to a certain extent at least, were also in the real or apparent interests of the great mass of the people. In individual cases these more radical demands were realized, but often only for the moment; the more moderate party again gained the upper hand, and what had eventually been one was wholly or partly lost again; the vanquished shrieked of treachery, or ascribed their defeat to accident. But in truth the position was mainly this: the achievements of the first victory were only safeguarded by the second victory of the more radical party; this having been attained, and, with it, what was necessary for the moment, the radicals and their achievements vanished once more from the stage.

All revolutions of modern times, beginning with the great English revolution of the seventeenth century, showed these features, which appeared inseparable from every revolutionary struggle. They appeared applicable, also, to the struggles of the proletariat for its emancipation; all the more applicable, since in 1848 there were few people who had any idea at all of the direction in which this emancipation was to be sought. The proletarian masses themselves, even in Paris, after the victory, were still absolutely in the dark as to the path to be taken. And yet the movement was there, instinctive, spontaneous, irrepressible. Was not this just the situation in which a revolution had to succeed, led certainly by a minority, but this time not in the interests of the minority, but in the real interests of the majority? If, in all the longer revolutionary periods, it was so easy to win the great masses of the people by the merely plausible and delusive views of the minorities thrusting themselves forward, how could they be less susceptible to ideas which were the truest reflex of their economic position, which were nothing but the clear comprehensible expression of their needs, of needs not yet understood by themselves, but only vaguely felt? To be sure, this revolutionary mood of the masses had almost always, and usually very speedily, given way to lassitude or even to a revulsion to its opposite, so soon as illusion evaporated and disappointment set in. But here it was not a question of delusive views, but of giving effect to the very special interests of the great majority itself, interests which at that time were certainly by no means clear to this great majority, but which must soon enough become clear in the course of giving practical effect to them; by their convincing obviousness. And if now, as Marx showed in the third article, in the spring of 1850, the development of the bourgeois republic that had arisen out of the "social" revolution of 1848 had concentrated the real power in the hands of the big bourgeoisie—monarchistically inclined as it was—and, on the other hand, had grouped all the other social classes, peasants as well as petty bourgeoisie, round the proletariat, so that, during and after the common victory, not they, but the proletariat grown wise by experience, must become the decisive factor—was there not every prospect here of turning the revolution of the minority into the revolution of the majority?

History has proved us, and all who thought like us, wrong. It has made it clear that the state of economic development on the Continent at that time was not, by a long way, ripe for the removal of capitalist production; it has proved this by the economic revolution which, since 1848, has seized the whole of the Continent, has really caused big industry for the first time to take root in France, Austria, Hungary, Poland and, recently, in Russia, while it has made Germany positively an industrial country of the first rank—all on a capitalist basis, which in the year 1848, therefore, still had great capacity for expansion. But it is just this industrial revolution which has everywhere for the first time produced clarity in the class relationships, which has removed a number of transition forms handed down from the manufacturing period and in eastern Europe even from guild handicraft, and has created a genuine bourgeoisie and a genuine large-scale industrial proletariat and pushed them into the foreground of social development. But, owing to this, the struggle of these two great classes, which, apart from England, existed in 1848 only in Paris and, at the most, a few big industrial centers, has been spread over the whole of Europe and has reached an intensity such as was unthinkable in 1848. At that time the many obscure evangels of the sects, with their panaceas; today the one generally recognized, transparently clear theory of Marx, sharply formulating the final aims of the struggle. At that time the masses, sundered and differing according to locality and nationality, linked only by the feeling of common suffering, undeveloped, tossed to and fro in their perplexity from enthusiasm to despair; today a great international army of socialists, marching irresistibly on and growing daily in number, organization, discipline, insight, and assurance of victory. If even this mighty army of the proletariat has still not reached its goal, if, a long way from winning victory with one mighty stroke, it has slowly to press forward from position to position in a hard, tenacious struggle, this only proves, once and for all, how impossible it was in 1848 to win social reconstruction by a simple surprise attack. . . .

It was believed that the militant proletariat had been finally buried with the Paris Commune [1871]. But, completely to the contrary, it dates its most powerful advance from the Commune and the Franco-German war. The recruitment of the whole population able to bear arms into armies that could be counted in millions, and the introduction of firearms, projectiles, and explosives of hitherto undreamed of efficacy created a complete revolution in all warfare. This, on the one hand, put a sudden end to the Bonapartist war period and insured peaceful industrial development, since any war other than a world war of unheard of cruelty and absolutely incalculable outcome had become an impossibility. On the other hand, it caused military expenditure to rise in geometrical progression, and thereby forced up taxes to exorbitant levels and so drove the poorer classes of people into the arms of socialism. . . .

The war of 1870–71 and the defeat of the Commune had transferred the center of gravity of the European workers' movement for the time being from France to Germany, as Marx foretold. In France it naturally took years to recover from the bloodletting of May 1871. In Germany, on the other hand, where industry was, in addition, furthered (in positively hothouse fashion) by the blessing of the French milliards and developed more and more quickly, social democracy experienced a much more rapid and enduring growth. Thanks to the understanding with which the German workers made use of the universal suffrage introduced in 1866, the astonishing growth of the Party is made plain to all the world by incontestable figures. 1871, 102,000; 1874, 352,000; 1877, 493,000 Social-Democratic votes. Then came recognition of this advance by high authority in the shape of the Anti-Socialist Law: the Party was temporarily disrupted; the number of votes sank to 312,000 in 1881. But that was quickly overcome, and then, though oppressed by the Exceptional Law, without press, without external organization, and without the right of combination or meeting, the rapid expansion really began: 1884, 550,000; 1887, 763,000; 1890, 1,427,000 votes. Then the hand of the state was paralyzed. The Anti-Socialist Law disappeared; socialist votes rose to 1,787,000, over a quarter of all the votes cast. The government and the ruling classes had exhausted all their expedients—uselessly, to no purpose, and without success. The tangible proofs of their impotence, which the authorities, from night watchman to the imperial chancellor, had had to accept—and that from the despised workers—these proofs were counted in millions. . . .

But the German workers did a second great service to their cause in addition to the first, which they rendered by their mere existence as the strongest, best disciplined and most rapidly growing Socialist Party. They supplied their comrades of all countries with a new weapon, and one of the sharpest, when they showed them how to use universal suffrage.

There had long been universal suffrage in France, but it had fallen into disrepute through the misuse to which the Bonapartist government had put it. After the Commune there was no workers' party to make use of it. Also in Spain it had existed since the republic, but in Spain boycott of the elections was ever the rule of all serious opposition parties. The Swiss experiences of universal suffrage, also, were anything but encouraging for a workers' party. The revolutionary workers of the Latin countries had been wont to regard the suffrage as a snare, as an instrument of government trickery. It was otherwise in Germany. *The Communist Manifesto* had already proclaimed the winning of universal suffrage, of democracy, as one of the first and most important tasks of the militant proletariat, and Lassalle had again taken up this point. When Bismarck found himself compelled to introduce the franchise as the only means of interesting the mass of the people in his plans, our workers immediately took it in earnest and sent August Bebel to the first constituent *Reichstag*. And from that day on they have used the franchise in a way which has paid them a thousandfold and has served as a model to the workers of all countries. . .—they have transformed it from a means of deception, which it was heretofore, into an instrument of emancipation. And if universal suffrage had offered no other advantage than that it allowed us to count our numbers every three years; that by the regularly established, unexpectedly rapid rise in the number of votes it increased in equal measure the workers' certainty of victory and the dismay of their opponents, and so became our best means of propaganda; that it accurately informed us concerning our own strength and that of all hostile parties, and thereby provided us with a measure of proportion for our actions second to none, safeguarding us from untimely timidity as much as from untimely foolhardiness—if this had been the only advantage we gained from the suffrage, then it would still have been more than enough. But it has done much more than this. In election agitation it provided us with a means, second to none, of getting in touch with the mass of the people, where they still stand aloof from us; of forcing all parties to defend their views and actions against our attacks before all the people; and, further, it opened to our representatives in the *Reichstag* a platform from which they could speak to their opponents in Parliament and to the masses without, with quite other authority and freedom than in the press or at meetings. Of what avail to the government and the bourgeoisie was their Anti-Socialist Law when election agitation and socialist speeches in the *Reichstag* continually broke through it?

With this successful utilization of universal suffrage, an entirely new mode of proletarian struggle came into force, and this quickly developed further. It was found that the state institutions, in which the rule of the bourgeoisie is organized, offer still further opportunities for the working class to fight these very state institutions. They took part in elections to individual diets, to municipal councils, and to industrial courts; they contested every post against the bourgeoisie in the occupation of which a sufficient part of the proletariat had its say. And so it happened that the bourgeoisie and the government came to be much more afraid of the legal than of the illegal action of the workers' party, of the results of elections than of those of rebellion.

For here, too, the conditions of the struggle had essentially changed. Rebellion in the old style, the street fight with barricades, which up to 1848 gave everywhere the final decision, was to a considerable extent obsolete. . . .

The chances . . . were in 1849 already pretty poor. Everywhere the bourgeoisie had thrown in its lot with the governments, "culture and property" had hailed and feasted the military moving against the insurrections. The spell of the barricade was broken; the soldier no longer saw behind it "the people," but rebels, agitators, plunderers, levelers, the scum of society; the officer had in the course of time become versed in the tactical forms of street fighting, he no longer marched straight ahead and without cover against the improvised breastwork, but went round it through gardens, yards, and houses. And this was now successful, with a little skill, in nine cases out of ten.

But since then there have been very many more changes, and all in favor of the military. If the big towns have become considerably bigger, the armies have become bigger still. Paris and Berlin have, since 1848, grown less than fourfold, but their garrisons have grown more than that. By means of the railways, the garrisons can, in twenty-four hours, be more than doubled, and in forty-eight hours they can be increased to huge armies. The arming of this enormously increased number of troops has become incomparably more effective. In 1848 the smooth-bore percussion muzzle-loader, today the small-caliber magazine breech-loading rifle, which shoots four times as far, ten times as accurately, and ten times as fast as the former. At that time the relatively ineffective round shot and grapeshot of the artillery; today the percussion shells, of which one is sufficient to demolish the best barricade. At that time the pickax of the sapper for breaking through walls; today the dynamite cartridge.

On the other hand, all the conditions on the insurgents' side have grown worse. An insurrection with which all sections of the people sympathize will hardly recur; in the class struggle all the middle sections will never group themselves round the proletariat so exclusively that the reactionary parties gathered round the bourgeoisie well-nigh disappear. The "people," therefore, will always appear divided, and with this a powerful lever, so extraordinarily effective in 1848, is lacking. Even if more soldiers who have seen service were to come over to the insurrectionists, the arming of them becomes so much the more difficult. The hunting and luxury guns of the gun-shops—even if not previously made unusable by removal of part of the lock by the police—are far from being a match for the magazine rifle of the soldier, even in close fighting. Up to 1848 it was possible to make the necessary ammunition oneself out of powder and lead; today the cartridges differ for each rifle, and are everywhere alike only in one point, that they are a special product of big industry, and therefore not to be prepared *ex tempore,* with the result that most rifles are useless as long as one does not possess the ammunition specially suited to them. And, finally, since 1848 the newly built quarters of the big towns have been laid out in long, straight, broad streets, as though made to give full effect to the new cannons and rifles. . . .

The time of surprise attacks, of revolutions carried through by small conscious minorities at the head of unconscious masses, is past. Where it is a question of a complete transformation of the social organization, the masses themselves must also be in it, must themselves already have grasped what is at stake, what they are going in for with body and soul. The history of the last fifty years has taught us that. But in order that the masses may understand what is to be done, long, persistent work is required, and it is just this work which we are now pursuing, and with a success which drives the enemy to despair.

In the Latin countries, also, it is being more and more recognized that the old tactics must be revised. Everywhere the unprepared onslaught has gone into the background, everywhere the German example of utilizing the suffrage, of winning all posts accessible to us, has been imitated. In France, where for more than a hundred years the ground has been undermined by revolution after revolution, where there is no single party which has not done its share in conspiracies, insurrections, and all other revolutionary actions; in France, where, as a result, the government is by no means sure of the army and where, in general, the conditions for an insurrectionary *coup de main* are far more favorable than in Germany —even in France the socialists are realizing more and more that no lasting victory is possible for them, unless they first win the great mass of the people, *i.e.,* in this case, the peasants. Slow propaganda work and parliamentary activity are being recognized here, too, as the most immediate

tasks of the Party. Successes were not lacking. Not only have a whole series of municipal councils been won; fifty socialists have seats in the Chambers, and they have already overthrown three ministries and a president of the Republic. In Belgium last year the workers enforced the franchise, and have been victorious in a quarter of the constituencies. In Switzerland, in Italy, in Denmark, yes, even in Bulgaria and Rumania the socialists are represented in the parliaments. In Austria all parties agree that our admission to the *Reichsrat* can no longer be withheld. We will get in, that is certain, the only question still in dispute is: by which door? And even in Russia, when the famous *Zemsky Sobor* meets, that national assembly to which young Nicholas offers such vain resistance, even there we can reckon with certainty on also being represented in it.

Of course, our foreign comrades do not renounce their right to revolution. The right to revolution is, after all, the only real "historical right," the only right on which all modern states without exception rest. . . .

But whatever may happen in other countries, German social democracy has a special situation and therewith, at least in the first instance, a special task. The two million voters whom it sends to the ballot box, together with the young men and women who stand behind them as nonvoters, form the most numerous, most compact mass, the decisive *"shock force"* of the international proletarian army. This mass already supplies over a fourth of the recorded votes; and as the by-elections to the *Reichstag,* the diet elections in individual states, the municipal council and industrial court elections demonstrate, it increases uninterruptedly. Its growth proceeds as spontaneously, as steadily, as irresistibly, and at the same time as tranquilly as a natural process. All government interventions have proved powerless against it. We can count even today on two and a half million voters. If it continues in this fashion, by the end of the century we shall conquer the greater part of the middle section of society, petty bourgeois and small peasants, and grow into the decisive power in the land, before which all other powers will have to bow, whether they like it or not. To keep this growth going without interruption until of itself it gets beyond the control of the ruling governmental system, not to fritter away this daily increasing shock force in advance guard fighting, but to keep it intact until the day of the decision, that is our main task. And there is only one means by which the steady rise of the socialist fighting forces in Germany could be momentarily halted, and even thrown back for some time: a clash on a big scale with the military, a bloodbath like that of 1871 in Paris. In the long run that would also be overcome. To shoot out of the world a party which numbers millions—all the magazine rifles of Europe and America are not enough for this. But the normal development would be impeded, the shock force would, perhaps, not be available at the critical moment, *the decisive struggle* would be delayed, protracted, and attended by heavy sacrifices.

The irony of world history turns everything upside down. We, the "revolutionaries," the "rebels"—we are thriving far better on legal methods than on illegal methods and revolt. The parties of order, as they call themselves, are perishing under the legal conditions created by themselves. They cry despairingly . . . legality is the death of us; whereas we, under this legality, get firm muscles and rosy cheeks and look like eternal life. And if we are not so crazy as to let ourselves be driven into street fighting in order to please them, then nothing else is finally left for them but themselves to break through the legality so fatal to them.

B. ANARCHISM

Anarchism had exponents in all countries but it seems to have had a particularly powerful appeal to Russians. Since anarchism was also condemned by many socialists as aristocratic, it is perhaps fitting that the student should read the work of a Russian aristocrat, Prince Peter Kropotkin. Kropotkin (1842–1921), who was also a noted geographer, embraced the anarchist creed in 1874. He was imprisoned by the Russian government but escaped in 1876 and spent almost all his life in exile. The selections which follow are from a pamphlet, originally published in 1896, entitled "Anarchism: Its Philosophy and Ideal." (4)

Educated men—"civilized," as Fourier used to say with disdain—tremble at the idea that society might some day be without judges, police, or jailers.

But, frankly, do you need them as much as you have been told in musty books? Books written, be it noted, by scientists who generally know well what has been written before them, but, for the most part, absolutely ignore the people and their everyday life.

If we can wander, without fear, not only in the streets of Paris, which bristle with police, but especially in rustic walks where you rarely meet passers-by, is it to the police that we owe this security? Or rather to the absence of people who care to rob or murder us? I am evidently not speaking of the one who carries millions about him. That one—a recent trial tells us—is soon robbed, by preference in places where there are as many policemen as lampposts. No, I speak of the man who fears for his life and not for his purse filled with ill-gotten sovereigns. Are his fears real?

Besides, has not experience demonstrated quite recently that Jack the Ripper performed his exploits under the eye of the London police—a most active force—and that he only left off killing when the population of Whitechapel itself began to give chase to him?

And in our everyday relations with our fellow citizens, do you think that it is really judges, jailers, and police that hinder antisocial acts from multiplying? The judge, ever ferocious, because he is a maniac of law, the accuser, the informer, the police spy, all those interlopers that live from hand to mouth around the law courts, do they not scatter demoralization far and wide into society? Read the trials, glance behind the scenes, push your analysis further than the exterior façade of law courts, and you will come out sickened.

Have not prisons—which kill all will and force of character in man, which enclose within their walls more vices than are met with on any other spot of the globe—always been universities of crime? Is not the court of a tribunal a school of ferocity? And so on.

When we ask for the abolition of the state and its organs we are always told that we dream of a society composed of men better than they are in reality. But no; a thousand times, no. All we ask is that men should not be made worse than they are, by such institutions!

Once a German jurist of great renown, Ihering, wanted to sum up the scientific work of his life and write a treatise, in which he proposed to analyze the factors that preserve social life in society. *Purpose in Law* (*Der Zweck im Rechte*), such is the title of that book, which enjoys a well-deserved reputation.

He made an elaborate plan of his treatise, and, with much erudition, discussed both coercive factors which are used to maintain society; wagedom and the different forms of coercion which are sanctioned by law. At the end of his work he reserved two paragraphs only to mention the two noncoercive factors—the feeling of duty and the feeling of mutual sympathy—to which he attached little importance, as might be expected from a writer in law.

But what happened? As he went on analyzing the coercive factors he realized their insufficiency. He consecrated a whole volume to their analysis, and the result was to lessen their importance! When he began the last two paragraphs, when he began to reflect upon the noncoercive factors of society, he perceived, on the contrary, their immense, outweighing importance; and, instead of two paragraphs, he found himself obliged to write a second volume, twice as large as the first, on these two factors: voluntary restraint and mutual help; and yet, he analyzed but an infinitesimal part of these latter—those which result from personal sympathy—and hardly touched free agreement, which results from social institutions.

Well, then, leave off repeating the formulae which you have learned at school; meditate on this subject; and the same thing that happened to Ihering will happen to you: you will recognize the infinitesimal importance of coercion, as compared to the voluntary assent, in society.

On the other hand, if by following the very old advice given by Bentham you begin to think of the fatal consequences—direct, and especially indirect—of legal coercion, then, like Tolstoy, like us, you will begin to hate the use of coercion, and you will begin to say that society possesses a thousand other means for preventing antisocial acts. If it neglects those means today, it is because, being educated by church and state, our cowardice and apathy of spirit hinder us seeing clearly on this point. When a child has committed a fault, it is so easy to punish it; that puts an end to all discussions! It is so easy to hang a man—especially when there is an executioner who is paid so much for each execution— and it dispenses us from thinking of the cause of crimes.

C.   SYNDICALISM

Although certain of the aspects of syndicalism may be found in the ideas of the Utopian socialist Robert Owen, the syndicalist movement first became of practical importance in France in the 1890's, and, in fact, the name is derived from *syndicat,* the French word for labor union. The movement spread to other countries, being especially powerful in Italy and Spain. In the United States syndicalism was represented by the I.W.W.—the Industrial Workers of the World. The following sympathetic account of the aims and methods of syndicalism is taken from "Syndicalism: The Modern Menace to Capitalism," a pamphlet written in 1913 by Emma Goldman. Miss Goldman (1869–1940) was born in Russia and came to the United States in 1886. She soon became famous in this country and abroad for her Left-wing activities, so famous that she served a year in prison for inciting a riot. (5)

In view of the fact that the ideas embodied in syndicalism have been practiced by the workers for the last half-century, even if without the background of social consciousness; that in this country five men had to pay with their lives because they advocated syndicalist methods as the most effective in the struggle of labor against capital; and that, furthermore, syndicalism has been consciously practiced by the workers of France, Italy, and Spain since 1895, it is rather amusing to witness some people in America and England now swooping down upon syndicalism as a perfectly new and never before heard-of proposition. . . .

Our bourgeois magazines are full of dissertations on syndicalism. One of our most conservative colleges has even gone to the extent of publishing a work of one of its students on the subject, which has the approval of a professor. And all this, not because syndicalism is a force and is being successfully practiced by the workers of Europe, but because—as I said before—it has official authoritative sanction.

As if syndicalism had been discovered by the philosophy of Bergson or the theoretic discourses of Sorel and Borth, and had not existed and lived among the workers long before these men wrote about it. The feature which distinguishes syndicalism from most philosophies is that it represents the revolutionary philosophy of labor conceived and born in the actual struggle and experience of the workers themselves—not in universities, colleges, libraries, or in the brain of some scientists. *The revolutionary philosophy of labor,* that is the true and vital meaning of syndicalism.

Already as far back as 1848 a large section of the workers realized the utter futility of political activity as a means of helping them in their economic struggle. At that time already the demand went forth for direct economic measures, as against the useless waste of energy along political lines. This was the case not only in France, but even prior to that in England, where Robert Owen, the true revolutionary socialist, propagated similar ideas.

After years of agitation and experiment the idea was incorporated by the first convention of the Internationale, in 1867, in the resolution that the economic emancipation of the workers must be the principal aim of all revolutionists, to which everything else is to be subordinated.

In fact, it was this determined radical stand which eventually brought about the split in the revolutionary movement of that day, and its division into two factions; the one, under Marx and Engels, aiming at political conquest; the other, under Bakunin and the Latin workers, forging ahead along industrial and syndicalist lines. The further development of those two wings is familiar to every thinking man and woman: the one has gradually centralized into a huge machine, with the sole purpose of conquering political power within the existing capitalist state; the other is becoming an ever more vital revolutionary factor, dreaded by the enemy as the greatest menace to its rule. . . .

The fundamental difference between syndicalism and the old trade-union methods is this: while the old trade unions, without exception, move within the wage system and capitalism, recognizing the latter as inevitable, syndicalism repudiates and condemns present industrial arrangements as unjust and criminal, and holds out no hope to the worker for lasting results from this system.

Of course syndicalism, like the old trade unions, fights for immediate gains but it is not stupid enough to pretend that labor can expect humane conditions from inhuman economic arrangements in society. Thus it merely wrests from the enemy what it can force him to yield; on the whole, however, syndicalism aims at, and concentrates its energies upon, the complete overthrow of the wage system. Indeed, syndicalism goes further: it aims to liberate labor from every institution that has not for its object the free development of production for the benefit of all humanity. In short, the ultimate purpose of syndicalism is to reconstruct society from its present centralized, authoritative, and brutal state to one based upon the free, federated grouping of the workers along lines of economic and social liberty.

With this object in view, syndicalism works in two directions: first, by undermining the existing institutions; secondly, by developing and educating the workers and cultivating their spirit of solidarity, to prepare them for a full, free life, when capitalism shall have been abolished.

Syndicalism is, in essence, the economic expression of anarchism. That circumstance accounts for the presence of so many anarchists in the syndicalist movement. Like anarchism, syndicalism prepares the workers along direct economic lines, as conscious factors in the great struggles of today, as well as conscious factors in the task of reconstructing society along autonomous industrial lines, as against the paralyzing spirit of centralization with its bureaucratic machinery of corruption, inherent in all political parties.

Realizing that the diametrically opposed interests of capital and labor can never be reconciled, syndicalism must needs repudiate the old rusticated, worn-out methods of trade unionism, and declare for an open war against the capitalist regime, as well as against every institution which today supports and protects capitalism.

As a logical sequence syndicalism, in its daily warfare against capitalism, rejects the contract system, because it does not consider labor and capital equals, hence cannot consent to an agreement which the one has the power to break, while the other must submit to without redress.

For similar reasons syndicalism rejects negotiations in labor disputes, because such a procedure serves only to give the enemy time to prepare his end of the fight, thus defeating the very object the workers set out to accomplish. Also, syndicalism stands for spontaneity, both as a preserver of the fighting strength of labor and also because it takes the enemy unawares, hence compels him to a speedy settlement or causes him great loss. . . .

As I have already stated, syndicalism has grown out of the disappointment of the workers with politics and parliamentary methods. In the course of its development syndicalism has learned to see in the state—with its mouthpiece, the representative system—one of the strongest supports of capitalism; just as it has learned that the army and the church are the chief pillars of the state. It is therefore that syndicalism has turned its back upon parliamentarianism and political machines, and has set its face toward the economic arena wherein alone gladiator labor can meet his foes successfully. . . .

Now, as to the methods employed by syndicalism—Direct Action, Sabotage, and the General Strike.

DIRECT ACTION—*Conscious individual or collective effort to protest against, or remedy, social conditions through the systematic assertion of the economic power of the workers.*

Sabotage has been decried as criminal, even by so-called revolutionary socialists. Of course, if you believe that property, which excludes the producer from its use, is justifiable, then sabotage is indeed a crime. But unless a socialist continues to be under the influence of our bourgeois morality—a morality which enables the few to monopolize the earth at the expense of the many—he cannot consistently maintain that capitalist property is inviolate. Sabotage undermines this form of private possession. Can it therefore be considered criminal? On the contrary, it is ethical in the best sense, since it helps society to get rid of its worst foe, the most detrimental factor of social life. . . .

By the GENERAL STRIKE, syndicalism means a stoppage of work, the cessation of labor. Nor need such a strike be postponed until all the workers of a particular place or country are ready for it. As has been pointed out by Pelloutier, Pouget, as well as others, and particularly by recent events in England, the general strike may be started by one industry and exert a tremendous force. It is as if one man suddenly raised the cry "Stop the thief!" Immediately others will take up the cry, till the air rings with it. The general strike, initiated by one determined organization, by one industry, or by a small, conscious minority among the workers, is the industrial cry of "Stop the thief," which is soon taken up by many other industries, spreading like wildfire in a very short time. . . .

These ideas and methods of syndicalism some may consider entirely negative, though they are far from it in their effect upon society today. But syndicalism has also a directly positive aspect. In fact, much more time and effort is being devoted to that phase than to the others. Various forms of syndicalist activity are designed to prepare the workers, even within present social and industrial conditions, for the life of a new and better society. To that end the masses are trained in the spirit of mutual aid and brotherhood, their initiative and self-reliance developed, and an *esprit de corps* maintained whose very soul is solidarity of purpose and the community of interests of the international proletariat. . . .

One of the most vital efforts of syndicalism is to prepare the workers, *now,* for their role in a free society. Thus the syndicalist organizations supply its members with textbooks on every trade and industry, of a character that is calculated to make the worker an adept in his chosen line, a master of his craft, for the purpose of familiarizing him with all the branches of his industry, so that when labor finally takes over production and distribution, the people will be fully prepared to manage successfully their own affairs. . . .

This method of applied education not only trains the worker in his daily struggle but serves also to equip him for the battle royal and the future, when he is to assume his place in society as an intelligent, conscious being and useful producer, once capitalism is abolished.

Nearly all leading syndicalists agree with the anarchists that a free society can exist only through voluntary association, and that its ultimate success will depend upon the intellectual and moral development of the workers who will supplant the wage system with a new social arrangement, based on solidarity and economic well-being for all. That is syndicalism, in theory and practice.

D.   REVISIONISM

Many socialists became convinced that certain of Marx's doctrines needed to be revised. This tendency can be observed quite early; a systematic body of revisionist doctrine, however, was not evolved until rather late in the nineteenth century. In this section are printed documents which reveal aspects of revisionist socialism as it appeared in three countries: England, Germany, and France.

1. *Revision—The Fabian Society.* The Fabian Society was organized in England in 1884. Since its members subscribed to a belief in "the inevitability of gradualness," it took its name from Fabius, the Roman general who won campaigns by playing a waiting game. Unlike most socialist groups the Society did not try to make of itself a mass organization but, since it attracted some of the most brilliant English writers of the day, it became an excellent vehicle for propaganda. The first selection printed below was written by Sidney Webb for *Fabian Essays,* published in 1889. The second selection contains questions which the Fabians wished candidates for Parliament to answer. (6)

[*Sidney Webb on the Historic Basis of Socialism*]

The main stream which has borne European society toward socialism during the past 100 years is the irresistible progress of democracy. De Tocqueville drove and hammered this truth into the reluctant ears of the Old World two generations ago; and we have all pretended to carry it about as part of our mental furniture ever since. But like most epigrammatic commonplaces, it is not generally realized; and de Tocqueville's book has, in due course, become a classic which everyone quotes and nobody reads. The progress of democracy is, in fact, often imagined, as by Sir Henry Maine, to be merely the substitution of one kind of political machinery for another; and there are many political

democrats today who cannot understand why social or economic matters should be mixed up
with politics at all. It was not for this that they
broke the power of the aristocracy: they were
touched not so much with love of the many as
with hatred of the few; and, as has been acutely
said—though usually by foolish persons—they are
radicals merely because they are not themselves
lords. But it will not long be possible for any
man to persist in believing that the political organization of society can be completely altered
without corresponding changes in economic and
social relations. De Tocqueville expressly pointed
out that the progress of democracy meant nothing less than a complete dissolution of the
nexus by which society was held together under
the old regime. This dissolution is followed by
a period of anarchic spiritual isolation of the individual from his fellows, and to that extent by
a general denial of the very idea of society. But
man is a social animal; and after more or less
interval there necessarily comes into existence a
new nexus, differing so entirely from the old-
fashioned organization that the historic fossil
goes about denying that it is a nexus at all, or
that any new nexus is possible or desirable. To
him, mostly through lack of economics, the progress of democracy is nothing more than the destruction of old political privileges; and, naturally
enough, few can see any beauty in mere dissolution and destruction. Those few are the purely
political radicals abhorred of Comte and Carlyle:
they are in social matters the empiricist survivals
from a prescientific age.

The mere Utopians, on the other hand, who
wove the baseless fabric of their visions of reconstructed society on their own private looms,
equally failed, as a rule, to comprehend the problem of the age. They were, in imagination, re-
suscitated Joseph the Seconds, benevolent despots
who would have poured the old world, had it
only been fluid, into their new molds. Against
their crude plans the statesman, the radical, and
the political economist were united; for they
took no account of the blind social forces which
they could not control, and which went on in-
exorably working out social salvation in ways un-
suspected by the Utopian.

In the present socialist movement these two
streams are united: advocates of social reconstruction have learnt the lesson of democracy,
and know that it is through the slow and gradual
turning of the popular mind to new principles
that social reorganization bit by bit comes. All
students of society who are abreast of their time,
socialists as well as individualists, realize that important organic changes can only be (1) democratic, and thus acceptable to a majority of the
people, and prepared for in the minds of all;

(2) gradual, and thus causing no dislocation, however rapid may be the rate of progress; (3) not
regarded as immoral by the mass of the people,
and thus not subjectively demoralizing to them;
and (4) in this country at any rate, constitutional and peaceful. Socialists may therefore be
quite at one with radicals in their political methods. Radicals, on the other hand, are perforce
realizing that mere political leveling is insufficient to save a state from anarchy and despair.
Both sections have been driven to recognize that
the root of the difficulty is economic; and there
is every day a wider consensus that the inevitable
outcome of democracy is the control by the people themselves, not only of their own political
organization, but, through that, also of the main
instruments of wealth production; the gradual
substitution of organized cooperation for the
anarchy of the competitive struggle; and the consequent recovery, in the only possible way, of
what John Stuart Mill calls "the enormous share
which the possessors of the instruments of industry are able to take from the produce." The
economic side of the democratic ideal is, in fact,
socialism itself. . . .

This new scientific conception of the social
organism has put completely out of countenance
the cherished principles of the political economist and the philosophic radical. We left them
sailing gaily into anarchy on the stream of
laissez faire. Since then the tide has turned. The
publication of John Stuart Mill's *Political Economy* in 1848 marks conveniently the boundary
of the old individualist economics. Every edition
of Mill's book became more and more socialistic.
After his death the world learnt the personal history, penned by his own hand, of his development from a mere political democrat to a convinced socialist.

The change in tone since then has been such
that one competent economist, professedly anti-
socialist, publishes regretfully to the world that
all the younger men are now socialists, as well as
many of the older professors. It is, indeed, mainly
from these that the world has learnt how faulty
were the earlier economic generalizations, and
above all, how incomplete as guides for social or
political action. These generalizations are accordingly now to be met with only in leading articles, sermons, or the speeches of ministers or
bishops. The economist himself knows them no
more.

The result of this development of sociology is
to compel a revision of the relative importance of
liberty and equality as principles to be kept in
view in social administration. In Bentham's celebrated "ends" to be aimed at in a civil code, liberty stands predominant over equality, on the
ground that full equality can be maintained only

by the loss of security for the fruits of labor. That exposition remains as true as ever; but the question for decision remains, how much liberty? Economic analysis has destroyed the value of the old criterion of respect for the equal liberty of others. Bentham, whose economics were weak, paid no attention to the perpetual tribute on the fruits of others' labor which full private property in land inevitably creates. In his view liberty and security to property meant that every worker should be free to obtain the full result of his own labor; and there appeared no inconsistency between them. The political economist now knows that with free competition and private property in land and capital, no individual can possibly obtain the full result of his own labor. The student of industrial development, moreover, finds it steadily more and more impossible to trace what is precisely the result of each separate man's toil. Complete rights of liberty and property necessarily involve, for example, the spoliation of the Irish cottier tenant for the benefit of Lord Clanricarde. What then becomes of the Benthamic principle of the greatest happiness of the greatest number? When the Benthamite comes to understand the law of rent, which of the two will he abandon? For he cannot escape the lesson of the century, taught alike by the economists, the statesmen, and the "practical men," that complete individual liberty, with unrestrained private ownership of the instruments of wealth production, is irreconcilable with the common weal. The free struggle for existence among ourselves menaces our survival as a healthy and permanent social organism. Evolution, Professor Huxley declares, is the substitution of consciously regulated coordination among the units of each organism, for blind anarchic competition. Thirty years ago Herbert Spencer demonstrated the incompatibility of full private property in land with the modern democratic state; and almost every economist now preaches the same doctrine. The radical is rapidly arriving, from practical experience, at similar conclusions; and the steady increase of the government regulation of private enterprise, the growth of municipal administration, and the rapid shifting of the burden of taxation directly to rent and interest, mark in treble lines the statesman's unconscious abandonment of the old individualism, and our irresistible glide into collectivist socialism.

It was inevitable that the democracy should learn this lesson. With the masses painfully conscious of the failure of individualism to create a decent social life for four fifths of the people, it might have been foreseen that individualism could not survive their advent to political power. If private property in land and capital necessarily keeps the many workers permanently poor (through no fault of their own) in order to make the few idlers rich (from no merit of their own), private property in land and capital will inevitably go the way of the feudalism which it superseded. The economic analysis confirms the rough generalization of the suffering people. The history of industrial evolution points to the same result; and for two generations the world's chief ethical teachers have been urging the same lesson. No wonder the heavens of individualism are rolling up before our eyes like a scroll; and even the bishops believe and tremble.

It is, of course, possible, as Sir Henry Maine and others have suggested, that the whole experience of the century is a mistake, and that political power will once more swing back into the hands of a monarch or an aristocratic oligarchy. It is, indeed, want of faith in democracy which holds back most educated sympathizers with socialism from frankly accepting its principles. What the economic side of such political atavism would be it is not easy to forecast. The machine industry and steam power could hardly be dismissed with the caucus and the ballot box. So long, however, as democracy in political administration continues to be the dominant principle, socialism may be quite safely predicted as its economic obverse, in spite of those freaks or aberrations of democracy which have already here and there thrown up a short-lived monarchy or a romantic dictatorship. Every increase in the political power of the proletariat will most surely be used by them for their economic and social protection. In England, at any rate, the history of the century serves at once as their guide and their justification.

[*Questions for Parliamentary Candidates: September 1900*]

Will you press at the first opportunity for the following reforms:—

I: A Labor Program

1. The extension of the Workmen's Compensation Act to seamen, and to all other classes of wage earners?
2. Compulsory arbitration, as in New Zealand, to prevent strikes and lock-outs?
3. A statutory minimum wage, as in Victoria, especially for sweated trades?
4. The fixing of "an eight-hours' day" as the maximum for all public servants; and the abolition, wherever possible, of overtime?
5. An Eight-Hours' Bill, without an option, for miners: and, for railway servants, a forty-eight hours' week?
6. The drastic amendment of the Factory Acts, to secure (*a*) a safe and healthy work place for

every worker, (*b*) the prevention of overwork for all women and young persons, (*c*) the abolition of all wage labor by children under fourteen, (*d*) compulsory technical instruction by extension of the half-time arrangements to all workers under eighteen?

7. The direct employment of labor by all public authorities whenever possible; and, whenever it is not possible, employment only of fair houses, prohibition of subcontracting, and payment of trade-union rates of wages?

8. The amendment of the Merchant Shipping Acts so as (*a*) to secure healthy sleeping and living accommodation, (*b*) to protect the seaman against withholding of his wages or return passage, (*c*) to insure him against loss by shipwreck?

II: A Democratic Budget

9. The further taxation of unearned incomes by means of a graduated and differentiated income tax?

10. The abolition of all duties on tea, cocoa, coffee, currants, and other dried fruits?

11. An increase of the scale of graduation of the death duties, so as to fall more heavily on large inheritances?

12. The appropriation of the unearned increment by the taxation and rating of ground values?

13. The nationalization of mining rents and royalties?

14. Transfer of the railways to the state under the Act of 1844?

III: Social Reform in Town and Country

15. The extension of full powers to parish, town, and county councils for the collective organization of the (*a*) water, (*b*) gas and (*c*) electric lighting supplies, (*d*) hydraulic power, (*e*) tramways and light railways, (*f*) public slaughterhouses, (*g*) pawnshops, (*h*) sale of milk, (*i*) bread, (*j*) coal, and such other public services as may be desired by the inhabitants? . . .

17. Amendment of the Housing of the Working Classes Act by (*a*) extension of period of loans to 100 years, treatment of land as an asset, and removal of statutory limitation of borrowing powers for housing. . . .

21. The compulsory provision by every local authority of adequate hospital accommodation for all diseases and accidents?

IV: The Children and the Poor

22. The prohibition of the industrial or wage-earning employment of children during school terms prior to the age of fourteen?

23. The provision of meals, out of public funds, for necessitous children in public elementary schools?

24. The training of teachers under public control and free from sectarian influences?

25. The creation of a complete system of public secondary education genuinely available to the children of the poor?

26. State pensions for the support of the aged or chronically infirm?

V: Democratic Political Machinery

27. An amendment of the registration laws, with the aim of giving every adult man a vote, and no one more than one vote?

28. A redistribution of seats in accordance with population?

29. The grant of the franchise to women on the same terms as to men?

30. The admission of women to seats in the House of Commons and on borough and county councils? . . .

32. The payment of all members of Parliament and of parliamentary election expenses out of public funds?

33. Triennial Parliaments?

34. All parliamentary elections to be held on the same day?

2. *Revisionism—Eduard Bernstein's Evolutionary Socialism.* A Continental socialist much influenced by the ideas of the Fabian Society was Eduard Bernstein (1850–1932), a German journalist and member of the German Social Democratic Party. In 1899 he wrote *Evolutionary Socialism,* a book which according to Bernstein expanded ideas contained in a letter written by him to a meeting of the Social Democratic Party in 1898. Portions of that letter follow. (7)

The views laid down by me in the series *Problems of Socialism* have lately been discussed in socialist papers and meetings, and a request has been made that the Party of German Social Democrats should state its position in regard to them. In case this happens and the Party agrees to the request, I am induced to make the following explanation.

The vote of an assembly, however significant it may be, naturally cannot disconcert me in my views, which have been gained from an examination of social phenomena. What I wrote in the *Neue Zeit* is the expression of a conviction from which I do not find myself induced to depart in any important particular.

But it is just as natural that a vote of the Party should find me anything but indifferent. And, therefore, it will be understood if I feel the paramount necessity of guarding myself against misconstruction of my conclusions and false deductions from them. As I am prevented from attending the Congress I send this written communication.

It has been maintained in a certain quarter that the practical deductions from my treatises would be the abandonment of the conquest of political power by the proletariat organized politically and economically. That is quite an arbitrary deduction, the accuracy of which I altogether deny.

I set myself against the notion that we have to expect shortly a collapse of the bourgeois economy, and that social democracy should be induced by the prospect of such an imminent, great, social catastrophe to adapt its tactics to that assumption. That I maintain most emphatically. . . .

No one has questioned the necessity for the working classes to gain the control of government. The point at issue is between the theory of a social cataclysm and the question whether with the given social development in Germany and the present advanced state of its working classes in the towns and the country, a sudden catastrophe would be desirable in the interest of the social democracy. I have denied it and deny it again, because in my judgment a greater security for lasting success lies in a steady advance than in the possibilities offered by a catastrophic crash.

And as I am firmly convinced that important periods in the development of nations cannot be leapt over I lay the greatest value on the next tasks of social democracy, on the struggle for the political rights of the working man, on the political activity of working men in town and country for the interests of their class, as well as on the work of the industrial organization of the workers.

In this sense I wrote the sentence that the movement means everything for me and that what is *usually* called "the final aim of socialism" is nothing; and in this sense I write it down again today. Even if the word "usually" had not shown that the proposition was only to be understood conditionally, it was obvious that it *could* not express indifference concerning the final carrying out of socialist principles, but only indifference —or, as it would be better expressed, carelessness —as to the form of the final arrangement of things. I have at no time had an excessive interest in the future, beyond general principles; I have not been able to read to the end any picture of the future. My thoughts and efforts are concerned with the duties of the present and the nearest future, and I only busy myself with the perspectives beyond so far as they give me a line of conduct for suitable action now.

The conquest of political power by the working classes, the expropriation of capitalists, are no ends in themselves but only means for the accomplishment of certain aims and endeavors. As such they are demands in the program of social democracy and are not attacked by me. Nothing can be said beforehand as to the circumstances of their accomplishment; we can only fight for their realization. But the conquest of political power necessitates the possession of political *rights;* and the most important problem of tactics which German social democracy has at the present time to solve, appears to me to be to devise the best ways for the extension of the political and economic rights of the German working classes.

3. *Revisionism—French "Reformist Socialism."* The following passages are selected from the preface to a collection of speeches published in 1903 by Alexandre Millerand (1859–1943), then a leader of the French socialists. In 1899 Millerand entered the French Cabinet as minister of commerce and industry, the first socialist since Louis Blanc to hold a Cabinet post. In his later life Millerand deserted the socialist cause; the sentiments expressed below, however, are typical of French "reformist socialism" in the 1890's. (8)

I touch here a subject which does not fail to excite and even to scandalize a certain number of our friends. The national interest, the solidarity of classes—are these questions about which a socialist has a right to be anxious without betraying the ideal which he claims to serve, the triumph of a humanity freed from class wars and from wars of nations?

History is made up of elements too numerous and complex for anyone to be able, without vanity, to claim to fix a hard-and-fast date for the triumph of his ideas. We fulfill our whole duty if we work in our station, within the limits of our strength, following the law of our nature, to prepare its victory. I have said how high the socialist ideal is, and how it is not enclosed in the narrow bounds which time and circumstances have fixed for any given nation. All the same, it spreads from men to their neighbors, and no bad way of working for its extension is to take pains first to win over one's fellow citizens.

How, then, can this propaganda be determined irrespectively of the environment wherein it is carried on? Can method and tactics be the same under different or even opposite regimes? If it is true that the republic is the political formula of socialism, it follows, of course, that in a country where socialism has achieved the immense step forward of realizing its political formula, its action and procedure, once it possesses republican forms and universal suffrage, will assume quite a special aspect and character. This means that it is not only the right but the imperative duty of social democracy in France to adapt its method to the conditions of the political regime in which it moves. It would betray the first of its duties if it took refuge in mere phrases of revolution in order to be saved the responsibilities and burdens implied by the reformist method and the pursuit of immediate results. It would, by the same act, sacrifice the primordial interests of the proletariat by declining the effort which should, little by little, realize the aggregate of improvements which I tried to resume in an exact summary.

But how will the French Socialist Party have the right to call the republican regime its own, how will it handle practically that incomparable instrument of reforms, if it affects keeping outside of the Republican Party's life and means to isolate itself in the barren part of the systematic critic? It will only win that authority over the nation without which our views cannot be realized, on condition that it remains neither alien nor indifferent to any of its emotions and aspirations. In domestic affairs it must take sides in the battle in which the Republic is engaged, and formulate its opinion, inspiring itself—as how should it else?—by its own ideal, but also by the needs, the thoughts, and the traditions of the republican democracy, which it continues and from which it inherits. It will not neglect either the good order and prosperity of the public finances, first condition of all social reform, or the maintenance and development of the national production. Public works, improvements destined to promote industry, commerce, and agriculture, judicious management and utilization of our colonial domain—all these are questions which will claim its scrutiny and retain its attention. It will be the attentive and zealous servant of the nation's greatness and prosperity.

Its patriotism—the more sincere because it hates the noisy declamations of Chauvinist politicians—has nothing to fear from its ardent love of peace and of mankind. Until that unknown date when the governments agree to lay aside in concert the heavy burden of military expenses, isolated disarmament would be worse than a folly; it would be a crime against the very ideal whose foremost soldier the socialists see France to be. While applying themselves to uphold and strengthen our diplomacy in the ways of peace, to draw from past conventions every effect of union and concord which they admit, and to get new treaties concluded tightening the bonds of friendship and solidarity between nations, they will watch no less carefully to preserve the country's independence unendangered by any aggression, through the power of its arms and the security of its alliances. While preparing for the future, they will not forget either the duties created for them by the past or the obligations imposed by the present. . . .

I have not dissimulated the end toward which it marches, and I am acquainted with the argument that socialism can, and indeed should, call itself "revolutionary," since in fact the disappearance of the wage system will be the most real and radical of revolutions. Words do not frighten me; but I dread equivocations. And what equivocation could be more unfortunate than that of a party masked by a title which contradicts formally its spirit and its method? If we reckon violence reprehensible as well as useless, if legal reform appear to us at once as our immediate objective and as the sole practical procedures to bring us nearer our distant goal, let us, then, have the courage, not a difficult courage, to call ourselves by our own name, "reformists," since reformists we are. Let us take our courage the whole way; and having declared for the reformist method, let us dare to accept its conditions and consequences. Long before yesterday the French Socialist Party gave the first place in its program to the capture of government; long before today it passed from theories to acts, and sent its campaigners into town halls, into departmental assemblies, into Parliament; it did not do so without resigning itself to the daily compromises which are the price of action, and allying itself with the parties near to it. Having gone so far, being persuaded more than ever of the utility and necessity of a method which has proved its value in experience, by what aberration should it desert that method at the very moment when it is becoming most effective? By what inconsistency should it consent to canvass every mandate, and yet rigorously forbid itself to join in the government, and take, along with the highest responsibilities, the most certain power?

Such an illogical course, if possible to continue, would soon ruin the credit and influence of the Party weak enough and sufficiently uncertain of itself to commit it. To put the people off to the mysterious date when a sudden miracle will change the face of the world, or day by day, reform by reform, by a patient and stubborn effort to win step by step all progress—those are the two methods which we must choose between.

Faithful to its principles and to the method which is its own, equally careful not to arouse chimerical hopes, and not to break its promises, French reformist socialism will be able to assume every responsibility; it will not decline any of the burdens imposed on it by its deep feeling of duty toward its ideal and toward its country.

IV
Nationalism

THE path of modern culture leads from humanity, through nationality, to bestiality.

GRILLPARZER, 1848

[81]

QUESTIONS FOR STUDY

PART I

1. Was Voltaire a nationalist? Explain.

2. Why was Rousseau's approach to the idea of a social contract important to the development of nationalism?

3. Must this approach necessarily produce nationalism?

4. How do Herder and Price differ? How are they alike?

5. Both modern liberalism and modern nationalism have roots in the eighteenth century. What roots do they have in common?

6. "The Declaration of the Rights of Man preferred the rights of the individual to the security of the group." Do you agree? Explain.

7. What state in the development of nationalism is revealed in the attitude of the early revolutionaries toward internal differences and foreign peoples? How has this changed by 1794?

8. What do you imagine would have been the reactions of Rousseau and Price to Jacobin nationalism?

PART II

9. According to Humboldt and Arndt why were the Germans a nationality?

10. What did Gneisenau believe were the relationships between liberalism and nationalism?

11. In this approach to national unification which was the more "realistic," Rotteck or Pfizer?

12. In comparing the *Fundamental Rights of the German People* with the French *Declaration of the Rights of Man* what similarities or differences in approach and emphasis are apparent? In what sense is each document the product of a particular time and place?

13. How do Gneisenau and Bismarck differ on the role of Prussia in German unification?

14. Explain the change in Treitschke's ideas on nationalism?

PART III

15. What are the ideals of fascism?

16. How does the fascist concept of the state differ from the liberal concept?

17. How does Hitler connect "aristocratic" authoritarianism at home with German domination abroad?

18. What would Rousseau have thought of Hitler's ideas?

19. How did Franco explain the evils in the Spanish state and society? What were his remedies?

20. What is there in common among the three varieties of integral nationalism? What differences are there, and how can those differences be explained?

21. What elements in integral nationalism can be found in eighteenth- and nineteenth-century nationalism?

Throughout history many ideological forces have operated to draw men together, to unite individuals for some common purpose. Before the modern era there were many varieties of "social cement": the imperial ideal of ancient Rome, the medieval Church's concept of a universal Christendom, the feudal concept of a highly integrated class structure. These unifying ideas in society have functioned over and beyond such basic needs as sustenance or government and have served to give purpose and method to the collective efforts of man at various periods in his history. In the modern period of Western civilization, one of the most universal and powerful examples of such a force at work has been nationalism. This Problem will introduce the student to the historical development of this most dynamic of the drives which motivate man as a social animal.

It may be unnecessary to point out the very controversial position of nationalism at the present time. A moment's reflection will convince the student that his own opinions on the subject are full of emotional overtones. In all probability he himself consciously or unconsciously considers nationalism to be either a "good" or a "bad" thing. He must, therefore, make every effort to distinguish between demonstrable fact, conjecture, and prejudice in analyzing this most disputed of phenomena.

Therefore, in the handling of such a controversial concept, precision and agreement on the meanings of the words used are of critical importance. The student must have a clear idea, for instance, of what "state," "nation," and "government" mean to him and his fellow students, for they will occur frequently in any discussion of nationalism. Though sometimes used interchangeably, they can and often do have separate meanings, the precise observance of which can do much for precision of argument. "Nation," for example, has two common meanings: the first is essentially political in implication and is synonymous with "state" or "country." "State" usually refers less to the people and more to the sovereign power in the community (whose implementation is the task of the "government"). A second meaning of "nation," in direct contrast to "state," suggests a group bound together by more than political ties, possibly by race, language, or common custom. The meaning of "nationality," a condition deriving from membership in a nation, depends in turn on the meaning of "nation" intended. "Nationalism" refers to an awareness of membership in a nation (here defined as a group bound together by more than political ties) and, especially, a desire to strengthen this peculiar consciousness of the group. It is this second definition of "nation," and its dependent variations, which provides the basic vocabulary for the study of nationalism. The student must not only make clear the precise meaning of such controversial words as he uses them himself, but he must also be sure of their meanings in the authors, ancient and modern, which he is reading.

Nationalism must be studied as a force working for group integration at a specific point in historical time. Of course certain natural tendencies are inherent in it—man's preference for a familiar environment, language, or custom rather than the unknown or strange—but modern nationalism is not a "natural" phenomenon in the sense that it is the product of "natural," immutable, or eternal laws. It is rather the growth and combination of many varied forces at a certain stage in history. Intermittent or vague symptoms of national feeling can be detected at very early periods in European history, but certain historical conditions which appeared in western Europe between the sixteenth and eighteenth century fused, magnified, and transformed these older feelings.

Three aspects of this transformation may be conveniently distinguished: the rise of the nation or nation-state; the parallel development of national feeling;

and, finally, the growth of the idea of nationalism. Most of European history after 1500 can be proved relevant to the first two points—the appearance of the nation-state and national feeling. Such developments as the rise of the centralized state, often embracing a sizeable amount of territory, the frequency of wars between these new states, the increasing prominence of the middle class, the secularization of culture, and the break-up of the universal Church by the Protestant Reformation all played their parts. Similarly, the growth of the idea of nationalism can be related to the main currents in political theory during the period. The latter had emancipated itself from its medieval dependence on theology, and subsequent efforts to provide a theoretical basis for royal sovereignty—whether it be Machiavelli, the Protestant reformers, or Thomas Hobbes—represented critical milestones on the road to national sovereignty.

The cumulative effect of these developments had become unmistakably evident in Europe by the middle of the eighteenth century. At that time, nationalism first appeared as a force vitally influencing European thought, society, and politics. From that point onward, with varying degrees of intensity, the phenomenon has grown and spread until its impact is felt in every quarter of the globe. The purpose of this Problem is to examine the progress of nationalism, from its first appearance as a powerful factor in history down to its most recent stage of growth in the present era, with a view to understanding its nature and its significance. The materials in Section A of Part I provide the student with an opportunity to observe the emergence of a variety of nationalistic ideas in the eighteenth century; in Section B the documents reveal the initial crushing impact of nationalism upon the Western world during the French Revolution. Part II deals with the development of the phenomenon in the nineteenth century. Since it would be impossible to examine its progress in all lands during that period, Germany has been chosen as a highly representative case study for this Part. Then in Part III the student encounters the consequent development of "integral nationalism" in twentieth-century Europe.

In embarking upon so comprehensive a treatment of so complex a phenomenon, the student must bear in mind two important considerations. First, against the background of his textbook reading, he should recognize the different pace at which nationalism developed in different countries. Like other ideologies, nationalism did not appear in all lands at the same time or with the same force, and the differences in time and intensity were of the greatest importance for the development of Western civilization. Second, against the background of his study of the earlier problems in this volume, he should be alert to observe the interaction among nationalism, liberalism, and socialism. The first two of these ideologies were born in the same period; the third grew up a little more than a century later. The growth of each intimately conditioned the growth of the others. For this there is superficial evidence in such classic phrases as "liberal nationalism" and "national socialism," but the connections among these are more profound than mere phrases can reveal. In the broadest sense, all the dominant ideologies of the modern world are the product of the interaction among these three. By bringing an understanding of nationalism to bear upon his knowledge of liberalism and socialism, the student will place himself in the best position to comprehend, to analyse, and to evaluate the ideological forces operating in the twentieth century.

THE PROBLEM

Part I.   NATIONALISM: EIGHTEENTH-CENTURY BEGINNINGS AND FRENCH REVOLUTIONARY EXPERIENCE

Although certain of the elements which go to make up modern nationalism may well be as old as man himself, the eighteenth century provided certain conditions and forces most conducive to the appearance of nations and national feeling. In Part I of this Problem the student can determine for himself not only the nature of eighteenth-century nationalism but also the effect of the French Revolution on this movement.

A.   NATIONAL FEELING IN EIGHTEENTH-CENTURY EUROPE

1. *Voltaire on La Patrie.* The central position of François Marie Arouet de Voltaire (1694–1778) in the French Enlightenment has already been stressed in Problem I. Although much of his reforming zeal was directed at the institutions of his own France, Voltaire's outlook embraced all Europe. As much at home in England or Prussia as in his native France, he spent his declining years as veritable patriarch of his own domain in Switzerland. Impatient with some of the definitions which Diderot was using in the big *Encyclopedia,* Voltaire began his own *Philosophic Dictionary* in 1752 and continued to add to it for the next twenty years. The selection which follows is his article on *"Patrie"* for this dictionary. (1)

A young journeyman pastrycook who had been to college, and who still knew a few of Cicero's phrases, boasted one day of loving his fatherland. "What do you mean by your fatherland?" a neighbor asked him. "Is it your oven? Is it the village where you were born and which you have never seen since? Is it the street where dwelled your father and mother who have been ruined and have reduced you to baking little pies for a living? Is it the town hall where you will never be a police superintendent's clerk? Is it the Church of Our Lady where you have not been able to become a choirboy, while an absurd man is archbishop and duke with an income of twenty thousand golden louis?"

The journeyman pastrycook did not know what to answer. A thinker who was listening to this conversation, concluded that in a fatherland of some extent there were often many thousand men who had no fatherland.

You, pleasure loving Parisian, who have never made any great journey save that to Dieppe to eat fresh fish; who know nothing but your var-

nished town house, your pretty country house, and your box at that Opera where the rest of Europe persists in feeling bored; who speak your own language agreeably enough because you know no other, you love all that, and you love further the girls you keep, the champagne which comes to you from Rheims, the dividends which the Hotel-de-Ville pays you every six months, and you say you love your fatherland!

In all conscience, does a financier cordially love his fatherland?

The officer and the soldier who will pillage their winter quarters, if one lets them, have they a very warm love for the peasants they ruin?

Where was the fatherland of the scarred Duc de Guise, was it in Nancy, Paris, Madrid, Rome?

What fatherland have you, Cardinals de La Balue, Duprat, Lorraine, Mazarin?

Where was the fatherland of Attila and of a hundred heroes of this type?

I would like someone to tell me which was Abraham's fatherland.

The first man to write that the fatherland is wherever one feels comfortable was, I believe, Euripides in his *Phaeton.* But the first man who left his birthplace to seek his comfort elsewhere has said it before him.

Where then is the fatherland? Is it not a good field, whose owner, lodged in a well-kept house, can say: "This field that I till, this house that I have built, are mine; I live there protected by laws which no tyrant can infringe. When those who, like me, possess fields and houses, meet in their common interest, I have my voice in the assembly; I am a part of everything, a part of the community, a part of the dominion; there is my fatherland"?

Well now, it is better for your fatherland to be a monarchy or a republic? For four thousand years has this question been debated. Ask the rich for an answer, they all prefer aristocracy;

question the people, they want democracy: only kings prefer royalty. How then is it that nearly the whole world is governed by monarchs? Ask the rats who proposed to hang a bell round the cat's neck. But in truth, the real reason is, as has been said, that men are very rarely worthy of governing themselves.

It is sad that often in order to be a good patriot one is the enemy of the rest of mankind. To be a good patriot is to wish that one's city may be enriched by trade, and be powerful by arms. It is clear that one country cannot gain without another loses, and that it cannot conquer without making misery. Such then is the human state that to wish for one's country's greatness is to wish harm to one's neighbors. He who should wish his fatherland might never be greater, smaller, richer, poorer, would be the citizen of the world.

> 2. *Jean-Jacques Rousseau (1712-78).* Rousseau was born in Geneva, Switzerland. He led a wandering, shiftless, undistinguished existence until 1750, in which year he published a prize-winning essay, *A Discourse on the Arts and Sciences,* which won him considerable public attention. He turned to politics with his *Discourse on Inequality* (1755), which was followed by *A Discourse on Political Economy* (1758) and by *The Social Contract* (1762). In the latter year he also published *Emile,* a novel dealing with education. Rousseau cannot be counted as a *philosophe,* for, although he used much of the jargon of the Enlightenment his work was less the product of reason than of emotion. Perhaps for this reason his books had an enormous circulation. He had an immense influence on the growth of democracy (in idea and in fact) and while not himself a nationalist, "the importance of his thought in the development of nationalism can hardly be exaggerated. It lay not only in its immediate influence on the French Revolution, but also and probably even more, in its effect upon the whole development of nineteenth-century political thought, above all in Germany. Rousseau provided the theoretical foundation upon which alone the nationalism of the nineteenth century could be built." The following quotations are from various works of Rousseau. (2)

The Social Contract, 1762

There will always be a great difference between subduing a multitude and ruling a society. Even if scattered individuals were successively enslaved by one man, however numerous they might be, I still see no more than a master and his slaves, and certainly not a people and its ruler; I see what may be termed an aggregation, but not an association; there is as yet neither public good nor body politic. The man in question, even if he has enslaved half the world, is still only an individual; his interest, apart from that of others, is still a purely private interest. If this same man comes to die, his empire, after him, remains scattered without it. . . .

I suppose men to have reached the point at which the obstacles in the way of their preservation in the state of nature show their power of resistance to be greater than the resources at the disposal of each individual for his maintenance in that state. That primitive condition can then subsist no longer; and the human race would perish unless it changed its manner of existence.

But as men cannot engender new forces, but only unite and direct existing ones, they have no other means of preserving themselves than the formation, by aggregation, of a sum of forces great enough to overcome the resistance. These they have to bring into play by means of a single motive power, and cause to act in concert.

This sum of forces can arise only where several persons come together: but, as the force and liberty of each man are the chief instruments of his self-preservation how can he pledge them without harming his own interests, and neglecting the care he owes to himself? This difficulty, in its bearing on my present subject, may be stated in the following terms—

"The problem is to find a form of association which will defend and protect with the whole common force the person and goods of each associate, and in which each, while uniting himself with all, may still obey himself alone, and remain as free as before." This is the fundamental problem of which the *Social Contract* provides the solution.

The clauses of this contract are so determined by the nature of the act that the slightest modification would make them vain and ineffective; so that, although they have perhaps never been formally set forth, they are everywhere the same and everywhere tacitly admitted and recognized, until, on the violation of the social compact, each regains his original rights and resumes his natural liberty, while losing the conventional liberty in favor of which he renounced it.

These clauses, properly understood, may be reduced to one—the total alienation of each associate, together with all his rights, to the whole community; for, in the first place, as each gives himself absolutely, the conditions are the same for all; and, this being so, no one has any interest in making them burdensome to others.

Moreover, the alienation being without reserve, the union is as perfect as it can be and no associate has anything more to demand: for, if the individuals retained certain rights, as there would be no common superior to decide between them and the public, each, being on one point his own judge, would ask to be so on all; the state of nature would thus continue, and the association would necessarily become inoperative or tyrannical.

Finally, each man, in giving himself to all, gives himself to nobody; and as there is no associate over whom he does not acquire the same right as he yields others over himself, he gains an equivalent for everything he loses, and an increase of force for the preservation of what he has.

If then we discard from the social compact what is not of its essence, we shall find that it reduces itself to the following terms—

"Each of us puts his person and all his power in common under the supreme direction of the general will, and, in our corporate capacity, we receive each member as an indivisible part of the whole."

At once, in place of the individual personality of each contracting party, this act of association creates a moral and collective body, composed of as many members as the assembly contains votes, and receiving from this act its unity, its common identity, its life and its will. This public person, so formed by the union of all other persons formerly took the name of *city*, and now takes that of *republic* or *body politic;* it is called by its members *state* when passive, *sovereign* when active, and *power* when compared with others like itself. Those who are associated in it take collectively the name of *people*, and severally are called *citizens*, as sharing in the sovereign power, and *subjects*, as being under the laws of the state. But these terms are often confused and taken one for another; it is enough to know how to distinguish them when they are being used with precision.

The passage from the state of nature to the civil state produces a very remarkable change in man, by substituting justice for instinct in his conduct, and giving his actions the morality they had formerly lacked. Then only, when the voice of duty takes the place of physical impulses and right of appetite, does man, who so far had considered only himself, find that he is forced to act on different principles, and to consult his reason before listening to his inclinations. Although, in this state, he deprives himself of some advantages which he got from nature, he gains in return others so great, his faculties are so stimulated and developed, his ideas so extended, his feelings so ennobled, and his whole soul so uplifted, that, did not the abuses of this new condition often degrade him below that which he left, he would be bound to bless continually the happy moment which took him from it for ever, and instead of a stupid and unimaginative animal, made him an intelligent being and a man.

Let us draw up the whole account in terms easily commensurable. What man loses by the social contract is his natural liberty and an unlimited right to everything he tries to get and succeeds in getting; what he gains is civil liberty and the proprietorship of all he possesses. If we are to avoid mistake in weighing one against the other, we must clearly distinguish natural liberty, which is bounded only by the strength of the individual, from civil liberty, which is limited by the general will; and possession, which is merely the effect of force or the right of the first occupier, from property, which can be founded only on a positive title.

We might, over and above all this, add, to what man acquires in the civil state, moral liberty, which alone makes him truly master of himself; for the mere impulse of appetite is slavery, while obedience to a law which we prescribe to ourselves is liberty. But I have already said too much on this head, and the philosophical meaning of the word liberty does not now concern us.

The first and most important deduction from the principles we have so far laid down is that the general will alone can direct the state according to the object for which it was instituted, *i.e.* the common good: for if the clashing of particular interests made the establishment of societies necessary, the agreement of these very interests made it possible. The common element in these different interests is what forms the social tie; and, were there no point of agreement between them all, no society could exist. It is solely on the basis of this common interest that every society should be governed.

I hold then that sovereignty, being nothing less than the exercise of the general will, can never be alienated, and that the sovereign, who is no less than a collective being, cannot be represented except by himself: the power indeed may be transmitted, but not the will. . . .

A Discourse on Political Economy, 1758

I. The first and most important rule of legitimate or popular government whose object is the good of the people, is therefore, as I have observed, to follow in everything the general will.

But to follow this will it is necessary to know it, and above all to distinguish it from the particular will, beginning with one's self: this distinction is always very difficult to make, and only the most sublime virtue can afford sufficient illumination for it. As, in order to will, it is necessary to be free, a difficulty no less great than the former arises—that of preserving at once the public liberty and the authority of government. . . . How can it be that all should obey, yet nobody take upon him to command, and that all should serve, and yet have no masters, but be the more free, as, in apparent subjection, each loses no part of his liberty but what might be hurtful to that of another? These wonders are the work of law. It is to law alone that men owe justice and liberty. It is this salutary organ of the will of all which establishes, in civil right, the natural equality between men. It is this celestial voice which dictates to each citizen the precepts of public reason, and teaches him to act according to the rules of his own judgment, and not to behave inconsistently with himself. It is with this voice alone that political rulers should speak when they command; for no sooner does one man, setting aside the law, claim to subject another to his private will, than he departs from the state of civil society, and confronts him face to face in the pure state of nature, in which obedience is prescribed solely by necessity. . . .

II. The second essential rule of public economy is no less important than the first. If you would have the general will accomplished, bring all the particular wills into conformity with it; in other words, as virtue is nothing more than this conformity of the particular with the general will, establish the reign of virtue.

If our politicians were less blinded by their ambition, they would see how impossible it is for any establishment whatever to act in the spirit of its institution, unless it is guided in accordance with the law of duty; they would feel that the greatest support of public authority lies in the hearts of the citizens and that nothing can take the place of morality in the maintenance of government. It is not only upright men who know how to administer the laws; but at bottom only good men know how to obey them. The man who once gets the better of remorse, will not shrink before punishments which are less severe, and less lasting, and from which there is at least hope of escaping: whatever precautions are taken, those who only require impunity in order to do wrong will not fail to find means of eluding the law, and avoiding its penalties. In this case, as all particular interests unite against the general interest, which is no longer that of any individual, public vices have a greater effect in enervating the laws than the laws in the repression of such vices: so that the corruption of the people and of their rulers will at length extend to the government, however wise it may be. The worst of all abuses is to pay an apparent obedience to the laws, only in order actually to break them with security. . . .

But when the citizens love their duty, and the guardians of the public authority sincerely apply themselves to the fostering of that love by their own example and assiduity, every difficulty vanishes; and government becomes so easy that it needs none of that art of darkness, whose blackness is its only mystery. . . .

It is not enough to say to the citizens, be good; they must be taught to be so; and even example, which is in this respect the first lesson, is not the sole means to be employed; patriotism is the most efficacious: for, as I have said already, every man is virtuous when his particular will is in all things conformable to the general will, and we voluntarily will what is willed by those whom we love. It appears that the feeling of humanity evaporates and grows feeble in embracing all mankind, and that we cannot be affected by the calamities of Tartary or Japan, in the same manner as we are by those of European nations. It is necessary in some degree to confine and limit our interest and compassion in order to make it active. Now, as this sentiment can be useful only to those with whom we have to live, it is proper that our humanity should confine itself to our fellow citizens, and should receive a new force because we are in the habit of seeing them, and by reason of the common interest which unites them. It is certain that the greatest miracles of virtue have been produced by patriotism: this fine and lively feeling, which gives to the force of self-love all the beauty of virtue, lends it an energy which, without disfiguring it, makes it the most heroic of all passions. . . .

Do we wish men to be virtuous? Then let us begin by making them love their country: but how can they love it, if their country be nothing more to them than to strangers, and afford them nothing but what it can refuse nobody? It would be still worse, if they did not enjoy even the privilege of social security, and if their lives, liberties, and property lay at the mercy of persons in power, without their being permitted, or it being possible for them to get relief from the laws. For in that case, being subjected to the duties of the state of civil society, without enjoying even the common privileges of the state of nature, and without being able to use their strength in their own defense, they would be in the worst condition in which freemen could possibly find themselves, and the word "country" would mean for them something merely odious and ridiculous. . . .

Should the public authority, by taking the place of the father, and charging itself with that important function, acquire his rights by discharging his duties, he would have the less cause to complain, as he would only be changing his title, and would have in common, under the name of *citizen*, the same authority over his children, as he was exercising separately under the name of *father*, and would not be less obeyed when speaking in the name of the law, than when he spoke in that of nature. Public education, therefore, under regulations prescribed by the government, and under magistrates established by the sovereign, is one of the fundamental rules of popular or legitimate government. If children are brought up in common in the bosom of equality; if they are imbued with the laws of the state and the precepts of the general will; if they are taught to respect these above all things; if they are surrounded by examples and objects which constantly remind them of the tender mother who nourishes them, of the love she bears them, of the inestimable benefits they receive from her, and of the return they owe her, we cannot doubt that they will learn to cherish one another mutually as brothers, to will nothing contrary to the will of society, to substitute the actions of men and citizens for the futile and vain babbling of sophists, and to become in time defenders and fathers of the country of which they will have been so long the children. . . .

3. *Johann Gottfried von Herder (1744–1803)*. Herder was in many ways a typical product of the eighteenth century. Teacher and preacher all his days, he was interested in theology, literature, archaeology, philosophy, and the classics, and the thirty-two volumes of his collected works are pervaded with a humanitarian nationalism characteristic of the time. Yet the impressionable Herder, under the emotional influence of religious Pietism and an early love of Rousseau, became one of the fathers of the *Sturm und Drang* movement, a peculiarly German version of the Romantic movement. Thus, at the threshold between the eighteenth and nineteenth centuries, Herder can say that "Patriotism and Enlightenment are the two poles round which all the moral culture of mankind revolves." The following quotations are from his *Materials for the Philosophy of the History of Mankind* (1784), whose very title reveals the unsystematic yet wide-ranging nature of Herder's thought. (3)

Nature has sketched with mountain ranges which she fashioned and with streams which she caused to flow from them the rough but substantial outline of the whole history of man. . . . One height produced nations of hunters, thus supporting and rendering necessary a savage state; another, more extended and mild, afforded a field to shepherd peoples and supplied them with tame animals; a third made agriculture easy and needful; while a fourth led to fishing and navigation and at length to trade. The structure of the earth, in its natural variety and diversity, rendered all such distinguishing conditions inescapable. . . . Seas, mountain ranges, and rivers are the most natural boundaries not only of lands but also of peoples, customs, languages, and empires, and they have been, even in the greatest revolutions in human affairs, the directing lines or limits of world history. If otherwise mountains had arisen, rivers flowed, or coasts trended, then how very different would mankind have scattered over this tilting place of nations. . . .

Nature brings forth families; the most natural state therefore is also one people, with a national character of its own. For thousands of years this character preserves itself within the people and, if the native princes concern themselves with it, it can be cultivated in the most natural way: for a people is as much a plant of nature as is a family, except that it has more branches. Nothing therefore seems more contradictory to the true end of governments than the endless expansion of states, the wild confusion of races and nations under one scepter. An empire made up of a 100 peoples and a 120 provinces which have been forced together is a monstrosity, not a state-body. . . .

Active human powers are the springs of human history, and, as man originates from and in one race, so his body, education, and mode of thinking are genetic. Hence that striking national character, which, deeply imprinted on the most ancient peoples, is unequivocally displayed in all their operations on the earth. As the mineral water derives its component parts, its operative power, and its flavor from the soil through which it flows, so the ancient character of peoples arose from the family features, the climate, the way of life and education, the early actions and employments, that were peculiar to them. The manners of the fathers took deep root and became the internal prototype of the descendants. The mode of thinking of the Jews, which is best known to us from their writings and actions, may serve as an example: both in the land of their fathers and in the midst of other nations they remain as they were, and even when mixed with other peoples they may be distinguished for some generations onward. It was and is the same with all other peoples of antiquity—Egyptians, Chinese, Arabs, Hindus, etc. The more secluded they lived, nay frequently the more they were oppressed, the more their character was confirmed, so that, if every one of these nations had remained in its place, the earth might have been regarded as a garden where in one plot one human national plant, in another, another, bloomed in its proper form and nature, where in this corner one kind of national animal, in that, another, pursued its course according to its instincts and character. . . .

Has a people anything dearer than the speech of its fathers? In its speech resides its whole thought-domain, its tradition, history, religion, and basis of life, all its heart and soul. To deprive a people of its speech is to deprive it of its one eternal good. . . . As God tolerates all the different languages in the world, so also should a ruler not only tolerate but honor the various languages of his peoples. . . . The best culture of a people cannot be expressed through a foreign language; it thrives on the soil of a nation most beautifully, and, I may say, it thrives only by means of the nation's inherited and inheritable dialect. With language is created the heart of a people; and is it not a high concern, amongst so many peoples—Hungarians, Slavs, Rumanians, etc.—to plant seeds of well-being for the far future and in the way that is dearest and most appropriate to them? . . .

The savage who loves himself, his wife, and his child with quiet joy and glows with limited activity for his tribe as for his own life is, it seems to me, a more genuine being than that cultured shade who is enchanted by the shadow of his whole species. . . . In his poor hut, the former finds room for every stranger, receives him as a brother with impartial good humor and never asks whence he came. The inundated heart of the idle cosmopolitan is a home for no one. . . .

No greater injury can be inflicted on a nation than to be robbed of her national character, the peculiarity of her spirit and her language. Reflect on this and you will perceive our irreparable loss. Look about you in Germany for the character of the nation, for their own particular cast of thought, for their own peculiar vein of speech; where are they? Read Tacitus; there you will find their character: "The tribes of Germany, who never degrade themselves by mingling with others, form a peculiar, unadulterated, original nation, which is its own archetype. Even their physical development is universally uniform, despite the large numbers of the people," and so forth. Now look about you and say: "The tribes of Germany have been degraded by mingling with others; they have sacrificed their natural disposition in protracted intellectual servitude; and, since they have, in contrast to others, imitated a tyrannical prototype for a long time, they are, among all the nations of Europe, the least true to themselves.". . .

If Germany were only guided by the forces of the age, by the leading strings of her own culture, our intellectual disposition would doubtless be poor and restricted; but it would be true to our own soil, fashioned upon its own model, and not so misshapen and cast down. . . .

(4) *Richard Price on Love of Country*. A Nonconformist minister of Welsh origin but English residence, Price (1723–91) approached the Enlightenment's ideal in the breadth and nature of his interests. As an ardent lover of civil and religious liberty, he was strongly opposed to the war with the American colonists. He both preached and wrote in the colonists' cause. A friend of Franklin, in 1778 he was actually invited by Congress to settle in America. The *Discourse on the Love of Our Country*, selections from which are reproduced below, was first delivered as a sermon in London in November 1789. In it Price also expressed his decided approval of the course of the French Revolution which had begun in the preceding May. (4)

The love of our country has in all times been a subject of warm commendations; and it is certainly a noble passion; but, like all other passions, it requires regulation and direction. There are mistakes and prejudices by which, in this instance, we are in particular danger of being misled. I will briefly mention some of these to you, and observe,

First, That by our country is meant, in this case, not the soil or the spot of earth on which we happen to have been born; not the forests and fields, but that community of which we are members; or that body of companions and friends and kindred who are associated with us under the same constitution of government, protected by the same laws, and bound together by the same civil polity.

Secondly, It is proper to observe, that even in this sense of our country, that love of it which is our duty, does not imply any conviction of the superior value of it to other countries, or any particular preference of its laws and constitution of government. Were this implied, the love of their country would be the duty of only a very small part of mankind; for there are few countries that enjoy the advantage of laws and governments which deserve to be preferred. To found, therefore, this duty on such a preference, would be to found it on error and delusion. It is, however, a common delusion. There is the same partiality in countries to themselves, that there is in individuals. All our attachments should be accompanied, as far as possible, with right opinions. We are too apt to confine wisdom and virtue within the circle of our own acquaintance and party. . . .

Thirdly, It is proper I should desire you particularly to distinguish between love of our country and that spirit of rivalship and ambition which has been common among nations. What has the love of their country hitherto been among mankind? What has it been but a love of domination; a desire of conquest, and a thirst for grandeur and glory, by extending territory, and enslaving surrounding countries? What has it been but a blind and narrow principle, producing in every country a contempt of other countries, and forming men into combinations and factions against their common rights and liberties? This is the principle that has been too often cried up as a virtue of the first rank: a principle of the same kind with that which governs clans of *Indians* or tribes of *Arabs,* and leads them out to plunder and massacre. . . . What is now the love of his country in a *Spaniard,* a *Turk,* or a *Russian?* Can it be considered as anything better than a passion for slavery, or a blind attachment to a spot where he enjoys no rights, and is disposed of as if he were a beast?

Let us learn by such reflections to correct and purify this passion, and to make it a just and rational principle of action. . . .

But I am digressing from what I had chiefly in view, which was, after noticing that love of our country which is false and spurious, to explain the nature and effects of that which is just and reasonable. With this view I must desire you to recollect that we are so constituted that our affections are more drawn to some among mankind than to others, in proportion to their degrees of nearness to us, and our power of being useful to them. It is obvious that this is a circumstance in the constitution of our natures which proves the wisdom and goodness of our Maker; for had our affections been determined alike to all our fellow-creatures, human life would have been a scene of embarrassment and distraction. Our regards, according to the order of nature, begin with ourselves; and every man is charged primarily with the care of himself. Next come our families, and benefactors, and friends; and after them our country. We can do little for the interest of mankind at large. To this interest, however, all other interests are subordinate. The noblest principle in our nature is the regard to general justice, and that good will which embraces all the world. I have already observed this; but it cannot be too often repeated. Though our immediate attention must be employed in promoting our own interest and that of our nearest connections: yet we must remember, that a narrower interest ought always to give way to a more extensive interest. In pursuing particularly the interest of our country, we ought to carry our views beyond it. We should love it ardently, but not exclusively. We ought to seek its good, by all the means that our different circumstances and abilities will allow; but at the same time we ought to consider ourselves as citizens of the world, and take care to maintain a just regard to the rights of other countries. . . .

B.   NATIONALISM AND THE FRENCH REVOLUTION

The French Revolution, in one sense, may be defined as the first large-scale attempt to put liberal and national ideals into practice. The two had common roots in the eighteenth century, and each was to dominate the other during a part of the Revolution. In the period between the convocation of the Estates General in 1789 and the abolition of the monarchy in September 1792, the liberal program was tried. Later the increased pace of the Revolution stimulated a more nationalist solution. Many factors entered into this development: the intrigues of the *émigrés;* the constant threat represented by the hostile courts of Europe culminating in the French declaration of war in April 1792; internal resistance, led by priests and conservative peasants, to revolutionary enactments, especially in the provinces of the north and west, breaking forth ultimately in open insurrections such as that of the Vendée in March 1793; the continued economic crisis, accompanied from the middle of 1791 by high prices, food shortages, and unemployment; the successive rise to power of political groups like the Girondins and the Jacobins, with a republican and equalitarian emphasis which gave a different interpretation of the liberal ideal from that of the early revolutionaries. Similarly, the student will note a contrast in the national ideal of the two periods.

1. *The Declaration of the Rights of Man and of the Citizen, August 1789.* This Declaration of the National Assembly later served as preamble to the Constitution of 1791. To the student of nationalism it affords a significant example of the extent to which liberal goals prevailed in the early phase of the Revolution. (5)

The representatives of the people of France, formed into a National Assembly, considering that ignorance, neglect, or contempt of human rights, are the sole causes of public misfortunes and corruptions of government, have resolved to set forth in a solemn declaration, these natural, imprescriptible, and inalienable rights: that this declaration being constantly present to the minds of the members of the body social, they may be forever kept attentive to their rights and duties; that the acts of the legislative and executive powers of government, being capable of being every moment compared with the end of political institutions, may be more respected; and also, that the future claims of the citizens, being directed by simple and incontestable principles, may always tend to the maintenance of the Constitution, and the general happiness.

For these reasons, the National Assembly doth recognize and declare, in the presence of the Supreme Being, and with the hope of His blessing and favor, the following *sacred* rights of men and citizens:

I. Men are born, and always continue, free and equal in respect of their rights. Civil distinctions, therefore, can be founded only on public utility.

II. The end of all political associations is the preservation of the natural and imprescriptible rights of man; and these rights are liberty, property, security, and resistance of oppression.

III. The nation is essentially the source of all sovereignty; nor can any individual, or any body of men, be entitled to any authority which is not expressly derived from it.

IV. Political liberty consists in the power of doing whatever does not injure another. The exercise of the natural rights of every man, has no other limits than those which are necessary to secure to every *other* man the free exercise of the same rights; and these limits are determinable only by law.

V. The law ought to prohibit only actions hurtful to society. What is not prohibited by the law, should not be hindered; nor should anyone be compelled to that which the law does not require.

VI. The law is an expression of the will of the community. All citizens have a right to concur, either personally, or by their representatives, in its formation. It should be the same to all, whether it protects or punishes; and all being equal in its sight, are equally eligible to all honors, places, and employments, according to their different abilities, without any other distinction than that created by their virtues and talents.

VII. No man should be accused, arrested, or held in confinement, except in cases determined by the law, and according to the forms which it has prescribed. . . .

VIII. The law ought to impose no other penalties but such as are absolutely and evidently necessary; and no one ought to be punished, but in virtue of a law promulgated before the offense, and legally applied.

IX. Every man being presumed innocent till he has been convicted, whenever his detention becomes indispensable, all rigor to him, more than is necessary to secure his person, ought to be provided against by the law.

X. No man ought to be molested on account of his opinions, not even on account of his *religious* opinions, provided his avowal of them does not disturb the public order established by the law.

XI. The unrestrained communication of thoughts and opinions being one of the most precious rights of man, every citizen may speak, write, and publish freely, provided he is responsible for the abuse of this liberty, in cases determined by the law.

XII. A public force being necessary to give security to the rights of men and of citizens, that force is instituted for the benefit of the community and not for the particular benefit of the persons to whom it is intrusted.

XIII. A common contribution being necessary for the support of the public force, and for defraying the other expenses of government, it ought to be divided equally among the members of the communtiy, according to their abilities.

XIV. Every citizen has a right, either by himself or his representative, to a free voice in determining the necessity of public contributions, the appropriation of them, and their amount, mode of assessment, and duration.

XV. Every community has a right to demand of all its agents an account of their conduct.

XVI. Every community in which a separation of powers and a security of rights is not provided for, wants a constitution.

XVII. The right to property being inviolable and sacred, no one ought to be deprived of it, except in cases of evident public necessity, legally ascertained, and on condition of a previous just indemnity.

2. *Fraternity and Federalism.* French national consciousness was in a formative period during the early months of the Revolution. A contributing factor was the idea of federation. The first Festival of the Federations was held on the first anniversary of Bastille Day, July 14, 1790. The federations which met then were local defense groups which had been formed throughout France during the unrest of the summer in 1789 and which had already then taken up some measure of contact with one another for mutual assistance. In addition all the national guards and army corps had been ordered present by the decree of May 27, 1790, which established the occasion as a national convocation. Following are two eyewitness accounts of the celebration. (6)

Meanwhile, more than 300,000 people of both sexes, from Paris and the environs, had been assembled since six in the morning at the Champ-de-Mars. Sitting on turf seats, which formed an immense circus, drenched, draggled, sheltering themselves with parasols from the torrents of rain which descended upon them, and at the least ray of sunshine adjusting their dresses, they waited, laughing and chatting, for the federates and the National Assembly.

A spacious amphitheater had been erected for the King, the royal family, the ambassadors, and the deputies. The federates, who first arrived, began to dance farandeles; those who followed joined them, forming a round which soon embraced part of the Champ-de-Mars. A sight worthy of the philosophic observer was that exhibited by this host of men, who had come from the most opposite parts of France, hurried away by the impulse of the national character, banishing all remembrance of the past, all idea of the present, all fear of the future, and indulging in a delicious thoughtlessness. Three hundred thousand spectators, of all ages and of both sexes, followed their motions, beating time with their hands, forgetting the rain, hunger, and the weariness of long waiting. At length, the whole procession having entered the Champ-de-Mars, the dance ceased, each federate repaired to his banner. The Bishop of Autun prepared to perform mass at an altar in the antique style, erected in the center of the Champ-de-Mars. Three hundred priests in white surplices, girt with broad tricolored scarfs, ranged themselves at the four corners of the altar. The Bishop of Autun blessed the oriflamme and the eighty-three banners: he struck up the *Te Deum*. Twelve hundred musicians played that hymn. . . .

The enthusiasm and the festivities were not confined to the day of the federation. During the stay of the federates at Paris, there was one continued series of entertainments, of dances, and of rejoicing. People again went to the Champ-de-Mars, where they drank, sang, and danced. M. de La Fayette reviewed part of the national guard of the departments and the army of the line. The King, Queen, and the Dauphin were present at this review. They were greeted with acclamations. The Queen, with a gracious look, gave the federates her hand to kiss, and showed them the Dauphin. The federates, before they quitted the capital, went to pay homage to the King: all of them testified the most profound respect, the warmest attachment. The chief of the Bretons dropped on his knee, and presented his sword to Louis XVI. "Sire," said he, "I deliver to you, pure and sacred, the sword of the faithful Bretons: it shall never be stained but with the blood of your enemies." "That sword cannot be in better hands than those of my dear Bretons," replied Louis XVI,

raising the chief of the Bretons, and returning him his sword. "I have never doubted their affection and fidelity. Assure them that I am the father, the brother, the friend, of all the French." The King, deeply moved, pressed the hand of the chief of the Bretons, and embraced him. A mutual emotion prolonged for some moments this touching scene. The chief of the Bretons was the first to speak. "Sire," he said "all the French, if I may judge from our hearts, love and will love you, because you are a citizen king."

3. *Liberal France and the War.* On April 20, 1792, the Legislative Assembly declared war on Austria, in part from internal political motives which made the rising Girondists the war party and in part in response to what the French felt to be a grave threat posed by the monarchical powers of Europe to the revolution in France. The following selection has been taken from this declaration of war. (7)

The National Assembly declared that the French nation, faithful to the principles consecrated by the Constitution "not to undertake any war with a view of making conquests, and never to employ its forces against the liberty of any people," takes up arms only for the maintenance of its liberty and independence; that the war which it is obliged to undertake is not a war of nation against nation, but the just defense of a free people against the unjust aggression of a king;

That the French will never confuse their brothers with their real enemies; that they will neglect nothing to soften the scourge of war, to care for and preserve property, and to cause the miseries inseparable from war to fall only on those who are allied against its liberty;

That it adopts in advance all foreigners who, renouncing the cause of its enemies, will come to stand under its banners and to consecrate their efforts to the defense of liberty; that it will even favor, by all the means in its power, their establishment in France. . . .

4. *Robespierre on the Aim of the Revolution.* On September 21, 1792, the Convention abolished the monarchy. The following June the Jacobin party asserted its triumph over its Gironde rivals in the Convention by arresting their leaders. The Jacobins determined the internal and foreign policy of the France during the Terror, the extreme phase of the Revolution which ended with their overthrow on July 27, 1794. Maximilian Robespierre (1758–94), in the very midst of the Terror, on February 5, 1794, set forth before

the Convention in the name of the Committee of Public Safety the following vision toward which his Jacobin group purportedly strove. (8)

It is time to mark clearly the aim of the Revolution. . . .

We wish an order of things where all low and cruel passions are enchained by the laws, all beneficent and generous feelings awakened; where ambition is the desire to deserve glory and to be useful to one's country; where distinctions arise only from equality itself; where the citizen is subject to the magistrate, the magistrate to the people, the people to justice; where the country secures the welfare of each individual, and each individual proudly enjoys the prosperity and glory of his country; where all minds are enlarged by the constant interchange of republican sentiments and by the need of earning the respect of a great people; where industry is an adornment to the liberty that ennobles it, and commerce the source of public wealth, not simply of monstrous riches for a few families.

We wish to substitute in our country morality for egotism, probity for a mere sense of honor, principle for habit, duty for etiquette, the empire of reason for the tyranny of custom, contempt for vice for contempt for misfortune, pride for insolence, large-mindedness for vanity, the love of glory for the love of money, good men for good company, merit for intrigue, talent for conceit, truth for show, the charm of happiness for the tedium of pleasure, the grandeur of man for the triviality of grand society, a people magnanimous, powerful, and happy for a people lovable, frivolous, and wretched—that is to say, all the virtues and miracles of the Republic for all the vices and puerilities of the monarchy.

We wish in a word to fulfill the course of nature, to accomplish the destiny of mankind, to make good the promises of philosophy, to absolve Providence from the long reign of tyranny and crime. May France, illustrious formerly among peoples of slaves, eclipse the glory of all free peoples that have existed, become the model to the nations, the terror of oppressors, the consolation of the oppressed, the ornament of the universe; and in sealing our work with our blood may we ourselves see at last the dawn of universal felicity gleam before us! That is our ambition. That is our aim.

5. *Jacobin Nationalism and the Individual.* The relationship of the state to its citizens is revealed in two famous Jacobin decrees of 1793, the *Levée en Masse* and the Law on Suspects. In the third selection here a young conscript soldier informs his mother of his feelings toward his country. (9)

[*The Levée en Masse, August 23, 1793*]

1. From this moment until that in which the enemy shall have been driven from the soil of the Republic, all Frenchmen are in permanent requisition for the service of the armies.

The young men shall go to battle; the married men shall forge arms and transport provisions; the women shall make tents and clothing and shall serve in the hospitals; the children shall turn old linen into lint; the aged shall betake themselves to the public places in order to arouse the courage of the warriors and preach the hatred of kings and the unity of the Republic.

2. The national buildings shall be converted into barracks, the public places into workshops for arms, the soil of the cellars shall be washed in order to extract therefrom the saltpeter.

3. The arms of the regulation caliber shall be reserved exclusively for those who shall march against the enemy; the service of the interior shall be performed with hunting pieces and side arms.

4. The saddle horses are put into requisition to complete the cavalry corps; the draft horses, other than those employed in agriculture, shall convey the artillery and the provisions.

5. The Committee of Public Safety is charged to take all the necessary measures to set up without delay an extraordinary manufacture of arms of every sort which corresponds with the ardor and energy of the French people. It is, accordingly, authorized to form all the establishments, factories, workshops, and mills which shall be deemed necessary for the carrying on of these works, as well as to put in requisition, within the entire extent of the Republic, the artists and workingmen who can contribute to their success. . . .

6. The representatives of the people sent out for the execution of the present law shall have the same authority in their respective districts, acting in concert with the Committee of Public Safety; they are invested with the unlimited powers assigned to the representatives of the people to the armies.

7. Nobody can get himself replaced in the service for which he shall have been requisitioned. The public functionaries shall remain at their posts.

[*The Law on Suspects, September 17, 1793*]

1. Immediately after the publication of the present decree all the suspect persons who are in the territory of the Republic and who are still at liberty shall be placed under arrest.

2. These are accounted suspect persons: 1st, those who by their conduct, their connections, their remarks, or their writings show themselves the partisans of tyranny or federalism and the

enemies of liberty; 2d, those who cannot, in the manner prescribed by the decree of March 21st last, justify their means of existence and the performance of their civic duties; 3d, those who have been refused certificates of civism; 4th, public functionaries suspended or removed from their functions by the National Convention or its commissioners and not reinstated, especially those who have been or shall be removed in virtue of the decree of August 14th last; 5th, those of the former nobles, all of the husbands, wives, fathers, mothers, sons or daughters, brothers or sisters, and agents of the *émigrés*, who have not constantly manifested their attachment to the revolution; 6th, those who have emigrated from France in the interval from July 1, 1789, to the publication of the decree of March 30–April 8, 1792, although they may have returned to France within the period fixed by that decree or earlier.

3. The committees of surveillance established according to the decree of March 21st last, or those which have been substituted for them, either by the orders of the representatives of the people sent with the armies and into the departments, or in virtue of special decrees of the National Convention, are charged to prepare, each in its district, the list of suspect persons, to issue warrants of arrest against them, and to cause seals to be put upon their papers. The commanders of the public force to whom these warrants shall be delivered shall be required to put them into execution immediately, under penalty of removal.

4. The members of the committee without being seven in number and an absolute majority of votes cannot order the arrest of any person.

9. The committees of surveillance shall send without delay to the committee of general security of the National Convention the list of the persons whom they shall have caused to be arrested, with the reasons for their arrest and the papers which shall have been seized with them as suspect persons.

10. The civil and criminal tribunals can, if there is need, cause to be arrested and sent into the above-mentioned jails persons accused of offenses in respect of whom it may have been declared that there was no ground for accusation, or who may have been acquitted of the accusations brought against them.

[*Conscript Joliclerc to his Mother, December 13, 1793*]

When *la patrie* calls us for her defense, we should fly to it as I should run to a good meal. Our life, our properties, and our talents do not belong to us. It is to the nation, to *la patrie* that all that belongs. Well do I know that you and all the other inhabitants of our village do not share these sentiments. They are insensible to the cries of this outraged *patrie*, and all they do for it they

do by compulsion. But I, who have been raised in liberty of conscience and of thought, who have always been a republican in my soul, although obliged to live in a monarchy, these principles of love for *la patrie*, for Liberty, for the Republic, have not only been engraved on my heart but are inlaid in it and they will remain in it so long as it will please that Supreme Being who govern all to maintain a breath of life in me. . . .

[*May 30, 1794*] About my lot? I am at my post, I am where I ought to be. . . . Should I perish there you ought to rejoice about it. Can one make a finer sacrifice than to sacrifice oneself for one's country? Can one sacrifice oneself for anything more glorious, more just, and more equitable? No, my dear mother. Think that I am at my post and you will be consoled. If your conscience makes you some reproach, sell even the last of your petticoats for *la patrie*. It should be our sole rudder, for it guides us and gives us happiness. I told you in my last letter that our Lieutenant David was in jail at Nantes. Well, he was guillotined with two of our captains about three weeks ago. . . .

6. *Jacobin Nationalism and Europe.* War was a constant factor conditioning the development of Jacobin nationalism. Hence it is not surprising that along with the internal effects of the heightened national consciousness went a changed conception of the relationships of revolutionary France to other nations. Jacobin views are illustrated in the Convention's occupation policy, quoted first below. (10)

[*Decree for Proclaiming the Liberty and Sovereignty of All Peoples, Passed by the Convention, December 15, 1792*]

The National Convention, after having heard the report of its united committees of finances, war, and diplomacy, faithful to the principles of the sovereignty of the people, which do not permit it to recognize any of the institutions which bring an attack upon it, and wishing to settle the rules to be followed by the generals of the armies of the Republic in the countries where they shall carry its arms, decrees:

1. In the countries which are or shall be occupied by the armies of the Republic, the generals shall proclaim immediately, in the name of the French nation, the sovereignty of the people, the suppression of all the established authorities and of the existing imposts and taxes, the abolition of the tithe, of feudalism, of seignorial rights, both feudal and *censuel*, fixed or precarious, of *banalités*, of real and personal servitude, of the privileges of hunting and fishing, of *corvées*, of the nobility, and generally of all privileges.

2. They shall announce to the people that they bring them peace, assistance, fraternity, liberty, and equality, and that they will convoke them directly in primary or communal assemblies, in order to create and organize an administration and a provisional judiciary; they shall look after the security of persons and property; they shall cause the present decree and the proclamation herewith annexed to be printed in the language or idiom of the country, and to be posted and executed without delay in each commune. . . .

4. The generals shall directly place under the safeguard and protection of the French Republic all the movable and immovable goods belonging to the public treasury, to the prince, to his abettors, adherents, and voluntary satellites, to the public establishments, to the lay and ecclesiastical bodies and communities; they shall cause to be prepared without delay a detailed list of them, which they shall dispatch to the executive council, and shall take all the measures which are in their power that these properties may be respected.

5. The provisional administration selected by the people shall be charged with the surveillance and control of the goods placed under the safeguard and protection of the French Republic; it shall look after the security of persons and property; it will cause to be executed the laws in force relative to the trial of civil and criminal suits and to the police and the public security; it shall be charged to regulate and to cause the payment of the local expenses and those which shall be necessary for the common defense; it may establish taxes, provided, however, that they shall not be borne by the indigent and laboring portion of the people.

6. When the provisional administration shall be organized the National Convention shall appoint commissioners from within its own body

to go to fraternize with it.

7. The executive council shall also appoint national commissioners, who shall repair directly to the places in order to cooperate with the generals and the provisional administration selected by the people upon the measures to be taken for the common defense, and upon the means employed to procure the clothing and provisions necessary for the armies, and to meet the expenses which they have incurred and shall incur during their sojourn upon its territory. . . .

9. The provisional administration selected by the people and the functions of the national commissioners shall cease as soon as the inhabitants after having declared the sovereignty and independence of the people, liberty, and equality, shall have organized a free and popular form of government.

10. There shall be made a list of the expenses which the French Republic shall have incurred for the common defense and of the sums which it may have received, and the French nation shall make arrangements with the government which shall have been established for that which may be due; and in case the common interest should require that the troops of the Republic remain beyond that time upon the foreign territory, it shall take suitable measures to provide for their subsistence.

11. The French nation declares that it will treat as enemies the people who, refusing liberty and equality, or renouncing them, may wish to preserve, recall, or treat with the prince and the privileged castes; it promises and engages not to subscribe to any treaty, and not to lay down its arms until after the establishment of the sovereignty and independence of the people whose territory the troops of the Republic have entered upon and who shall have adopted the principles of equality, and established a free popular government.

Part II.

NATIONALISM AND LIBERALISM IN GERMANY, 1808-70

Long after other peoples of western Europe had formed themselves into effective national states, Germany remained a divided land, and the idea of nationalism was foreign to most Germans. Thus Germany has been chosen as a case study in nineteenth-century nationalism, since here one can see the development of nationalistic ideas as Germans sought to form a united state, and here one can observe the tensions between liberalism and nationalism which that striving created. For the effective beginnings of nationalism in Germany one must look to the French Revolution. For the first time, intellectuals and average citizens alike began to think seriously of political affairs and to question the validity of existing conditions in Germany. This tendency to reflection increased sharply when Napoleon proceeded to impose revolutionary principles and institutions upon the German states.

At the height of his power, the Emperor controlled most of the German lands, and his sense of order led him not only to destroy the ramshackle imperial structure but also to reduce the number of competing sovereignties in Germany from three hundred to thirty-eight. At the same time, by introducing into the territories under his control the civil liberties which had been won in France, Napoleon laid the basis for German liberalism of the nineteenth century. Finally, the growing burden of French domination aroused a spirit of resentment which soon took the form of a desire for German unification and the expulsion of the foreigner. Thus Napoleon was father not only of German liberalism but of German nationalism as well. When the tide turned against the Emperor, the patriots who led the successful risings in Germany were for the most part inspired by the hope that they were ushering in an age in which Germany would retain the liberties of the Revolution while standing before the world as a unified national state. These hopes were not fulfilled in 1815. Once Napoleon was defeated, the great powers, including Austria and Prussia, gave no encouragement to national or liberal aspirations; the German states were organized into a jerry-built confederation; and the German princes once more based their policies on self-interest and ruthlessly suppressed all criticism of the existing system. Nevertheless the desires for national unity and for liberal institutions persisted and grew. The documents which follow indicate the nature of that growth and demonstrate the relationships between liberal and nationalistic ideas.

A.   GERMAN NATIONALISM: THE FIRST PHASE

1. *Humboldt on German Nationality.* Wilhelm von Humboldt (1767–1835), minister of education in Prussia, 1809–10, was the moving genius in the series of educational reforms which culminated in the foundation of the University of Berlin. Deeply concerned about the status of Germany after Napoleon should be defeated, he sent in December 1813 the following memorandum to Stein, onetime head of the Prussian ministry. (11)

When we speak of the future condition of Germany, we must guard against restricting ourselves to the point of view which wishes to protect Germany from France. Although, indeed, the independence of Germany is threatened only from that direction, such a one-sided attitude can never serve as a model in laying foundations for a continually beneficent status for a great nation. Germany must be strong and free, not only to be able to protect herself against this and that neighbor, or indeed against any enemy, but for this reason: namely, that, because only a nation which is strong externally preserves within itself the spirit from which all inner blessings flow, so it must be strong and free in order to nourish that self-reliance which is necessary even when not subjected to trial, in order to pursue its national development peacefully and undisturbed, and in order to continue to maintain the advantageous position which it has assumed in the midst of the European nations. . . .

The feeling that Germany is a unit . . . rests not wholly upon community of custom, language, and literature . . . but on the memory of rights and liberties enjoyed in common, glory won and dangers suffered in common, and on the memory of a closer bond which our ancestors fashioned and which still lives, if only in the yearning of their descendants. [The continuance of] the isolated existence of self-devoted German states (even if the very small ones were ceded to the larger) would merely increase the number of states which find it impossible, or exceedingly difficult, to maintain complete self-reliance; and it would increase it in a manner dangerous to the European balance of power; it would bring the larger German states, even Austria and Prussia, into danger, and it would gradually undermine the German nationality as a whole.

In the way in which nature unites individuals, and separates humanity into nations, there is an exceedingly profound and mysterious means of keeping the individual, who is nothing in himself, and the race, which is valuable only in the individual, in the right path toward the gradual and proportionate development of their strength; and although politics need never operate according to such views, yet it must not presume to act in opposition to the natural disposition of things. And Germany wishes now . . . to be thought of by its inhabitants and to be regarded by the foreigner, as one nation, one people, one state.

There can be then only one question: how shall we make a unit of Germany once again? . . .

2. *Arndt on German Nationality.* Ernst Moritz Arndt (1769–1860), a native of Swedish Pomerania, became early in life an ardent German patriot, and his verse and prose soon made him the lyric champion of the forces which rose against Napoleon. As early as 1802, he was preaching the necessity of German unity under the leadership of a strong state, and after Jena he pinned his hopes upon Prussian resurgence and Prussian leadership. Disillusioned by the reaction in Prussia after 1815, he carried on the fight for a united and liberal Germany and lived to be hailed as a national hero by the assembly at Frankfurt in 1848. "The German Fatherland," verses from which follow, was written in 1813. (12)

What is the German's Fatherland?
The Prussian, or the Swabian kind?
Where Rhenish grapes bloom ripe and full?
Where curves his flight the Baltic gull?
Ah, no! no! no!
His Fatherland must greater grow!

What is the German's Fatherland?
Point out to me its farthest bound!
Wherever rings the German tongue
And praises God the German song,
There shall it be!
There, German, make your Germany!

There shall the German's country lie,
Where scorn meets Gallic frippery,
Where France reaps hatred from the land,

    And German clasps a German hand!
    There shall it be!
    There is the whole of Germany!

    There is the whole of Germany!
    O God, regard it from on high;
    Grant German courage to us all
    That we may love it true and well.
    There shall it be!
    There is the whole of Germany!

3. Gneisenau — *Liberalism and National Unity.* Neithardt August von Gneisenau (1760–1831) was chief of the Prussian general staff during the war of emancipation. Like Stein he himself was not a Prussian; like Stein, he took as his goal a Germany founded on "unity, strength, and nationality." His liberal views won for him the name "the Jacobin of the Prussian army" and eventually, after

1815, caused a breach between him and the Prussian court. The first of the following selections is from a memorandum which he submitted to the King of Prussia in 1808; the second is taken from a letter to Ernst Moritz Arndt in 1814. (13)

[Prussia and Reform]

If the people [of Germany] are to come to the vigorous defense of a fatherland, it is both reasonable and politic that we should supply them with a fatherland. And this is particularly necessary because of those peoples who have not until now lived beneath the Prussian scepter but who may cleave to us for the liberation of the common German fatherland. A free constitution, an administration with a simple organization will make them desirous of living with us under common laws. . . . When we, by proclamation and deed, have given the German nation the happy hope of beneficent state reform, there is no doubt that a great part of the nation will rise to defend our cause against our oppressor. . . . Then we shall see more than fifteen million men fighting for one national goal, their independence. The interest which the royal family has aroused in Germany by its misfortune will be increased, if the house of Brandenburg, to whose regent they are indebted for such liberal principles, places itself at the head of the union for German independence and German freedom.

[Letter to Arndt, August 28, 1814]

By word and by pen I have demonstrated and urged the necessity of granting a constitution to Prussia, in the near future, if not immediately. Even the mere considerations of political science demand this. There is no firmer bond than a good constitution, for uniting to our old territories the inhabitants of those lands which are acquired. Moreover, we must in this way win for ourselves the support of popular opinion in Germany. By such an action we shall gain primacy over their spirits. Only a threefold superiority of military, constitutional, and scientific power can keep us erect among our mighty neighbors. From a Montgelas [the chief adviser of the King of Bavaria], from a King of Württemberg, from the other governments of the Confederation of the Rhine, no one dare expect liberal adjustments; they are ill disposed toward us. Therefore we must wean away from them the hearts of their subjects—for the most part new subjects—by granting to our own subjects a good constitution and estimable laws. . . .

B. THE LIBERAL DILEMMA AND THE REVOLUTION OF 1848

1. *The Liberal Dilemma.* The latent conflict between liberal and national aspirations, apparent since the days of the French Revolution, was most marked among the liberals of south Germany. Two attitudes to this conflict appear below. The first selection was written in 1836 by the Baden historian Karl von Rotteck (1775–1840), the second was written in 1832 by Paul Pfizer (1801–67), a native of Stuttgart and, for a brief period during the revolutionary disturbances of 1848, minister to the King of Württemburg. (14)

[*Karl von Rotteck on the Constitutional System*]

How may a people express its general will in a reliable way? What is the natural and unprejudiced organ for this? In quite small states it is the *Landesgemeinde*—that is, the assembly of all citizens who are (politically) of age, the majority of whom, with full authority, make decisions in the name of the people or express wishes or demands. In greater states, this can happen only by means of a body freely elected from the bosom of the nation, a body which, in so far as the electoral law is a rational one, represents the whole by nature and in actuality and which can be legally regarded as identical with it. In this natural and true national representation, which has to represent the interests and the rights of the people to the government, lies the essence of the constitutional system. Such a representation is, therefore, immeasurably removed from the aristocratic feudal estates. . . . Those estates represent merely the castes or corporations to which they belong, or by which they were appointed, namely the nobility and the clergy. The so-called third estate, that is, the mass of the nation, appears there in the most paltry representation in the person of deputies of single towns and in the most subordinate position. . . .

The representation of the whole people by means of an assembly stemming from it by free election, which seems so obvious an idea, is a development of the most recent times. But it alone is capable of giving reality to the idea of a genuine popular will and transforming a repressive state (*Gewaltstaat*) into a state of laws (*Rechtsstaat*). Not what the personal or individual will of the regent desires is law in the state, but only what is determined by the general will of those subjects politically of age. Ruling individuals, even those of the most honorable disposition, can go astray because of diverse preju-

dices; and they can be untrue and impure—that is, they can follow personal ends instead of the common good. Therefore, if the nation is not to be put at the mercy of chance vagaries of individual intelligence and character, it must be freely permitted to express its convictions, its needs, its desires, and its will—that is, it must be granted a natural and therefore reliable organ for such expression.

[*Pfizer on the Aims of German Liberalism*]

Freedom within and independence from without, a personal liberty and nationality—these are the two poles toward which all the life of the century is directed. . . .

After centuries in which all the rights of peoples were bound up in the rights and the personality of princes, we have finally convinced ourselves that peoples do not exist for the sake of princes, but princes for the sake of the peoples, and that the peoples possess in themselves rights which exist independently of the person of the ruling monarch. According to the former conceptions, the ruler of a land was in a true sense the lord and proprietor of his land and people; he bartered, sold, and pawned his realm and could say quite rightfully of himself: I am the state! But since we have drawn a distinction between the rights of princes and those of the people, since we have recognized more reasonably that the well-being of a whole country or people is to be preferred to the interest of *one* prince or *one* family, the principle of nationality has begun to dominate the history of the European states. Nations have now taken the place which was formerly occupied by monarchies or dynasties.

True, many think that, with the downfall of that medieval type of princely power, the antagonism between countries and peoples also loses its meaning and that a common bond will, in the future, unite all humanity and so bring back the golden age, where difference of rank and descent no longer matter but are replaced by absolute freedom and equality. But just as in a perfect organism it is right that each physical part have its own purpose, form, and function . . . so in the organism of humanity it is fitting that each nation discharge and fulfill its characteristic task, and that, in this pursuit, it be neither disturbed nor restrained by the might of others or their lust for power. Germany, home of thinking and feeling, home of the most profound inner contemplation, will always be so antithetical to France, the land of agitation and outward show, as to make it impossible for her to remain comfortable under French hegemony, and even if all the peoples of our continent should be united not merely by international law but by positive constitutional law, this antithesis would continue, however tempered and appeased. . . .

Germany is not greatly aided by the mere axioms of civil liberty, however meritorious and necessary their propagation may be. Despite the urge for liberty on the part of individuals, the Germans will always play a sorry role, and their only recompense abroad for their enthusiasm will be a pitying smile at their well-meaning, though weak nature, until they desire freedom as a nation. . . . It is, of course, foolish to demand that Germans wholly forget about freedom within until they have secured independence from without; but it is just as wrong, if not more so, to wish to sacrifice the latter to the former. . . .

Constitutional Germany is therefore required to advance the work of humanity on its own, and, as far as it is able, to be active in the cause of the unity *and* the freedom of the German nation.

> 2. *1848 — The Fundamental Rights of the German People*. After 1840 nationalistic and liberal agitation increased in intensity, and the inevitable explosion came in March 1848, one month after the successful revolution in Paris. When revolution won the upper hand in both Vienna and Berlin, middle-class liberals and intellectuals seized the opportunity to create the union they had long desired and summoned a national constituent assembly to meet in Frankfurt. This body, which included representatives from all the German states and from Austria and German Bohemia, began its work in May 1848, and, in the course of the next year, drafted and published a constitution for the nation. The first part of the Assembly's work was devoted to writing a charter of liberties for the German people. Selections from this charter are printed below. (15)

The following fundamental rights shall be guaranteed to the German people. They shall serve as a standard for the constitutions of the separate German states, and no constitution or legislation of any German state may ever set aside or limit them.

ARTICLE I 1. The German people consists of the citizens of the states which make up the German Reich. 2. Every German has the rights of German citizenship. He may exercise these rights in every German state. The election laws of the Reich determine the right to vote in elections for the Reich's assembly. 3. Every German has the

right to sojourn or establish his residence in any part of the territory of the Reich, to acquire real estate of any description and to control the same, to engage in any trade, to enjoy the rights of local citizenship. The government of the Reich shall establish for the whole of Germany the conditions governing sojourn and residence by a law of residence and those respecting trades by trade regulations. 4. No German state may make a distinction in matters of civil and criminal law and procedural rights between its citizens and other Germans which would place the latter in the category of aliens. . . .

ARTICLE II 7. No privilege of rank is valid before the law. Nobility is abolished as a rank. All privileges of rank are abolished. All Germans are equal before the law. All titles, in so far as they do not pertain to an office, are abolished. . . .

ARTICLE III 8. The freedom of the individual is inviolable. The arrest of a person shall take place, except in case of his being apprehended in the deed, only on the authority of a court order stating the cause. . . . Everyone accused shall be released on presentation of bail. . . . 10. The home is inviolable. The searching of a domicile is permissible only: *i.* on authority of a judicial order stating reasons, which order must be presented to the parties concerned immediately or within the following twenty-four hours; *ii.* in case of pursuit of an offender caught in the act on the part of legally authorized officials. . . . 11. The confiscation of letters and papers may be undertaken only on authority of a judicial order stating reasons, except in case of arrest or of searching of a domicile. . . . 12. The privacy of letters is guaranteed. . . .

ARTICLE IV 13. Every German has the right to express his opinion freely in speaking, writing, printing, or pictorial representation. . . . Laws governing the press will be proclaimed by the Reich.

ARTICLE V 14. Every German has full freedom of belief and of conscience. . . . 15. Every German is unrestricted in the common practice of his religion at home or in public. . . .

ARTICLE VI 22. Science and the teaching of science are free. 23. Instruction and the system of education are under the supervision of the state and are, with the exception of religious instruction, freed from the supervision of the clergy as such. 24. Every German is free to establish, to lead, and to give instruction in institutions for instruction and education, if he has given evidence of his qualifications to do so to the proper authorities of the state. Instruction at home is not restricted in any way. 25. Sufficient provision shall everywhere be made for the education of German youth through public schools. . . . 28. Everyone is free to choose his occupation and to prepare himself for it, how and where he wishes.

ARTICLE VII 29. Every German has the right to apply in writing to the authorities, to the representatives, and to the *Reichstag* with requests and complaints. . . .

ARTICLE VIII 31. Germans have the right to assemble peacefully and without arms; no special permission to do so is required. Public assemblies in the open may be forbidden in times of urgent danger in the interest of public order and safety. . . .

ARTICLE IX 34. Private property is inviolable. Expropriation may take place only in the interest of the public welfare, only according to law and on the basis of just compensation. Ecclesiastical property shall be protected by legislation. . . . 36. Every relationship of bondage or serfdom is ended forever. . . . 41. All feudal relations are to be annulled. . . . 43. Taxation shall be so regulated that the privileged position of some occupations and property shall cease in the community and the state.

ARTICLE X 44. All legal jurisdiction proceeds from the state. There shall be no patrimonial courts. 45. Judicial power will be exercised independently by the courts. Cabinet and ministerial jurisdiction is inadmissible. None may be withdrawn from his legal court. Extraordinary courts shall never take place. 46. There shall be no privileged juridical position of persons or of property. . . . 51. The execution and administration of justice shall be separated and be independent of each other. Cases of conflict of jurisdiction between administrative and judicial authorities in the individual states are decided by a court determined by law. 52. Judicial power on the part of administrative authorities ceases. All violations of law are determined by the courts. The police authorities have no power to punish. 53. Legal decisions of German courts are equally valid and effective in all German states. A law of the nation will determine details.

ARTICLE XI 54. The fundamental principles of the constitution of every community are: *i.* the election of its head officer and representative; *ii.* the independent administration of its community affairs including the local police, under the legally appointed supervision of the state; *iii.* that all matters pertaining to public administration be open to the public; *iv.* the rule that all negotiations will be public. . . .

ARTICLE XII 56. Every German state shall have a constitution with representation of the people. Ministers are responsible to the representatives of the people. 57. The representatives of the people have a decisive voice in legislation, in taxation, in the regulation of affairs of state.

ARTICLE XIII 58. The non-German speaking races of Germany are guaranteed their racial development, namely the equal right of their languages in the regions which they occupy, their rights in church affairs, in instruction, in local government, and in administration of justice.

ARTICLE XIV 59. Every German citizen abroad is under the protection of the Reich.

C. THE ACHIEVEMENT OF NATIONAL UNITY

1. *Bismarck's Solution.* The Frankfurt Assembly, having agreed upon a constitution uniting all of non-Austrian Germany, offered the imperial crown to Friedrich Wilhelm IV of Prussia. The King contemptuously rejected the offer, and, in the latter half of 1849, the Assembly collapsed. The possibility of eventual national unification seemed remote, but in the 1860's help appeared from an unexpected quarter. In 1848, Otto von Bismarck (1815–98) was a typical Prussian squire, with little interest in the question of national unification, and in 1850 he expressed actual satisfaction when Austria defeated the Prussian government's attempt to form a union of the north German states. As Prussia's representative in the federal Diet from 1853 to 1859, however, Bismarck became convinced that a struggle between Austria and Prussia for dominance was inevitable. His objective thenceforth was to prepare Prussia for the coming conflict; and, when he became minister president of Prussia in 1862 that objective determined the domestic policy which he followed. When the Prussian liberals asserted the right of parliamentary control over the Prussian army and refused to vote funds for its support unless their claims were granted, Bismarck refused to admit their competence to limit royal policy and levied the necessary funds with a brutal unconcern for their protests. The following selections from Bismarck's papers illustrate the principles and objectives of his policy. (16)

[*A Letter to Minister von Manteuffel, 1856*]

The soul of a Prusso-Austrian alliance, even in time of greatest common danger, would be the opposite of all that makes an alliance strong. Mutual political distrust, military and political jealousy, the suspicion of each that, in the case of good fortune, the other would seek to prevent the aggrandizement of his ally by separate engagements with the enemy and that, in the case of bad fortune, he would seek to secure his own safety—all of these things would now, between us, be stronger and more crippling than in any badly assorted alliance of the past. No general would grant the victory to the other until it was too late. In our history we have the treaties of Vossem and St. Germain, we have the memory of our fate at the Congress of Vienna, which justify us in being distrustful of the advantages of the Austrian alliance, and the policy of the last two years shows us that the prefidious tactics of Vienna have not changed in practice. Perhaps they would give us guarantees by means of a personal exchange of obligations . . . but the traditional policy of Austria and her jealousy of us would not be obviated by that, and I could trust the old fox in its new coat just as little as when it had its mangy summer hair. Because of the policy of Vienna, Germany is clearly too small for us both; as long as an honorable arrangement concerning the influence of each in Germany cannot be concluded and carried out, we will both plough the same disputed acre, and Austria will remain the only state to whom we can permanently lose or from whom we can permanently gain. Through the Concordat and what is involved with it, this historically inevitable friction has been even more pronounced and understanding even more difficult. But even without that we have a great number of conflicting interests which neither of us can abandon without abandoning the mission in which he essentially believes and which cannot be untangled by diplomatic correspondence. Even the strongest pressure from without, the most pressing danger to the existence of both was unable to forge this weapon in 1813 and 1849. For a thousand years intermittently—and since Charles V every century—the German dualism has regularly adjusted the reciprocal relations [of the two powers] by a thorough internal war; and in this century also no other means than this can set the clock of evolution at the right hour.

With this reasoning I by no means intend to draw the conclusion that we should regulate our policy so as to force the decision between Austria and us under the most favorable circumstances possible. I wish only to express my conviction that, in the not too distant future, we shall have to fight for our existence against Austria and that it is not within our power to avoid that, since the course of events in Germany has no other solution.

[A Speech to the Budget Commission, 1862]

Our blood is too hot; we prefer to wear armor which is too heavy for our slender body; but we should use it nonetheless. The eyes of Germany are fixed not upon Prussia's liberalism, but upon her armed might. Bavaria, Württemberg, and Baden may indulge in liberal experiments; therefore, no one will assign to them Prussia's role. Prussia must harbor and maintain her strength for the favorable moment—a moment which has already, on one occasion, slipped by; Prussia's boundaries, as drawn by the Vienna treaties, are not suitable for a healthy state life. The great questions of the day will not be decided by speeches or by majority decisions—that was the mistake of 1848 and 1849—but by blood and iron!

[A Letter to Graf von der Goltz, 1863]

I reject completely your view that a "question of Prussian policy which is extremely simple in itself" will be beclouded by the dust raised by the Danish affair. . . . The question is whether we are a great power or a German federal state and whether we, in the first capacity, are to rule according to the monarchical principle, or—as is generally the case in the second capacity—by means of professors, district judges, and pettystate babblers. The pursuit of the phantom of popularity "in Germany" has cost us our position in Germany and in Europe, and we will not win it back by being carried along by the stream, in the hope of directing it, but by standing firmly on our own feet, and being *first* a great power and *then* a federal state. . . . You believe that there is something in "German public opinion," in the legislative chambers, newspapers, etc., which could help and support us in a policy of union or hegemony. I hold this to be a radical error, a thing of fantasy! Our strength can be derived, not from our policy with regard to the chambers or the press, but only from our military policy as a great power, and we have not lasting strength enough to squander it on false fronts. . . .

2. *The War of 1866.* Bismarck put his principles into practice in the wars of 1864 and 1866. The first of these, waged in collaboration with Austria, was fought ostensibly to protect the rights of German inhabitants of Schleswig and Holstein, provinces bound by historical ties and international treaty to the Danish crown. Once Denmark was defeated, however, the Germanic powers annexed the Duchies. Austria's decision to assume the administration of Holstein was fatal to her position in Germany. It enabled Bismarck, by a series of skillfully planned incidents, to force war upon Austria in 1866. The causes of the war are analyzed dispassionately by Moltke, the Prussian chief of staff, in the selection from his memoirs which follows. **(17)**

The war of 1866 was entered on not because the existence of Prussia was threatened, nor was it caused by public opinion and the voice of the people; it was a struggle, long foreseen and calmly prepared for, recognized as a necessity by the Cabinet, not for territorial aggrandizement, for an extension of our domain, or for material advantage, but for an ideal end—the establishment of power. Not a foot of land was exacted from conquered Austria, but she had to renounce all part in the hegemony of Germany.

The imperial family alone were to blame if the old empire had now for centuries allowed domestic politics to override German national politics. Austria had exhausted her strength in conquests south of the Alps, and left the western German provinces unprotected, instead of following the road pointed out by the course of the Danube. Its center of gravity lay out of Germany; Prussia's lay within it. Prussia felt itself called upon and strong enough to assume the leadership of the German races. The regrettable but unavoidable exclusion of one of them from the new empire could only be to a small extent remedied by a subsequent alliance. But Prussia has become immeasurably greater without Austria, than it was before with Austria.

3. *The Waning of the Liberal Opposition.* Since the failure of the 1848 revolution, German liberals had been torn between their growing conviction that Prussian leadership was the only means to national unity and their distrust of Prussian internal policy. The Prussian victories in 1864 and 1866 were decisive in overcoming liberal scruples. Within Prussia itself the liberal opposition which had fought since the early 1860's for the establishment of parliamentary control over the military budget capitulated completely after the victory over Austria. In September 1866, the Prussian parliament—in an action which has been described as the definitive collapse of German liberalism—voted Bismarck an indemnity for his unconstitutional collection of taxes since 1862. The selections by Treitschke, a prominent liberal spokesman, reflect the progressive victory of national feeling over liberal principles. (18)

[Heinrich von Treitschke, 1860]

Not only is a federation of states including Austria and Prussia an absurdity. No! A federal state which includes monarchies is equally absurd—a child can understand that. There is only one salvation: *one state,* a monarchical Germany under the Hohenzollern dynasty. Expulsion of the princely houses, annexation to Prussia—there, plainly and bluntly, is my program! Who is there

who thinks for a moment that this will come about peacefully? But is the unity of Germany under Emperor William I an idea which is not worth a few hundred thousand lives? To me, in the face of this idea, my life is not worth a shilling. This idea is worth *understanding* and it is worth *spreading.* I believe that it will come to life, but, I fear—only after infinite suffering.

[Heinrich von Treitschke, 1861]

For Germany as it is I find only one salvation: a monarchy, one and indivisible. Any talk of a federal state made up of monarchies seems to me a *contradictio in adjecto,* any hope of a republic is stupidity, as long as these ideas have no reality in the minds of our people. Prussia has, therefore, no choice. With the help of the German people, she must *conquer by force.* And for that very reason the crisis in Prussia must come finally to a salutary conclusion. I hope that the people will do their duty and elect the most democratic chamber possible. Then, as befits a sound people, issues will be clear. Let their opponents try a Junker ministry or a *coup d'état;* the time is not ripe for such madness. Circumstances are propitious for a last decisive break with Junkerdom. For that is the Achilles' heel of the north, just as ultramontanism is in the south. . . . If Prussia takes this one daring step, she is halfway to the German throne.

[Heinrich von Treitschke, 1861]

In south German newspapers it has become almost commonplace to state that the achievement of the national idea is unthinkable until it is certain that Prussia will subordinate herself to the future central administration. To me that seems a singularly unfortunate way of expressing a thing which will come as a matter of course. But, our next goal is the formation of a united German military administration. With regard to this military question, the present state of affairs is such that we inhabitants of the middle states must, in every case of danger, call to Prussia: "Save us! Help us!" If we are to be reasonable, then, there can be no question here of a subordination of Prussia; it is plain that we are forced to call upon the Prussian army to be the strong central point of a union of the rest of Germany's fighting forces. It is, of course, to be hoped that future events will bring in their train constitutional forms, through which the other German peoples will be able to exert upon the policy of the Prussian Crown a constitutional influence similar to that already granted by law to the representatives of the Prussian people. And if our highest hopes succeed, if the imperial idea comes again to life, the German Crown will be borne not by some unknown "pure-German" entity, but by the house of Hohenzollern which cannot cast off its Prussian traditions like a suit of old clothes. Then, indeed, Prussia would "subordinate" herself to the central administration of Germany, but the Prussian Crown would have the right to use its monarchical veto against the German Parliament and, by exercising this prerogative it would not betray its Prussian traditions. It is well not to close one's eyes to these realities.

[Heinrich von Treitschke, 1865]

The aggrandizement of Prussia, which is proceeding step by step, scarcely corresponds to our ideals, but it seems to us a lesser evil—indeed, a stroke of fortune—compared with Germany's condition today. In any case, it is within Prussia's power to make a tremendous step forward toward the goal of the unity of the fatherland; and no mortal can say whether or when there will be an opportunity of ending our dismemberment by general mediation.

4. *The Triumph of Nationalism.* The Prussian victory over France in 1870 not only created the emotional atmosphere which made political unification possible but also further weakened liberal antagonism to Prussian militarism. The extent of Treitschke's retreat from the liberal position is demonstrated by his "What We Demand from France," written in August, 1870. (19)

In view of our obligation to secure the peace of the world, who dares object that the people of Alsace and Lorraine do not wish to belong to us? In face of the sacred necessity of these great days, the doctrine of the right of self-determination for all branches of the German race—that alluring solution proposed by demagogues without a country—becomes a pitiable and a shameful

thing. These provinces are ours by the right of the sword, and we shall dispose of them by a higher right—the right of the German nation, which cannot allow its lost children to remain forever alien to the German Empire. We Germans, knowing Germany and France, know better than these unfortunates themselves what is to the advantage of the people of Alsace, who, because of the misleading influence of their French life, have no knowledge of the new Germany. Against their will we shall restore them to their true selves. With joyful wonder, we have watched the immortal progress of the moral forces of history in the awful changes of these days, and we have done so too often to be capable of belief in the unconditional value of mere popular disinclination. The spirit of a nation embraces not only contemporary generations, but those also who are before and behind it! We appeal from the misguided wills of those who now live in Alsace to the desires of those who lived there before them. We call upon all those stout Germans who once set the seal of our spirit upon the speech and the customs, the art and the communal life of the upper Rhine—and, before the nineteenth century comes to an end, the world will recognize that the spirit of Erwin von Steinbach and Sebastian Brandt still lives and that, though we set at naught the will of the present generation of Alsatians, we did so merely in obediance to the dictates of national honor.

For two centuries, ever since the birth of the Prussian state, we have been struggling to liberate the lost German lands from foreign domination. It is not the object of this national statecraft to force into our new Empire every acre of German land which we surrendered in the days of our weakness . . . But we dare not suffer the complete and systematic destruction of the German nationality before our very eyes; we dare not suffer its degradation to a state of vassalage. . . .

Part III.   INTEGRAL NATIONALISM

The recognition of the principle of "national self-determination" at the Versailles Peace Conference in 1919 and the formation of several new national states apparently marked the culmination of nineteenth-century liberal nationalism. But even before 1919 a new brand of nationalism had appeared, called by Charles Maurras, one of its first proponents, "integral nationalism." Integral nationalism, says Maurras, means "the exclusive pursuit of national policies, the absolute maintenance of national integrity, and the steady increase of national power." Yet this represents no sudden break with the past. Certain elements of integral nationalism may be traced back to earlier varieties, and such factors as imperialism, social Darwinism, and the instruments of modern propaganda contributed to the development of the new nationalism. The documents which follow represent three examples of successful integral nationalism, "successful" in that in each case the government of the state acknowledged integral nationalism to be its program. The student should observe the similarities and dissimilarities among the movements and, by setting each movement against its historical background, should attempt to discover the reasons therefor.

A.   ITALY

In one sense a study of the origins of fascism in Italy is a study of Italy's history since 1870. The ineffectiveness, if not the corruption, of Italian parliamentarianism, the perennial governmental deficits, the underlying poverty of the country, the disappointments in the realm of foreign affairs—these are some of the roots of the fascist movement. In the years immediately following World War I these difficulties were present in an aggravated form. Many Italians felt that Italy had not obtained her share of territories at Versailles; inflation and unemployment were severe; and the government, hindered by the presence of extreme socialists in the Chamber, seemed powerless to act. It was this confused, anarchical situation which allowed the fascist regime to come into power. The leader of the movement, Benito Mussolini (1883–1945), had begun his political career as a revolutionary socialist. As editor of the socialist newspaper *Avanti,* he opposed the entry of Italy into the war but he soon changed his views and entered the army himself as a private soldier. Ousted by the socialists for his change of view on the war, Mussolini founded his own newspaper, the *Populo d'Italia,* and his own political party, the *Fasci di Combattimento,* and in 1922 made the famous "march on Rome," an act which led King Victor Emmanuel III to ask Mussolini to form a ministry. The selections printed below are taken from the article on "Fascism" in the 1932 edition of the *Italian Encyclopedia.* Although signed by Mussolini, the article was prepared by Giovanni Gentile (1875–1944), an Italian philosopher. (20)

And above all, fascism, the more it considers and observes the future and the development of humanity quite apart from political considerations of the moment, believes neither in the possibility nor the utility of perpetual peace. It thus repudiates the doctrine of pacifism—born of a renunciation of the struggle and an act of cowardice in the face of sacrifice. War alone brings up to its highest tension all human energy and puts the stamp of nobility upon the peoples who have the courage to meet it. All other trials are substitutes, which never really put men into the position where they have to make the great decision—the alternative of life or death. Thus a doctrine which is founded upon this harmful postulate of peace is hostile to fascism. And thus hostile to the spirit of fascism, though accepted for what use they can be in dealing with particular political situations, are all the international leagues and societies which, as history will show, can be scattered to the winds when once strong national feeling is aroused by any motive—sentimental, ideal, or practical. . . .

Such a conception of life makes fascism the complete opposite of that doctrine, the base of so-called scientific and Marxian socialism, the materialist conception of history; according to which the history of human civilization can be explained simply through the conflict of interests among the various social groups and by the change and development in the means and instruments of production. . . . And if the economic conception of history be denied, according to which theory men are no more than puppets, carried to and fro by the waves of chance, while the real directing forces are quite out of their control, it follows that the existence of an unchangeable and unchanging class war is also denied—the natural progeny of the economic conception of history. And above all fascism denies that class war can be the preponderant force in the transformation of society. . . .

After socialism, fascism combats the whole complex system of democratic ideology and repudiates it, whether in its theoretical premises or in its practical application. Fascism denies that the majority, by the simple fact that it is a majority, can direct human society; it denies that numbers alone can govern by means of a periodical consultation, and it affirms the immutable, beneficial, and fruitful inequality of mankind, which can never be permanently leveled through the mere operation of a mechanical process such as universal suffrage. The democratic regime may be defined as from time to time giving the people the illusion of sovereignty, while the real effective sovereignty lies in the hands of other concealed and irresponsible forces. Democracy is a regime nominally without a king, but it is ruled by many kings—more absolute, tyrannical, and ruinous than one sole king even though a tyrant. . . .

Fascism has taken up an attitude of complete opposition to the doctrines of liberalism, both in the political field and the field of economics. There should be no undue exaggeration (simply with the object of immediate success in controversy) of the importance of liberalism in the last century, nor should what was but one among many theories which appeared in that period be put forward as a religion for humanity for all time, present and to come. Liberalism only flourished for half a century. . . .

Given that the nineteenth century was the century of socialism, of liberalism, and of democracy, it does not necessarily follow that the twentieth century must also be a century of socialism, liberalism, and democracy: political doctrines pass, but humanity remains; and it may rather be expected that this will be a century of authority, a century of the Left, a century of fascism. For if the nineteenth century was a century of individualism (liberalism always signifying individualism) it may be expected that this will be the century of collectivism, and hence the century of the state. . . .

In 1929, at the first five-yearly assembly of the fascist regime, I said:

"For us fascists, the state is not merely a guardian, preoccupied solely with the duty of assuring the personal safety of the citizens; nor is it an organization with purely material aims, such as to guarantee a certain level of well-being and peaceful conditions of life; for a mere council of administration would be sufficient to realize such objects. Nor is it a purely political creation, divorced from all contact with the complex material reality which makes up the life of the individual and the life of the people as a whole. The state, as conceived of and as created by fascism, is a spiritual and moral fact in itself, since its political, juridical, and economic organization of the nation is a concrete thing: and such an organization must be in its origins and development a

manifestation of the spirit. The state is the guarantor of security both internal and external, but it is also the custodian and transmitter of the spirit of the people, as it has grown up through the centuries in language, in customs, and in faith. And the state is not only a living reality of the present, it is also linked with the past and above all with the future, and thus transcending the brief limits of individual life, it represents the immanent spirit of the nation. . . .

For fascism, the growth of empire, that is to say the expansion of the nation, is an essential manifestation of vitality, and its opposite a sign of decadence. Peoples which are rising, or rising again after a period of decadence, are always imperialist; any renunciation is a sign of decay and of death. Fascism is the doctrine best adapted to represent the tendencies and the aspirations of a people, like the people of Italy, who are rising again after many centuries of abasement and foreign servitude. But empire demands discipline, the coordination of all forces and a deeply felt sense of duty and sacrifice: this fact explains many aspects of the practical working of the regime, the character of many forces in the state, and the necessarily severe measures which must be taken against those who would oppose this spontaneous and inevitable movement of Italy in the twentieth century, and would oppose it by recalling the outworn ideology of the nineteenth century—repudiated wheresoever there has been the courage to undertake great experiments of social and political transformation: for never before has the nation stood more in need of authority, of direction, and of order. If every age has its own characteristic doctrine, there are a thousand signs which point to fascism as the characteristic doctrine of our time. For if a doctrine must be a living thing, this is proved by the fact that fascism has created a living faith; and that this faith is very powerful in the minds of men is demonstrated by those who have suffered and died for it.

Fascism has henceforth in the world the universality of all those doctrines which, in realizing themselves, have represented a stage in the history of the human spirit.

B.

GERMANY

The conservative nationalist state created by Bismarck collapsed with its military defeat in World War I. The German revolution of 1918 produced the democratic Weimar Republic, but from the onset the new republic faced great difficulties. Disastrous inflation and the peculiar ring-around-the-rosy of reparations prevented the government from ever building a sound economic foundation, and it was always subject to attacks from the radical Left and the reactionary Right. The chief supporters of the old empire remained in being: the army, the bureaucracy, big business, and the landed aristocracy retained economic and administrative power and maintained a nationalist ideology, an ideology exacerbated by territorial losses, reparations, and the war-guilt clauses of the Versailles

Treaty. Conservative nationalism, frustrated by defeat, sought to rehabilitate itself by finding new concepts and new allies. A potent ally was to be the National Socialist Workers Party, founded in 1919 in Munich. The seventh member of this small party was Adolf Hitler (1889–1945), an Austrian by birth, a draftsman by profession, and, at that time, an ex-corporal employed by the army in espionage work. In 1923 Hitler joined an army clique in an unsuccessful attempt to overthrow the republic. He was sentenced to detention in a fortress and there wrote *Mein Kampf*. Hitler, himself uneducated and intellectually incoherent, was assisted in his writing by Rudolf Hess, a fellow prisoner. *Mein Kampf* became the bible of the nazi movement. The first selection is from *Mein Kampf;* the rest, from Hitler's speeches. (21)

German Austria must return to the great German motherland, and not because of economic considerations of any sort. No, no: even if from the economic point of view this union were unimportant, indeed, if it were harmful, it ought nevertheless to be brought about. *Common blood belongs in a common Reich.* As long as the German nation is unable even to band together its own children in one common state, it has no moral right to think of colonization as one of its political aims. Only when the boundaries of the Reich include even the last German, only when it is no longer possible to assure him of daily bread inside them, does there arise, out of the distress of the nation, the moral right to acquire foreign soil and territory. The sword is then the plow, and from the tears of war there grows the daily bread for the generations to come. . . .

The question of the "nationalization" of a people is first of all a question of creating sound social conditions as the fundamental possibility for educating the individual. For only those who, through education and schooling, get to know the cultural and economic, and above all the political, greatness of their own country can and will be proud of being allowed to call themselves members of this nation. Moreover, I can only fight for what I love; only love what I can respect; only respect what I know. . . .

Like a woman, whose psychic feeling is influenced less by abstract reasoning than by an undefinable, sentimental longing for complementary strength, who will submit to the strong man rather than dominate the weakling, thus the masses love the ruler rather than the suppliant, and inwardly they are far more satisfied by a doctrine which tolerates no rival than by the grant of liberal freedom; they often feel at a loss what to do with it, and even easily feel themselves deserted. They neither realize the impudence with which they are spiritually terrorized, nor the outrageous curtailment of their human liberties, for in no way does the delusion of this doctrine dawn on them. Thus they see only the inconsiderate force, the brutality and the aim of its manifestations to which they finally always submit. . . .

The Jewish doctrine of Marxism rejects the aristocratic principle in nature; instead of the eternal privilege of force and strength, it places the mass of numbers and its dead weight. Thus it denies the value of the individual in man, disputes the meaning of nationality and race, depriving mankind of the assumption for its existence and culture. As the basis of the universe it would lead up to the end of all order conceivable to man. And as in this greatest discernible organism only chaos could be the result of the application of such a law, so on this earth the decline of its inhabitants would be the result. . . .

Democracy of the west today is the forerunner of Marxism, which would be inconceivable without it. It is democracy alone which furnishes this universal plague with the soil in which it spreads. In parliamentarianism, its outward form of expression, democracy created a "monstrosity of filth and fire" (*Spottgeburt aus Dreck und Feuer*) in which, to my regret, the "fire" seems to have burned out for the moment. . . .

The parliamentary principle of decision by majority, by denying the authority of the person and placing in its stead the number of the crowd in question, sins against the aristocratic basic idea of nature, whose opinion of aristocracy, however, need in no way be represented by the present-day decadence of our upper ten thousand. . . .

One thing we must and may never forget: here, too, a majority can never replace the Man. It is not only always a representative of stupidity, but also of cowardice. Just as a hundred fools do not make one wise man, an heroic decision is not likely to come from a hundred cowards. . . .

It will be easiest to understand this absurd and dangerous human error if one compares the democratic parliamentarianism with true Germanic democracy.

The characteristic of the first is that a number of, say five hundred, men, and recently also women, are elected, who are entrusted with the final decision on everything. They alone practically represent the government, for though they elect the cabinet which to all outward appearances seems to take on the guidance of the state's affairs, this is nevertheless mere pretense. In reality, this so-called government cannot take one step without having first obtained the consent of the general assembly. Therefore, it cannot be held responsible for anything at all, as it is not the government which has the ultimate decision, but the majority of parliament. In all cases, therefore, the government is only the executive of the will of the majority. We would judge its political ability only by the skill it shows either in adapting itself to the will of the majority, or in winning it over. But then it sinks from the height of a real government to that of a beggar appealing to the majority. Its most important task now consists of securing either the favor of the majority, from case to case, or of taking upon itself the formation of a more gracious new majority. If it succeeds in this, then it may continue to "rule" for a short time longer, but if it does not, it must go. Whether its intentions are right or not is of no consequence. . . .

This system is opposed by the true Germanic democracy of the free choice of a leader with the latter's obligation to take over fully all responsibility for what he does or does not do. There will be no voting by a majority on single questions, but only the decision of the individual who backs it with his life and all he has.

If the objection were raised that under such circumstances no one could be found ready to devote himself to such a hazardous task, there can be one reply:

God be thanked, this is just the meaning of Germanic democracy, that no unworthy climber or moral shirker can come in the back way to rule his fellow citizens, but that the greatness of the position to be assumed will discourage incompetents and weaklings. . . .

[The Basis of Expansionism, May 1, 1927]

From this standpoint there is only one hypothesis left for the German people, namely, that in this world population represents the changing element, while soil and territory represent an unchanging element. This means that at present soil and territory are limited in this world. Germany is the fatherland of 62,000,000 people who live together on an area which is 450,000 kilometers square. This is a ridiculous figure when one considers the size of the other nations in the world today. This is especially noticeable when one looks at a globe map of the world on which Germany completely disappears. Unfortunately the great mass of our German people does not have the logical insight to draw the necessary conclusions from this fact. Instead, the great mass of our German people prefers to chase after certain phantoms. Moreover, the population can increase in a short time; it can perhaps reach 68,000,000 or 70,000,000, and yet the area on which it lives will remain the same. . . .

The only thing left for a people to do, then, is to attempt an adjustment in the relationship between the area on which it lives, that is, its reservoir of subsistence, and its population. The first method (limitation of the population) is the one which seems the easier. If we cannot expand the soil, then we decrease the population. There are certain parties in Germany who advocate this method. . . . Just a few weeks ago the "German" press announced that we had now received permission to send Germans to Canada again and that the first quota had actually been reached. It was said that this was an important and obvious success of our foreign policy. The success of German foreign policy, therefore, consists in chasing our best human material out of Germany.

The other way [to solve our problem] is to bring the soil into consonance with the population, even if it must be done by war. This is the natural way which Providence has prescribed. Providence has given the world unto man, not so that he should degenerate into pacifism, but so that in the eternal struggle with one another the strength and vigor of man should be preserved and so that some day the greatest freedom might belong to the most vigorous and most mighty people. The German people adopted this natural course a few times in its history, when, in trying to expand the soil in order to bring it into consonance with the population, it occupied the region southeast of the Rhine and then northeast of the Rhine, thus acquiring some territory for the German people. If this policy had not been followed at that time our people today would constitute a ridiculously small state with a ridiculously small population. . . .

[Racial Purity, January 30, 1937]

The main plank in the National Socialist program is to abolish the liberalistic concept of the individual and the Marxist concept of humanity and to substitute therefor the folk community, rooted in the soil and bound together by the bond of its common blood. This is a very simple statement, but it involves a principle that has tremendous consequences. This is probably the first time and this is the first country in which the people are being taught to realize that, of all tasks which we have to face, the noblest and most sacred for mankind is that each racial species must preserve the purity of the blood which God has given it. . . . The greatest revolution which National Socialism has brought about is that it has rent asunder the veil which hid from us the knowledge that all human failures and mistakes are due to the conditions of the time and therefore can be remedied, but that there is one error which cannot be remedied once men have made it, namely, the failure to recognize the importance of conserving the blood and the race free from intermixture and thereby the racial aspect and character which are God's gift and God's handiwork. It is not for men to discuss the question of why Providence created different races, but rather to recognize the fact that it punishes those who disregard its work of creation.

Unspeakable suffering and misery have come upon mankind because they lost this instinct which was grounded in a profound intuition; and this loss was caused by a wrong and lopsided education of the intellect. Among our people there are millions and millions of persons living today for whom this law has become clear and intelligible. What individual seers and the still unspoiled natures of our forefathers saw by direct perception has now become a subject of scientific research in Germany. I can prophesy here that, just as the knowledge that the earth moves around the sun led to a revolutionary alteration in the general world-picture, so the blood-and-race doctrine of the National Socialist Movement will bring about a revolutionary change in our knowledge and therewith a radical reconstruction of the picture which human history gives us of the past and will also change the course of that history in the future.

This will not lead to an estrangement between nations; but, on the contrary, it will bring about for the first time a real understanding of one an-other. At the same time, however, it will prevent the Jewish people from intruding themselves among all the other nations as elements of internal disruption, under the mask of honest world-citizens, and thus gaining power over these nations.

We feel convinced that the consequences of this revolutionizing vision of truth will bring about a radical transformation in German life. For the first time in our history, the German people have found the way to a higher unity. . . . From that chaos of disunion which had been caused by tribal, dynastic, philosophical, religious, and political strife, the German nation has arisen and has unfurled the banner of a reunion which symbolically announces, not a political triumph, but the triumph of the racial principle. . . . The National Socialist Movement limits its sphere of internal activity to those individuals who belong to one people and it refuses to allow the members of a foreign race to wield an influence over our political, intellectual, or cultural life. We refuse to accord to the members of a foreign race any predominant position in our national economic system. In this folk-community, which is based on the bond of blood, and in the results which National Socialism has obtained by making the idea of this community understood among the public, lies the most profound reason for the marvelous success of our Revolution.

C.   SPAIN

In 1936, the year of the outbreak of the Spanish civil war, Spain was a sadly divided nation. Certain divisions, such as the separatist movements in the provinces, were centuries old, and the strife between clericals and anticlericals also had its roots deep in the past. Political and economic causes of disunity were, however, of more recent origin. The political history of Spain had for decades been a history of sudden and radical changes. From 1923 to 1930 the Spanish monarchy was ruled by a military dictator, Primo de Rivera. In 1931 the monarchy fell, and a republic was proclaimed. The constitution of the republic was an exceedingly liberal document, and the advanced legislation passed by the republicans in their first eighteen months of office promised to do more for the Spanish people than had been accomplished by the monarchy in half a century. But this legislation alienated the vested interests in Spain: the Church, the army, and the aristocracy.

The Church was disestablished; many army officers were retired on pension; and the great landed estates were confiscated for the benefit of the peasants. The parties of the Right and Center coalesced, and in 1933 their victory at the polls ushered in a period of reaction. It was also a period of violence, for the workers, sensing the trend toward dictatorship, on several occasions rose in revolt. In July 1936 the murder of a royalist leader touched off the civil war; in that same month General Francisco Franco (1892–   ), a relatively obscure officer who had formerly been chief of staff, flew to Morocco and organized a mutiny in the Foreign Legion and the Moorish troops. In October Franco was named chief of state by the insurgents, and conducted the insurgent cause through more than two years of bloody warfare. The following speech was delivered by Franco three months after he became chief of state. (22)

Spain, Spain, Spain—land of heroic deeds, of heroic greatness, home of ascetics and of Quixotes, land of nobles, has awakened with new vitality and strength. It is a national movement, this wakening of a people who did not know themselves, and felt strange and out of place. Undermined by the hidden forces of revolution, little by little it was succumbing to the criminal designs of alien committees that, under the mask of democracy, and brandishing the strong weapon of materialism was undermining all there was of nobility and spirituality in our ancient homeland.

Liberty, fettered by the license of government partisans; equality, destroyed by those who in the government proclaimed themselves to be belligerents; fraternity, given the lie by daily assassinations of men of the opposition, with the complacency and complicity of the authorities and the government; these exist again.

Hidden pacts with Russian communism, secret agreements with foreign nations behind the back of the constitution and the laws, persecution of the constitution and the laws, persecution without truce of everything representing any spiritual or moral value, or that did not yoke itself to the tumbril of Muscovite revolution—this was the Spain of yesterday: the Spain of workers criminally exploited by their employers, of the tubercular without sanatoriums, of the hearths without fires, of political bosses, of social injustice, or children with no schools, of Spaniards without a fatherland, of men without a God.

For peace and the country's welfare, for the rational and just betterment of working and middle classes, for liberty of conscience and respect for religion and tradition, for the tranquillity and prosperity of the home, for our threatened civilization, and the prestige of our flag, for the independence of our country, for a new Spain, a free Spain, a great Spain, our soldiers are fighting today this Russo-communistic invasion.

This new Spain will represent a great national family, one without masters or vassals, without poor or potentate. Social justice will be the basis of our new empire, without destructive and suicidal class warfare, without meddlesome interferences from abroad that are so incompatible with our national dignity. We want a fraternal Spain, an industrious and working Spain, where parasites can find no lodging. A Spain without chains and tyrannies: a nation without destructive Marxism and communism: a state for the people and not a people for the state. A Spain without parties in continual conflict, without parliamentary preponderancies or irresponsible assemblies. We want a Spain great, strong, and united, one with authority, direction, and order. Our progress must be firm and unhesitating: and we must go progressively and constantly on to our goal of a great organic Spain. . . .

We must awaken in all Spaniards the love of country, pride in realizing their Spanish birth, by creating conditions of life for all social classes that will permit them to appreciate without pain or rancor the political greatness of the new state. . . .

This is our commission—love of our country, honor, love for the people, deep Catholic sentiment, and a complete faith in the destiny of Spain.

In the order of religion, to the angry persecution of the Marxists and communists of whatever represents the existence of spirituality, of faith, or of religious worship, we oppose the sentiment of a Catholic Spain, with her saints and martyrs, with her secular institutions, her social justice, her Christian charity, and that great comprehensive soul which, in the Golden Ages of our history when a vigorous and deep-rooted Catholicism was the reconstructing arm of our historic unity, suffered, under the tolerant guardianship of the Catholic state, the mosques and synagogues to be gathered within the soul of Catholic Spain.

This great national movement demands of everyone faith and enthusiasm, and includes the sacrifice of everything that in this holocaust of our land can be spared. If we are to make a Spain for everyone, everyone must sacrifice himself for Spain and put aside shades of difference and details that might roughen the facets that in a new Spain must be limpid and glittering.

Union and collaboration with the state must be disinterested, self-sacrificing, without materialistic aims or self-seeking. Law and the family must be its principal cells. Family, laws, corporations, municipalities, province, region, will be the principal wheels of progress of this new state. . . .

This is the Spain that, honored by the recognition of those countries which understand the threat of communism and the sanctity of our crusade for the defense of civilization, salutes the world. Spain which nobly thanks those other nations for their spiritual assistance, those other nations which, without official manifestation, weep for the profanation of churches and the martyrdom of our brethren at the hands of blood-maddened hordes, as if our churches were the very ones in which they kneel in worship and the blood of our martyred were that of their own.

Spain that unites in intimate communion with the plans of her chief!

Spaniards all: Long live Spain!

V

The Legacy of the Nineteenth Century— Communism and Socialism

CIVILIZATION means restriction; and so does socialism. So far from being anarchy, it is the very antithesis of it. Anarchy is the goal of liberalism, if liberalism could ever be persuaded to be logical. So the scarecrow of anarchy, at least, need not frighten away any would-be convert to socialism. There remains, it is true, the other scarecrow, revolution; and that, I admit, has more life in it. Socialism *is* revolutionary; but so is liberalism, or was, while it was anything.

G. LOWES DICKINSON

CONTENTS

[111]

QUESTIONS FOR STUDY

PART I

1. Why, according to Lenin, is the dictatorship of the proletariat the most important item in Marxist doctrine?

2. How did Lenin describe the dictatorship of the proletariat? What form does it take?

3. In what way was Trotsky's theory of "permanent revolution" a response to Russia's peculiar situation in respect to a socialist revolution?

4. How do the decrees of the Russian Revolution square with communist theory?

5. How does Radek resolve the dilemma in Russian foreign policy? Has the Soviet Union followed the foreign policy outlined by Radek?

6. In what ways does a soviet system differ from a parliamentary system? Does Stalin claim that the soviet system is more liberal? More democratic?

7. What is the role of the Communist Party in the soviet system? How does it modify the character of this system?

8. What is the fundamental "self-contradiction" in the communist state? How does Stalin resolve it?

9. Why did Bukharin confess? How does his confession of faith compare with Condorcet's (see Problem I)? With Carnot's (see Problem III)?

PART II

10. How does Bauer's left-wing socialism differ from Russian communism? What accounts for the difference?

11. What contributions does Bauer make to socialist theory?

12. Compare Bauer and Blum. Are they in fundamental agreement?

13. How does Blum answer the challenge posed by fascism?

14. According to Blum, what is the basic drive behind socialism?

15. What is Crossman's answer to the problems raised for a socialist government by fascism in the sphere of international relations?

16. According to Attlee, what is the socialist position in the modern world?

17. Judging from the British example, does socialist doctrine change its character in any respect when it is applied?

18. What are the basic similarities and differences between communism and the different varieties of socialism studied in this Problem?

[112]

If liberal democracy constituted the focal issue of political struggle in Europe during the nineteenth century, then it may well be said that socialism plays an analogous role in the twentieth. Just as the nineteenth-century liberals sought to realize the credo of the eighteenth century, so European socialists have in our century carried to the daily struggle of the political arena the ideas developed by their predecessors. To be sure, socialist parties were founded throughout Europe during the period from 1875 to 1900 but they had not yet achieved the mass support that was to make them an important political factor. Since 1900 the advance in the sphere of political organization has been remarkable, but general socialist theory has hardly progressed beyond the lines laid down by Marx and Engels, the Fabians, and Bernstein. The most notable development in the socialist picture in the last fifty years, aside from the gigantic increase in numbers, has been the embodiment of the old theoretical differences in separate, hostile party frameworks. The secession of radicals from the socialist movement has created the conflict of Communist and Socialist parties which characterizes the European political scene today.

This rise of communism was indissolubly bound up with the activities of Vladimir Lenin (1870–1924). He gave to the movement the specific interpretation of Marxism which is its theory and he built the Russian party organization which is its primary instrument. For Lenin, who was primarily a man of action, theory and practice were closely connected, and he developed the independent communist movement from intraparty conflicts on concrete issues, first within Russia and later on an international scale. In the Russian arena, he fought the Economists (the Russian Revisionists) and then split with the Mensheviks, who represented in Russia the dominant line of European socialism. These socialists claimed Marxist orthodoxy but interpreted it to mean that the socialist parties must include the great masses of the workers and that the socialist revolution must await the ripening of revolutionary consciousness in these masses under the impact of capitalist development. The Bolshevik faction, formed in 1903 under Lenin's leadership on the issue of party organization, opposed this view by championing Lenin's idea of the party as a small, centralized, highly disciplined corps of intellectual elite who, armed with Marxist theory and ever-conscious of the revolutionary goal of the movement, must bring about revolution by direction from above. Behind this tactical conflict lay a crucial difference in general approach. While the socialists would put off the seizure of power until the economic evolution predicted by Marx had prepared a democratic basis for revolution in the workers, the Bolsheviks emphasized the revolutionary aspect of Marxism and would seize political power at the first opportunity, whether the workers were ripe for it or not. In Russia the cleavage became final when in 1905 it was embodied in doctrine: the Mensheviks announced that in the coming democratic revolution they would help the bourgeoisie to power in order to create the conditions for capitalist evolution; Lenin advanced the slogan of the "democratic dictatorship of the proletariat and peasantry" to signify the Bolsheviks' intention of leading the democratic revolution and taking over political power directly from czarism itself.

The split became world-wide with the break-up of the Second International on the issue of World War I. Until 1914 a balance of radical universal doctrine and moderate practical activity in internal affairs had reconciled the extremes and maintained the unity of the organization, thanks to the absence of any critical international issue requiring positive decisions. In 1907 and 1912 international socialist congresses had even agreed on manifestoes which called wars "imperialist" conflicts, pledged the socialist parties to work for peace within their own countries and threatened that revolutions might result from war. The practical decisions required by the actual outbreak of the war put the doctrine to the test and, as in Russia, the underlying divergences asserted themselves. The bulk of the socialist parties, committed to the evolutionary process of their respective nations, supported their governments' war effort for defensive purposes. The Bolsheviks and the few kindred extremists from other countries demanded that the revolutionary situation created by the "imperialist" war be used by each socialist party to begin the civil war in its own country. A pacifistic middle group, forerunners of the Left-wing socialists of the future, wavered uneasily between these groups and proposed that the socialists intervene for immediate peace on any terms. The unity of the socialist movement was at an end, and the emergence of these three groups by 1917 set the stage for the struggle over the fate of Europe.

The documents selected for this Problem show the basic forms which have been developed to adapt the socialist idea to conditions of the twentieth century and some of the concrete policies which have been adopted when exponents of the idea have come to power. Part I is concerned with the theory and practice of communism. Part II deals similarly with socialism. The student should compare the doctrines and should note the direction which each has taken when applied. Are communism and socialism merely two variant aspects of the same fundamental attitude toward society or do they embody profoundly different values and ways of life? The student should come to some decision on this question.

Part I.

COMMUNISM

The history of twentieth-century communism is focussed inevitably upon Russia. Not only did the outstanding theoreticians of European communism, Lenin and Trotsky, come out of the Russian social democratic movement, not only was the Russian Communist Party the first modern communist party (the Communist Party proclaimed by Marx and Engels in 1848 was an abortive venture), but the triumph of this party in November 1917, before its counterparts in the other countries even acquired independent organization, gave it the prestige which permitted its complete domination of world communism down to the present day. Moreover, the institutionalization of communism in Russia has enabled observers to assess the creative powers of the movement in a manner which is impossible with the oppositional activities of communist parties elsewhere. Part 1 of this Problem, consequently, will concentrate upon certain aspects of Russian communism and its creature, the Third, or Communist, International.

A.

THE COMMUNIST THEORY

1. *Leninism.* The founder and undisputed leader of the Russian Communist Party untill his death in 1924, Vladimir Lenin (a revolutionary pseudonym; his real name was Vladimir Il'ich Ulianov), laid down what remains the authoritative doctrine of communism. Primarily a tactician rather than a political philosopher, Lenin felt that he was merely executing the letter and the spirit of Marxist theory. Consequently, his activity until World War I was concerned with the problems of organizing the party and setting forth the tactics which would furnish the fittest instruments for the conquest of power. With the war, however, Lenin saw the arrival of the long-awaited revolutionary situation and, in his *Imperialism, the Highest Stage of Capitalism* (1917) and *State and Revolution* (1917), he gave the theoretical basis to his views on the nature of internationalist capitalist society (see Problem XI) and to the form of the communist revolution in Russia. The selections which follow are from *State and Revolution.* (1)

The main point in the teaching of Marx is the class struggle. This has very often been said and written. But this is not true. Out of this error, here and there, springs an opportunist distortion of Marxism, such a falsification of it as to make it acceptable to the bourgeoisie. The theory of the class struggle was *not* created by Marx, but by the bourgeoisie *before* Marx and is, generally speaking, *acceptable* to the bourgeoisie. He who recognizes *only* the class struggle is not yet a Marxist; he may be found not to have gone beyond the boundaries of bourgeois reasoning and politics. To limit Marxism to the teaching of the class struggle means to curtail Marxism—to distort it, to reduce it to something which is acceptable to the bourgeoisie. A Marxist is one who *extends* the acceptance of class struggle to the acceptance of the *dictatorship of the proletariat.* Herein lies the deepest difference between a Marxist and an ordinary petty or big bourgeois. On this touchstone it is necessary to test a *real* understanding and acceptance of Marxism. . . .

Opportunism *does not lead* the recognition of class struggle up to the main point, up to the period of *transition* from capitalism to communism, up to the period of *overthrowing* and completely abolishing the bourgeoisie. In reality, this period inevitably becomes a period of unusually violent class struggles in their sharpest possible forms and, therefore, the state during this period inevitably must be a state that is democratic *in a new way* (for the proletariat and the poor in general) and dictatorial *in a new way* (against the bourgeoisie).

Further, the substance of the teachings of Marx about the state is assimilated only by one who understands that the dictatorship of a *single* class is necessary not only for any class society generally, not only for the *proletariat* which has overthrown the bourgeoisie, but for the entire *historic period* which separates capitalism from "classless society," from communism. The forms of bourgeois states are exceedingly variegated, but their essence is the same: in one way or another, all these states are in the last analysis inevitably a *dictatorship of the bourgeoisie.* The transition from capitalism to communism will certainly bring a great variety and abundance of political forms, but the essence will inevitably be only one: *the dictatorship of the proletariat.* . . .

In capitalist society, under the conditions most favorable to its development, we have more or less complete democracy in the democratic republic. But this democracy is always bound by the narrow framework of capitalist exploitation, and consequently always remains, in reality, a democracy for the minority, only for the possessing classes, only for the rich. Freedom in capitalist society always remains just about the same as it was in the ancient Greek republics: freedom for the slaveowners. The modern wage slaves, owing to the conditions of capitalist exploitation, are so much crushed by want and poverty that "democracy is nothing to them," "politics is nothing to them"; that, in the ordinary peaceful course of events, the majority of the population is debarred from participating in social and political life. . . .

But from this capitalist democracy—inevitably narrow, subtly rejecting the poor, and therefore hypocritical and false to the core—progress does not march onward, simply, smoothly and directly, to "greater and greater democracy," as the liberal professors and petty-bourgeois opportunists would have us believe. No, progress marches onward, *i.e.* toward communism, through the dictatorship of the proletariat; it cannot do otherwise, for there is no one else and no other way to *break the resistance* of the capitalist exploiters.

But the dictatorship of the proletariat—*i.e.*, the organization of the vanguard of the oppressed as the ruling class for the purpose of crushing the oppressors—cannot produce merely an expansion of democracy. *Together* with an immense expansion of democracy which *for the first time* becomes democracy for the poor, democracy for the people, and not democracy for the rich folk, the dictatorship of the proletariat produces a series of restrictions of liberty in the case of the oppressors, the exploiters, the capitalists. We must crush them in order to free humanity from wage slavery; their resistance must be broken by force; it is clear that where there is suppression there is also violence, there is no liberty, no democracy. . . .

Democracy for the vast majority of the people, and suppression by force, *i.e.*, exclusion from democracy, of the exploiters and oppressors of the people—this is the modification of democracy during the *transition* from capitalism to communism. . . .

Democracy is of great importance for the working class in its struggle for freedom against the capitalists. But democracy is by no means a limit one may not overstep; it is only one of the stages in the course of development from feudalism to capitalism, and from capitalism to communism. . . .

Democracy is a form of the state—one of its varieties. Consequently, like every state, it consists in organized, systematic application of force against human beings. This on the one hand. On the other hand, however, it signifies the formal recognition of the equality of all citizens, the equal right of all to determine the structure and administration of the state. This, in turn, is connected with the fact that, at a certain stage in the development of democracy, it first rallies the proletariat as a revolutionary class against capitalism, and gives it an opportunity to crush, to smash to bits, to wipe off the face of the earth the bourgeois state machinery—even its republican variety: the standing army, the police, and bureaucracy; then it substitutes for all this a *more* democratic, but still a state machinery in the shape of armed masses of workers, which becomes transformed into universal participation of the people in the militia. . . .

Accounting and control—these are the *chief* things necessary for the organizing and correct functioning of the *first phase* of communist society. *All* citizens are here transformed into hired employees of the state, which is made up of the armed workers. *All* citizens become employees and workers of *one* national state "syndicate." All that is required is that they should work equally, should regularly do their share of work, and should receive equal pay. The accounting and control necessary for this have been *simplified* by capitalism to the utmost, till they have become the extraordinarily simple operations of watching, recording and issuing receipts, within the reach of anybody who can read and write and knows the first four rules of arithmetic.

When the *majority* of the people begin everywhere to keep such accounts and maintain such control over the capitalists (now converted into employees) and over the intellectual gentry, who still retain capitalist habits, this control will really become universal, general, national; and there will be no way of getting away from it, there will be "nowhere to go."

The whole of society will have become one office and one factory, with equal work and equal pay.

But this "factory" discipline, which the proletariat will extend to the whole of society after the defeat of the capitalists and the overthrow of the exploiters, is by no means our ideal, or our final aim. It is but a *foothold* necessary for the radical cleansing of society of all the hideousness and foulness of capitalist exploitation, *in order to advance further.*

From the moment when all members of society, or even only the overwhelming majority, have learned how to govern the state *themselves,* have taken this business into their own hands, have "established" control over the insignificant minority of capitalists, over the gentry with capitalist leanings, and the workers thoroughly demoralized by capitalism—from this moment the need for any government begins to disappear. The more complete the democracy, the nearer the moment when it begins to be unnecessary. The more democratic the "state" consisting of armed workers, which is "no longer a state in the proper sense of the word," the more rapidly does *every* state begin to wither away.

For when *all* have learned to manage, and independently are actually managing by themselves social production, keeping accounts, controlling the idlers, the gentlefolk, the swindlers, and similar "guardians of capitalist traditions," then the escape from this national accounting and control will inevitably become so increasingly difficult, such a rare exception, and will probably be accompanied by such swift and severe punishment (for the armed workers are men of practical life, not sentimental intellectuals, and they will scarcely allow anyone to trifle with them), that very soon the *necessity* of observing the simple, fundamental rules of everyday social life in common will have become a *habit.*

The door will then be wide open for the transition from the first phase of communist society to its higher phase, and along with it to the complete withering away of the state.

2. *Trotskyism.* Another, though subordinate, contribution to communist theory was added in 1917 when Leon Trotsky (1879–1940), né Lev Bronstein, joined the Bolsheviks. He had previously played the role of a lone wolf, for his theory of "permanent revolution," developed during the revolution of 1905, had found approval with neither Mensheviks nor Bolsheviks. In 1917, however, Trotsky and Lenin were in agreement in their estimate of the Russian situation. Trotsky, who was deported from Russia by Stalin in 1929, later insisted that Lenin endorsed his theory, but Stalin, who claims the Lenin heritage, has denied this. Whatever the merits of the case, "permanent revolution" is now a divergent communist line. The selections which follow are from Trotsky's *The Permanent Revolution,* which was written in 1930, the first year of his exile. (2)

The permanent revolution, in the sense which Marx attached to the conception, means a revolution which makes no compromise with any form of class rule, which does not stop at the democratic stage, which goes over to socialist measures and to war against the reaction from without, that is, a revolution whose every next stage is anchored in the preceding one and which can only end in the complete liquidation of all class society.

To dispel the chaos that has been created around the theory of the permanent revolution, it is necessary to distinguish three lines of thought that are united in this theory.

First, it embraces the problem of the transition of the democratic revolution into the socialist. This is really the historical origin of the theory. . . .

If the traditional view was that the road to the dictatorship of the proletariat led through a long period of democracy, the theory of permanent revolution established the fact that for backward countries the road to democracy passed through the dictatorship of the proletariat. By that alone, democracy does not become a regime anchored within itself for decades, but rather a direct introduction to the socialist revolution. Each is bound to the other by an unbroken chain. In this way, there arises between the democratic revolution and the socialist transformation of society a permanency of revolutionary development.

The second aspect of the "permanent" theory already characterizes the socialist revolution as such. For an indefinitely long time and in constant internal struggle, all social relations are transformed. The process necessarily retains a political character, that is, it develops through collisions of various groups of society in transformation. Outbreaks of civil war and foreign wars alternate with periods of "peaceful" reforms. Revolutions in economy, technique, science, the family, morals, and usages develop in complicated reciprocal action and do not allow society to reach equilibrium. Therein lies the permanent character of the socialist revolution as such.

The international character of the socialist revolution, which constitutes the third aspect of the theory of the permanent revolution, results from the present state of economy and the social structure of humanity. Internationalism is no abstract principle but a theoretical and political reflection of the character of world economy, of the world development of productive forces, and the world scale of the class struggle. The socialist revolution begins on national grounds. But it cannot be completed on these grounds. The maintenance of the proletarian revolution within a national framework can only be a provisional state of affairs, even though, as the experience of the Soviet Union shows, one of long duration. In an isolated proletarian dictatorship, the internal and external contradictions grow inevitably together with the growing successes. Remaining isolated, the proletarian state must finally become a victim of these contradictions. The way out for it lies only in the victory of the proletariat of the advanced countries. Viewed from this standpoint, a national revolution is not a self-sufficient whole: it is only a link in the international chain. The international revolution presents a permanent process, in spite of all fleeting rises and falls.

B.   THE COMMUNIST REVOLUTION

In February 1917 the czarist autocracy in Russia broke down under the pressure of a long and losing war. As in the revolution of 1905, the spearheads of the revolt were the striking workers in Moscow and St. Petersburg and the soviets, or factory committees, which rose spontaneously to represent their demands. Although a provisional government dominated by middle-class liberals and supported by the constitutionally elected Russian parliament, the Duma, took over the state, the soviets spread, took up connections with one another, and formed the Congress of Soviets of Workers', Soldiers', and Peasants' Delegates, which the provisional government was too weak to dissolve in the months that followed. Hence when, in April and May, the Bolshevik leaders streamed back into St. Petersburg from exile and Siberia, they found a revolutionary instrument at hand. At first the Bolsheviks were a minority in the Congress, but their demands for immediate peace and confiscation of the land in favor of the peasants coincided with the deepest desires of the people, and they gained support within the revolutionary elements of Russian society. Despite an abortive putsch in July 1917, which drove them underground, and a shift to the Left within the provisional government, which transferred the premiership to Kerensky, a Socialist Revolutionary (an agrarian socialist party founded in 1900), in August, the Bolsheviks won a majority in the Second Congress of Soviets, which met on November 6, 1917. With the convocation of this body the Bolshevik Revolution was begun and was carried through to a successful conclusion under conditions of foreign and civil war, foreign intervention, and economic dislocation. The communists exploited the chaos in Russia to make a clean sweep of former authorities and institutions and to replace them with those of a communist state. Following are some of the decrees which established this state. (3)

I. The Land Decree of Council of People's Commissars, November 8, 1917

The final settlement of the land question belongs to the national Constituent Assembly.

The most equitable settlement is as follows:

1. The right of private ownership of land is abolished forever. Land cannot be sold, bought, leased, mortgaged, or alienated in any manner whatsoever. All lands—state, appanage, cabinet, monastery, church, entail, private, communal, peasant, and any other lands—pass to the nation without indemnification and are turned over for the use of those who till them. Persons who have suffered from the loss of property will be entitled to public aid only during the time necessary for their readjustment to the changed conditions of existence.

2. All the underground resources, such as ores, petroleum, coal, salt, etc., as well as forests and waters which have national importance, are transferred for the exclusive use of the state. All small streams, lakes, forests, etc., are transferred for the use of the land communities, on condition that they be administered by the organs of local self-government.

3. Holdings under intensive agriculture—orchards, gardens, plantations, nurseries, etc.—are not to be divided, but turned into model farms and handed over to the state or the community, depending upon size and importance. Small private estates, city and village land in fruit or truck gardens, are to be left in possession of their present owners, but the size of these holdings and the amount of tax to be paid on them shall be determined by law.

4. Stud farms, state and private farms for breeding thoroughbred stock, poultry, etc., shall be confiscated, nationalized, and turned over either for the exclusive use of the state or the land community, depending upon their size and importance. The question of indemnification is to be settled by the Constituent Assembly.

5. The entire livestock, tools, etc., of the confiscated lands shall be turned over for the exclusive use of the state or land community, depending upon size and importance, without indemnification, but this does not apply to the small landholding peasants.

6. All Russian citizens (male and female) who are willing to till the land, either by themselves or with the assistance of their families or in collective groups, are entitled to the use of the land, as long as they are able to cultivate it. Hired labor is not permitted. . . .

7. The land is to be divided equally among the toilers, according to needs of labor capacity, depending on local conditions. Each community

is to decide for itself how its land is to be apportioned, whether it is to be held collectively or as homesteads or artels.

8. All the alienated land goes into one national fund. Its distribution among the toilers is carried out by local and central self-governing bodies, beginning with the democratic organization in villages and cities and ending with the central regional institutions. This fund is subject to periodical redistribution, based on the rise in population, the increase in production, and the methods of cultivation. . . .

II. Decree on the Establishment of the Supreme Council of National Economy, December 14, 1917

1. The supreme council of national economy is established . . . attached to the soviet of people's commissars.

2. The work of the supreme council of national economy is to organize the national economy and state finances. With that in view the supreme council of national economy will draw up general standards and plans for the regulation of the economic life of the country, coordinating and unifying the activities of the local and central regulating organs . . . that are attached to the people's commissariats . . . the All-Russian soviet of workers' control, the factory shop committees, and the trade unions.

3. The supreme council of national economy has the right to confiscate, requisition, sequester, and consolidate various branches of industry, commerce, and other enterprises in the field of production, distribution, and state finance.

4. The supreme council of national economy is to take charge of all existing institutions for the regulation of the economic life and has the right to reorganize them. . . .

III. Decree on Establishment of the Extraordinary Commission to Fight Counterrevolution [Cheka], December 20, 1917

The duties of the commission will be:

1. To persecute [sic] and break up all acts of counterrevolution and sabotage all over Russia, no matter what their origin.

2. To bring before the revolutionary tribunal all counterrevolutionists and saboteurs and to work out a plan for fighting them. . . .

The commission will be formed tomorrow. . . . The commission is to watch the press, saboteurs, strikers, and the Socialist Revolutionists of the right. . . .

IV. Decree on the Nationalization of Banks, December 27, 1917

In the interests of a proper organization of the national economy, a thorough eradication of bank speculation and a complete emancipation of the toiling masses from exploitation by the banking capitalists, and in order to found a single unified state bank for the Russian Republic which shall serve the interest of the people and the poorest classes, the central executive committee decrees that:

1. Banking is hereby declared a state monopoly.

2. All existing private joint-stock banks and other banking houses are to become a part of the state bank. . . .

V. Decree of the Soviet of People's Commissars on the Rights and Duties of Soviets, January 7, 1918

1. Soviets of workers', soldiers', and peasants' deputies, being local organs, are quite independent in regard to questions of a local character, but must always act in accord with the decrees and decisions of the central soviet government as well as of the larger bodies (*uezd, gubernia,* and regional soviets) of which they form a part.

2. Upon the soviets, as organs of government, devolve the tasks of administration and service in every sphere of local life, viz., administrative, economic, financial, and educational.

3. In the field of administration the soviets must carry out all decrees and decisions of the central government, undertake to give to the people the widest information about those decisions, issue obligatory ordinances, make requisitions and confiscations, impose fines, suppress counterrevolutionary organs of the press, make arrests, and dissolve public organizations which incite active opposition or the overthrow of the soviet government.

Note: The soviets must report to the central soviet government regarding all measures undertaken by them and concerning most important local events. . . .

VI. Decree of the Soviet of People's Commissars on the Nationalization of Large-scale Industry, June 28, 1918

For the purpose of combating decisively the economic disorganization and the breakdown of the food supply, and of establishing more firmly the dictatorship of the working class and the village poor, the soviet of people's commissars has resolved:

1. To declare all of the following industrial and commercial enterprises which are located in the Soviet Republic, with all their capital and property, whatever they may consist of, the property of the Russian Socialist Federated Soviet Republic. . . .

[At this point there is given a long list of the most important mines, mills, factories, etc.]

5. The entire personnel of every enterprise—technicians, workers, members of the board of directors, and foremen—shall be considered employees of the Russian Socialist Federated Republic. . . . Those who leave their posts . . . are liable to the revolutionary tribunal and to the full penalty of the law.

6. All private capital belonging to members of the boards of directors, stockholders, and owners of the nationalized enterprises will be attached pending the determination of the relation of such capital to the turnover capital and resources of the enterprises in question. . . .

8. The supreme council of national economy is authorized to formulate at once and send to all nationalized plants detailed instructions on the organization of management and the problems of labor organization connected with the carrying out of the present decree. . . .

C. THE COMMUNIST STATE

The Russian communists were equipped with a well-developed ideology when they began their task of constructing a socialist society. However, both in foreign policy and internal institutions, the Soviet regime has had to cope with the basic necessities of the modern state while attempting to realize the communist ideal. The student should try to decide to what extent the Soviet regime represents the necessary implications of communist doctrine and to what extent it is a distortion of the communist ideal.

1. *The International Policy of Communism.* In the field of foreign relations the potential conflict between the interests of the communist state and the international interests of communism was resolved in favor of the former with the triumph of Stalin. The policy of socialism in one country triumphed over Trotsky's doctrine of permanent revolution. Stalin and his followers still maintain, however, that their policy is in the service of world communism. The following selection gives the official Russian line, as of 1933, on this issue. It is taken from an article on Russian foreign policy written for American consumption by Karl Radek. (4)

Foreign policy is a function of domestic policy. It solves problems which result from the development of a given society, a given state, under definite historical conditions. . . .

It is silly to say that geography plays the part of fate, that it determines the foreign policy of a state. Czarist policy originated not in geographical conditions, but in the privileges of the Russian nobility and the demands of young Russian capitalism. The questions raised by geography are dealt with by each social formation in its own way; that way is determined by its peculiar economic and political aims. . . .

The main object for which Soviet diplomacy is fighting is *peace*. Now this term "peace" is much abused. There is no diplomat whose official pronouncements do not use this term reverently over and over again, even though he is a representative of one of those imperialistic nations which are most active in preparing war. But those who are incapable of understanding the specific place occupied by the struggle for peace in Soviet foreign policy are altogether incapable of understanding that policy in whole or in part. Why is the struggle for peace the central object of Soviet policy? Primarily because the Soviet Union—to use the expression of Lenin—"has everything necessary for the building up of a socialist society.". . .

Does the Soviet Union need war in order to build up socialism? It does not. Certain capitalist circles have stubbornly asserted since the Soviet Union was founded that it would seek a solution of its difficulties in war; these assertions are repudiated by the history of the Soviet Union during its sixteen years of life. Even at the moment when we were particularly ill equipped to undertake the building-up of socialism, immediately after we had assumed governmental responsibilities, we readily accepted the heaviest sacrifices in order to give peace to the country. We deeply believed—and this was of great importance—that we had in our hands everything necessary for building up a socialist society. Now we know that the problem of building socialism in the Soviet Union admits of a practical solution and that a considerable part of the problem has been already solved. The peace policy of the Soviet Union therefore rests on the granite foundation of triumphant socialist construction.

The enemies of the Soviet Union attempt to undermine the importance of this fact from two directions. Some of them accuse the Soviet Union of having given up its international aims. These aims, in their opinion, would demand military intervention by the Soviet Union to aid the emancipation of the international proletariat and of the colonial peoples. Others, on the contrary, maintain that, because the Bolshevik Party which controls the Soviet Union is inherently an international party, all the peace declarations of the Soviet Union are purely provisional and hence, that having reached a certain economic level which enables it to wage an aggressive war, the Soviet Union will repudiate its peace declarations and assume the initiative in a war. The best way of answering both these accusations is to quote the statement made by Stalin in December 1926: . . .

"And what is meant by 'victory on the world scale'? Does it mean that such a victory is equivalent to the victory of socialism in a single country? No, it does not. Lenin in his writings carefully distinguished the victory of socialism in a single country from victory 'on the world scale.' What Lenin really means when he speaks of 'victory on the world scale' is that *the success of socialism in our country, the victory of consolidating socialism in our country, has such an immense international significance that it (the victory) cannot be limited to our country alone but is bound to call forth a powerful movement toward socialism in all capitalist countries,* and even if it does not coincide with the victory of the proletarian revolution in other countries, it must in any event lead to a strong proletarian movement of other nations toward the victory of world revolution. Such is the revolutionary outlook according to Lenin, if we think in terms of the outlook for the victory of the revolution, which after all is the question in which we in the Party are interested.". . .

The Soviet Union is opposed to imperialism. It is opposed to an imperialistic war. It recognizes as equitable only one war, the war for the defense of socialism, the war of the enslaved peoples for their liberation. This point of view determines our attitude toward imperialism, as a system, and toward the consequences of its policy which find their expression in the preparation of a new war. It also dictates our attitude toward imperialistic alliances which evolve during the process of preparing a new war for the redistribution of the world.

The Soviet Union takes no part in the struggle for the redistribution of the world.

The words of Stalin at the sixteenth congress of the Communist Party of the Soviet Union— "We do not want a single bit of foreign land; but at the same time not an inch of our land shall ever be yielded to anyone else"—these words are the exact expression of the policy of the Soviet Union. . . .

The Soviet Union is confronted both in Europe and the Far East with hostile camps which are preparing war against one another. It holds toward them a position of neutrality, and endeavors to guarantee its own peace by a policy of non-interference in their affairs and by entering into mutual obligations of nonaggression with all sides. These obligations have been stated concretely and precisely in the pact containing the definition of the aggressor. The Soviet government has definitely undertaken not to move its armed forces by land, sea, or air across the frontiers of states which have assumed similar obligations, and also not to intervene directly or indirectly in their domestic affairs. All this indicates to the world that the policy of peace and neutrality on which the Soviet Union has embarked is not a mere diplomatic gesture, but a concrete political obligation in the earnestness of which should be beyond question. . . .

The Soviet Union does not close the door to the possibility of a deal, an agreement, with imperialistic powers which are waging a struggle against other imperialistic powers, if the latter attack the Soviet Union; but in entering into such an agreement the Soviet Union would not accept any responsibility for the specific purposes pursued by the imperialistic powers parties to the agreement. Never and under no conditions would it participate in the plundering of other nations, because participation in such a plunder would be contrary to the international solidarity of the workers. But against attacking imperialism an agreement is permissible with any opponent in order to defeat an enemy invading Soviet territory.

2. *The Internal Structure of the Communist State.* The basic institutions of the Soviet state, the organizations which for communists combine proletarian dictatorship and proletarian democracy, are the Communist Party and the system of soviets. The role of the Party, which changed its name from the Bolshevik faction of the Russian Social Democratic Party to the Russian Communist Party in March 1918, was officially recognized as a state institution in the constitution of 1936. The following selections, delivered in 1924, show Stalin's conceptions of the role of soviets and Party in the communist state, and, Trotsky's dissenting analysis of the nature of soviet democracy. (5)

[Stalin on the Soviets]

The victory of the dictatorship of the proletariat signifies the suppression of the bourgeoisie, the destruction of the bourgeois state machinery, and the displacement of bourgeois democracy by proletarian democracy. That is clear. But what organizations are to be employed for this colossal undertaking? There can hardly be any doubt that the old forms of proletarian organization which grew up with bourgeois parliamentarism as their base are not equal to this task. What new forms of proletarian organization are required to break up the machinery, to displace bourgeois democracy by proletarian democracy, and, above all, to serve as the foundation of the state power of the proletariat?

This new form of organization of the proletariat is the soviets.

Why are the soviets stronger than the old forms of organization? Because the soviets are absolutely *all-embracing* mass organizations of the proletariat and because they and they alone embrace all workers without exception.

The soviets are the *only* mass organizations that take in all the oppressed and exploited, workers and peasants, soldiers and sailors; and for this reason the vanguard of the masses of the proletariat can most easily and most completely bring to fruition its political direction of the struggle of the masses.

The soviets are *the most powerful organs* of the revolutionary mass struggle, of the mass political demonstrations, and of the mass uprising; they are organs capable of breaking the omnipotence of finance capital and its political satellites.

The soviets are the organizations which organize the masses themselves directly, *i.e., the most democratic,* signifying the most authoritative, organizations of the masses, that provide them with the maximum facilities for participating in the building up of the new state and its administration; they develop to their fullest extent the revolutionary energy, the initiative and the creative faculties of the masses in the struggle for the destruction of the old system, in the struggle for the new proletarian system.

The soviet power is the unification and the crystallization of the local soviets into one general state organization, into a state organization of the proletariat as the vanguard of the oppressed and exploited masses and, as the ruling class, their unification into the soviet republic.

The soviet power is in essence the fact that the largest and most revolutionary mass organizations of precisely those classes that were oppressed by the capitalists and landed proprietors now constitute the *"permanent* and *sole* foundation of all state power, of the entire state apparatus"; . . .

For this reason the soviet power is a *new form* of state organization different in principle from the old bourgeois democratic and parliamentary form. . . .

The soviet power combines the legislative and executive functions in a single state body and replaces territorial electoral divisions by units of production, *i.e.,* factories and workshops, and thereby connects the workers and the laboring masses in general directly with the apparatus of state administration and teaches them how to administer the country. . . .

The soviet republic is thus the political form,

so long sought and finally found, within the framework of which the economic emancipation of the proletariat and the complete victory of socialism is to be accomplished. The Paris Commune handed it down to us in embryonic form. The soviet power is its development and culmination.

[Stalin on the Party]

The Party must first of all constitute the *vanguard* of the working class. The Party must absorb all the best elements of the working class, their experience, their revolutionary spirit, and their unbounded devotion to the cause of the proletariat. But in order that it may really be the vanguard, the Party must be armed with a revolutionary theory, with a knowledge of the laws of the movement, with a knowledge of the laws of the revolution. . . . The Party cannot be a real party if it limits itself to registering what the masses of the working class think or experience, if it drags along at the tail of the spontaneous movement, if it does not know how to overcome the inertia and the political indifference of the spontaneous movement; or if it cannot rise above the ephemeral interests of the proletariat, if it cannot raise the masses to the level of the class interests of the proletariat. . . . The Party is the political leader of the working class. . . .

The Party is not only the vanguard of the working class. If it really desires to lead the struggle of the class it must at the same time be the *organized* detachment of its class. . . .

But the Party is not merely the *sum total* of Party organizations. The Party at the same time represents a single *system* of these organizations, their formal unification into a single whole, permitting of higher and lower organs of leadership of the submission of the minority to the majority, where decisions on questions of practice are obligatory upon all members of the Party. . . .

The Party is the organized detachment of the working class. But the Party is not the only organization of the working class. The proletariat has in addition a great number of other organizations which are indispensable in its struggle against the capitalist system. . . . Most of these organizations are nonparty. . . . The question then arises: Who is to determine the line, the general direction along which the work of all these organizations is to be conducted? Where is that central organization with the necessary experience to work out such a general line and also able, because of its authority, to prevail upon all these organizations to carry out this line, so as to attain unity of direction and preclude the possibility of working at cross purposes?

This organization is the Party of the proletariat. . . .

The Party is the highest form of class organization of the proletariat.

This does not mean, of course, that nonparty organizations like trade unions, operatives, etc., must be formally subordinated to Party leadership. It means simply that the members of the Party who belong to these organizations and doubtless exercise influence in them, should do all they can to persuade these nonparty organizations to draw nearer to the Party of the proletariat in their work and voluntarily accept its political guidance. . . .

The proletariat needs the Party not only to achieve the dictatorship, it needs it still more to maintain and extend its dictatorship in order to attain complete victory for socialism. . . .

Now what is meant by "maintaining" and "extending" the dictatorship? It means to imbue these millions of proletarians with the spirit of discipline and organization; it means making the proletarian masses immune against the deteriorating influences of petty-bourgeois spontaneity and petty-bourgeois habits; . . . it means assistance must be given to the masses of the proletarians in educating themselves so that they may become a force capable of abolishing classes and of preparing the ground for the organization of socialist production. But it is impossible to accomplish all this without a Party, which is strong by reason of its cohesion and discipline. . . .

The proletariat needs the Party *for* the achieving and maintenance of the dictatorship. The Party is the instrument of the dictatorship of the proletariat.

From this it follows that when classes disappear and the dictatorship of the proletariat will die out, the Party will also die out. . . .

Achievement and maintenance of the dictatorship of the proletariat are impossible without a party strong in its cohesion and iron discipline. But iron discipline in the Party is impossible without unity of will and without absolute and complete unity of action on the part of all members of the Party. This does not mean of course that there will never be any conflict of opinion within the Party. On the contrary, iron discipline does not preclude but presupposes criticism and conflicts of opinion within the Party. Least of all does it mean that this discipline must be "blind" discipline. On the contrary, iron discipline does not preclude but presupposes conscious and voluntary submission, for only conscious discipline can be truly iron discipline. But after a discussion has been closed, after criticism has run its course and a decision has been made, unity of will and unity of action become indispensable conditions without which Party unity and iron discipline in the Party are inconceivable. . . .

It follows that the existence of factions is incompatible with Party unity and with its iron discipline. . . .

The Party is synonymous with unity of will, which leaves no room for any factionalism or division of Party control.

[*Trotsky on the Internal Structure of the Communist State*]

However you may interpret the nature of the present soviet state, one thing is indubitable: at the end of its second decade of existence, it has not only not died away, but not begun to "die away." Worse than that, it has grown into a hitherto unheard of apparatus of compulsion. The bureaucracy not only has not disappeared, yielding its place to the masses, but has turned into an uncontrolled force dominating the masses. The army not only has not been replaced by an armed people, but has given birth to a privileged officers' caste, crowned with marshals, while the people, "the armed bearers of the dictatorship," are now forbidden in the Soviet Union to carry even non-explosive weapons. With the utmost stretch of fancy it would be difficult to imagine a contrast more striking than that which exists between the schema of the workers' state according to Marx, Engels, and Lenin, and the actual state now headed by Stalin. While continuing to publish the works of Lenin (to be sure, with excerpts and distortions by the censor), the present leaders of the Soviet Union and their ideological representatives do not even raise the question of the causes of such a crying divergence between program and reality. . . .

The Soviet Union is a contradictory society halfway between capitalism and socialism, in which: (*a*) the productive forces are still far from adequate to give the state property a socialist character; (*b*) the tendency toward primitive accumulation created by want breaks out through innumerable pores of the planned economy; (*c*) norms of distribution preserving a bourgeois character lie at the basis of a new differentiation of society; (*d*) the economic growth, while slowly bettering the situation of the toilers, promotes a swift formation of privileged strata; (*e*) exploiting the social antagonisms, a bureaucracy has converted itself into an uncontrolled caste alien to socialism; (*f*) the social revolution, betrayed by the ruling party, still exists in property relations and in the consciousness of the toiling masses; (*g*) a further development of the accumulating contradictions can as well lead to socialism as back to capitalism; (*h*) on the road to capitalism the counterrevolution would have to break the resistance of the workers; (*i*) on the road to socialism the workers would have to overthrow the bureaucracy. In the last analysis, the question will be decided by a struggle of living social forces, both on the national and the world arena.

3. *Stalin and the Communist "Contradictions."* Joseph Stalin, in 1934, gave the following resolution to the knotty logical problems posed by the attempted synthesis of nationalism and internationalism and of dictatorship and democracy: (6)

It may seem strange that we, who are in favor of the fusion of national cultures in the future into one common culture (both in form and content), with a single, common language, are at the same time in favor of the blossoming of national cultures at the present time, in the period of the dictatorship of the proletariat. But there is nothing strange in this. The national cultures must be permitted to develop and expand and to reveal all their potential qualities, in order to create the conditions necessary for their fusion into a single, common culture with a single, common language. The blossoming of cultures national in form and socialist in content under a proletarian dictatorship in one country, with the object of their fusion into a single, common, socialist (both in form and content) culture, with a single, common language, when the proletariat is victorious throughout the world and socialism becomes an everyday matter—such is the dialectical nature of the Leninist presentation of the question of national culture.

It may be said that, presented in this way, the question is "self-contradictory." But is there not the same sort of "self-contradiction" in our treatment of the question of the state? We are in favor of the withering away of the state, yet we are at the same time in favor of strengthening the dictatorship of the proletariat, which represents the most powerful and mighty of all forms of state power which have hitherto existed. The supreme development of the power of the state, with the object of preparing the way for the withering away of state power—such is the Marxist formula. Is that "self-contradictory"? Yes, it is "self-contradictory." But this contradiction is a living thing, and it is a complete reflection of Marxian dialectics. . . .

The same must be said of the formula of national culture: the blossoming of national cultures (and languages) in the period of the dictatorship of the proletariat in one country, with the object of preparing the way for their dying away and fusion into a single, common, socialist culture (and a single, common language) in the period of the victory of socialism all over the world.

Whoever has failed to understand this peculiarity and this "self-contradictory" nature of our transitional times, whoever has failed to understand this dialectical character of historical processes is lost to Marxism.

4. *The Communist Testament.* On March 12, 1938, Nikolai Bukharin, a veteran Bolshevik and outstanding communist ideologist, arose to make his last plea before the military collegium of the Supreme Court of the U.S.S.R. where, together with nineteen others, he was being tried for treason in one of the periodic public purges instituted by the Russian communist leaders during the 1930's. Having admitted, and substantiated by voluntary testimony, during the course of the trial, the bulk of the charges brought against him (including conspiracy with Trotsky against the Soviet state), Bukharin, foreseeing that this would be his last utterance (he was subsequently executed), sought to explain the ultimate motivations of his confession, his final act of loyalty to the communist state. The selection which follows is taken from Bukharin's speech and demonstrates the hold exercised by Russian communism over its followers. (7)

I shall now speak of myself, of the reasons for my repentance. Of course, it must be admitted that incriminating evidence plays a very important part. For three months I refused to say anything. Then I began to testify. Why? Because while in prison I made a revaluation of my entire past. For when you ask yourself: "If you must die, what are you dying for?"—an absolutely black vacuity suddenly rises before you with startling vividness. There was nothing to die for, if one wanted to die unrepented. And, on the contrary, everything positive that glistens in the Soviet Union acquires new dimensions in a man's mind. This in the end disarmed me completely and led me to bend my knees before the Party and the country. And when you ask yourself: "Very well, suppose you do not die; suppose by some miracle you remain alive, again what for? Isolated from everybody, an enemy of the people, in an inhuman position, completely isolated from everything that constitutes the essence of life. . . ." And at once the same reply arises. And at such moments, Citizen Judges, everything personal, all the personal incrustation, all the rancor, pride, and a number of other things, fall away, disappear. And, in addition, when the reverberations of the broad international struggle reach your ear, all this in its entirety does its work, and the result is the complete internal moral victory of the U.S.S.R. over its kneeling opponents. I happened by chance to get Feuchtwanger's book from the prison library. There he refers to the trials of the Trotskyites. It produced a profound impression on me; but I must say that Feuchtwanger did not get at the core of the matter. He stopped halfway, not everything was clear to him; when, as a matter of fact, everything is clear. World history is a world court of judgment: A number of groups of Trotskyite leaders went bankrupt and have been cast into the pit. That is true. But you cannot do what Feuchtwanger does in relation to Trotsky in particular, when he places him on the same plane as Stalin. Here his arguments are absolutely false. For in reality the whole country stands behind Stalin; he is the hope of the world; he is a creator. Napoleon once said that fate is politics. The fate of Trotsky is counterrevolutionary politics.

I am about to finish. I am perhaps speaking for the last time in my life.

Part II.   SOCIALISM

Socialism, as a specific labor movement in contradistinction to communism, had suffered a major decline since the First World War. In large measure this has been the result of the internal divisions between the moderate and radical wings of the socialist movement. In the First World War and the immediate postwar period, however, three factors arose to destroy the prewar balance of moderate action and radical doctrine: the attitude of the socialists toward the war itself, the conduct of socialists in the revolutionary years of 1918 and 1919, and the triumph of communism, as an avowedly new movement, in Russia. The policies adopted by the dominant elements within the socialist parties of western and central Europe revealed clearly their fundamental moderate character: they supported their nations in war, they refused to drive the chaotic postwar situation to socialist revolution, and they rejected the dictatorial means employed by the Russian communists. The result was the split not only into socialist and communist parties in each country but, within the socialist movement which remained, again into moderate and radical groups.

In the interwar period the Right and Left wings within the socialist movement existed within the same socialist party, with the Right, or revisionist, wing usually dominant. At the present time the respective influence of the two wings within socialism varies with the focus of power in each country, so that it is again split internationally, with the socialist Left wing dominant in eastern Europe and in Italy while the Right controls the parties in the rest of western Europe. The general position of the socialist parties in the interwar period must be gleaned largely from theoretical and programmatic writings, for until the victory of the Labour Party in Great Britain in 1945 there has been no purely socialist government in Europe (except for an inconsequential few chaotic weeks in Germany at the turn of 1918–19). When socialist governments were in power, as in England in 1924 and 1929 and in France in 1936, they were simply the leaders of coalitions which included middle-class parties.

A.   LEFT-WING SOCIALISM

The economic and social turmoil brought about by the war and the victory of communism in Russia brought the achievement of socialism from the realm of a distant Utopia to the sphere of imminent possibility. Socialists everywhere began seriously to concern themselves with the concrete means of bringing the socialist society into existence. While they devoted much attention to the more or less technical problems of socialization and planning, the primary issue was the general political problem of evolution versus revolution as means to power, democracy versus dictatorship. In the years 1916 to 1920 the radical wing of socialism was on the rise, for the revolutionaries who were to go communist after 1920 and the pacifists who objected to the support of the war effort given by the moderate majorities of most socialist parties were allied within the framework of socialism and received increased strength from the economic and social dislocations of 1918 and 1919. The Austrian socialists gave the outstanding theoretical formulation to the noncommunist radical position, which found a majority in the Party and which has kept the communist secession weak down to the present time. The ideologist of the Party was Otto Bauer (1881–1938), whose primary contributions to socialist theory had lain in fields neglected by socialists and exploited by Lenin—*i.e.* the problem of nationalism and the agrarian problem. Though an active party leader, Bauer, unlike Lenin, was not a man of action and was not able to translate his doctrine into reality. The following selections are from pamphlets written in 1919 and 1920. (8)

We must construct the socialist society gradually, progressing consciously, in planned organizational work, from one step to the next. Each of the successive measures which are to lead us to the socialist society must be well considered; it must not only regulate the distribution of goods more justly but perfect their production; it may not destroy the capitalistic organization of production without at the same time setting up a socialist organization which can direct production at least as well. The political revolution was the work of power; the social revolution can only be the work of constructive, organizational labor. The political revolution was the work of a few hours; the social revolution will have to be the result of bold but prudent labor of many years. This conception has nothing to do with the illusions of the narrow-minded revisionism or reformism of yesterday and the day before yesterday. It believed that society can peacefully "grow into" socialism without any violent revolution being necessary to it at all. This was certainly an error. For the social revolution assumes the conquest of political power by the proletariat; and the proletariat could and can not conquer the state power except with revolutionary means. But once political power is conquered, then a wholly new task is placed before the proletariat which can no longer be mastered with the means which are fitting for the political revolution. For the political revolution can only, as Marx said, "set free the elements of the future society"; but to construct the new society from these elements is a task which can be fulfilled not in street fighting, not in civil war, but only in creative work of legislation and administration. . . .

The social factors of power which determine the power of a class are primarily: first, the numbers of members of the class; second, the type, strength, and capacity of its organization; third, its place in the process of production and distribution . . . ; fourth, the strength of its political interest . . . ; fifth, the height of its education . . . the attracting power of its ideology.

The means of material power over which a class disposes is the quantity of useable arms it commands, the quantity and quality of weapons, the quality of its leadership, and organization for this armed power.

Democracy is that form of state within which the distribution of power in the state is determined exclusively by the social factors of power and is not displaced in favor of another class through the application of material means of power. . . . Democracy is a mere form; whether this form is filled with capitalistic, peasant, or proletarian content depends on the social factors of power. Democracy is an instrument of class domination; but this instrument can, according to the degree of development of the social factors of power, fall into the hands of various classes. . . . Naturally every state, including the democratic, rests on violence. But the democratic state uses the force of arms only for the purpose of executing its laws and decrees against resisting minorities. The content of these laws and decrees, however, is determined not through the violence of a class but exclusively through the social factors of power. . . . All nondemocratic forms of state depend on a situation in which a class sets up and maintains, by means of violence, a constitution which gives it more and other classes less power than corresponds to the social factors of power. . . . Like every other nondemocratic constitution Soviet dictatorship also depends on a class, in this case the proletariat, forcing on society by force of arms a constitution which secures a greater power to the ruling class than it could have in a democratic constitution, *i.e.*, in the free play of the social factors of power. . . . Like every other nondemocratic constitution Soviet dictatorship can be founded only through the violent subordination of the ruled classes, *i.e.*, through civil war. . . . In western and central Europe the proletariat stands against an incomparably stronger bourgeoisie, an incomparably more hostile bourgeoisie, a completely different kind of peasantry. Here therefore the Soviet dictatorship can be carried through only with still more terrible instruments of violence, in a still more terrible civil war than in Russia. . . . If Soviet dictatorship is hardly possible here in the long run, the proletariat also does not need it to conquer power. While in Russia the proletariat forms only a small minority of the population, in every modern industrial state it is the majority of the population. Therefore here, unlike Russia, power in the state can be conquered on the basis of democracy and with democratic means. . . . However, even when the proletariat conquers political power with democratic means, the bourgeoisie will resist its rule. It will rise against the democratic state, it will refuse obedience to its laws, it will sabotage its administration as soon as the democracy will have become a proletarian democracy. Even a democratic parliament will have to claim dictatorial means of power for itself, it will have to break the sabotage and perhaps the active resistance of the bourgeoisie with dictatorial, perhaps also with terrorist means as soon as this parliament will have become the instrument of domination of the working class. This too can be named a dictatorship of the proletariat; but it is an entirely different dictatorship than that of Bolshevism. It is not a dictatorship against democracy, but a dictatorship of democracy. Here violence does not seek to compel a legal distribution of power which is in opposition to the social distribution of power, but it simply secures the distribution of power determined by the social factors of power against the resistance of a minority. . . .

Certainly it is in no way certain that history will permit the proletariat to set up its dictatorship only after the conquest of political power with democratic means, *i.e.,* in the form of the dictatorship of a democratic parliament and local democratic bodies of self-administration. It can easily happen that the development of the class struggles may force the proletariat to a transitional dictatorship in a phase in which it can not yet rule with democratic means. In the period of the decisive class struggles between the bourgeoisie and the proletariat the class conflict is intensified everywhere. The sharpness of the class struggle may rupture democracy. A situation can prevail in which neither the bourgeoisie nor the proletariat is strong enough to rule the other with democratic means. . . . If the democratic apparatus can no longer function, either the bourgeoisie or the proletariat must set up its class rule by violent means. The dictatorship of the proletariat will in this case become the only way to prevent the brutal, counterrevolutionary dictatorship of the bourgeoisie. In this case the dictatorship of the proletariat will have to take other forms than where the proletariat has already taken over the legislating corporations of democracy. Here the distatorship of the proletariat can

not take the form of a dictatorship of democracy, but only the form of a dictatorship of proletarian class organizations. These class organizations can be workers' soviets as in Russia, local self-administrative bodies as in 1871 in Paris, or even trade unions. . . .

But it is a question not of the form of a proletarian dictatorship, but of its social content. If the proletariat proclaims the dictatorship as a permanent form of its class rule, as the political instrument for the overcoming of the capitalistic order of society, then the dictatorship will destroy the whole continuity of the economic process and the social administration, and inevitably all those enormous social and economic convulsions must strike, under which the dictatorship in western and central Europe must collapse. But if the proletariat sees the dictatorship only as a means and proclaims it only as a means of saving democracy from the impending danger of an antidemocratic counterrevolution or of ending a conflict in which democracy has collapsed, and proclaims the intention of leading the state back to democratic forms after the fulfillment of this task, then these dangers can, under proper circumstances, be avoided. The enormous task of the regrouping and the rationalization of production and distribution, and the professional and geographical regrouping of labor can, in western and central Europe, be carried through only on the basis of local and professional self-government, with the cooperation and cocontrol of all groups of the people who fulfill important functions in the social labor process. Dictatorship can here only secure democracy against counterrevolutionary dangers or defend it against uprisings by minorities, but it cannot hope to solve the tasks which only democracy can solve. . . .

B. RIGHT-WING SOCIALISM

With the extreme revolutionary elements drained off from the socialist movement into the new communist parties and with the stabilization of conditions in Europe, the moderates asserted their dominance over most of the socialist parties from the early 1920's. Save in Austria, the Left-wing elements who remained within the socialist movement formed relatively inconsequential minorities within the socialist parties: the return of the leaders of the German Independent Social Democratic Party to the moderate German Social Democratic Party in 1922 was a sign of the times. In the two decades that followed, the preponderance of the moderates within socialism was buttressed as a defensive reaction to the rising strength of the extremes of the Right and of the Left—fascism and communism. The leading moderate parties have been the British and the French socialist parties, both with revisionist traditions going back to their inception around the turn of the century, the British under Fabian influence and the French under the leadership of Jaures and Millerand. The most striking testament of moderate socialist faith was penned by Leon Blum, veteran socialist intellectual and premier of the Popular Front government in France in 1936, while he sat in prison during 1941 awaiting trial by the facsist regime which had taken over his defeated country. His book, *For All Mankind,* was smuggled out and printed by the French underground press in 1943. (9)

If today all our impressions can be summed up in one, and that one of a general collapse of French society, the ultimate reason is that the framework of that society was bourgeois, and that framework has given way. . . .

A ruling class and a political system have succumbed under the impact of events, as if they had gone down in the upheaval of revolution. That has happened before in French history without the country's being any the worse for it. Feudal aristocracy, monarchy based on divine right, both disappeared. Today, since a country cannot live without laws, France is faced with the immediate task of creating new institutions. There is nothing new about the principles on which these institutions will be based; they are known and laid down in advance. The French people are almost unanimous in their hope that the world war will end in a world-wide victory for democracy. The constitutional problem, therefore, is essentially a simple one. A weak and perverted bourgeois democracy has collapsed, and must be replaced by a true democracy, an energetic and competent democracy, popular instead of capitalist, strong instead of weak.

I am no constitution-maker; that is a task I leave to the specialists. But I have, I think, established two incontrovertible truths in the course of these arguments. The first is that parliamentary government is by no means necessarily either the only or the purest form of democracy; the second is that the faults for which the French parliamentary system is so often blamed are in reality the shortcomings and the vices of the French bourgeoisie. I do not intend to try to define what should be the role of the representative or parliamentary principle in a popular democracy. I claim only that, whatever be the function allotted to the legislative chambers when the distribution of powers in the future republic takes place, there can be no question of any attack on the elective principle nor on universal suffrage, which is the very symbol of democracy. To attempt to get rid of them would be to attack the deepest roots of French political tradition. On the other hand, the representative principle, using that term in its narrowest sense—that is, in the sense of the wholesale delegation of popular sovereignty to an elected house, and its expression through the sole medium of legislative assemblies—will, in all probability, not survive the experiment in bourgeois democracy that has now lasted more than a century. . . .

The second point I want to make is that this popular democracy will be, indeed can only be, a social democracy. That is the condition of future stability. There can, in logic, be no divorce between political and economic authority. The political power of the bourgeois class was derived from its economic power. It has now been stripped of that political power, and if economic power—which the bourgeoisie proved no less incapable of using for the good of the community —were to remain in its hands, then France would be exposed to the most dangerous risks. There would, almost certainly, be a new period of disturbance and impotence, a new series of upheavals, perhaps even of revolutions. Yet, although, up to now, the bourgeoisie has made only fumbling and hesitating attempts to use its economic privileges, it still retains legal and theoretical possession of them. This disequilibrium must be removed. There must be progressive, legal expropriation, carried out by peaceful means, but none the less ruthless in its action. Indeed, it will be, in reality, not expropriation but appropriation. Our task today is to rewrite the phrase used by Thiers and Dufaure of the Third Republic so that it reads, "The people's republic will be a social republic or it will be nothing."

There is, indeed, no way of evading the social problem when the facts themselves render its solution so urgent. How shall we continue to tolerate a system in which men have neither sufficient food, nor healthy houses, nor the wherewithal to protect their families from hunger, cold, illness, and vice? . . .

At a given stage of material evolution, just as at a given stage of scientific research, the same problems present themselves to the minds of all. Like fascism and nazism before it, the political system that calls itself the "national revolution" itself declares that they must be solved. But I cannot say too clearly or too often that France intends to solve them by herself and by democratic methods. In France at least, political and social democracy are inseparable terms. Political democracy cannot survive if it does not develop into social democracy; social democracy would be neither true nor stable if it were not based on political democracy. The French people will not consent to sacrifice the great human ideals laid down in 1789 to the major imperatives that material reality has added to them since then, or vice versa; they want to combine economic order and social equality with political, civil, and personal liberty. The task is a difficult one, but they intend to see it through themselves, using the political power that they have won in a hard struggle and that nothing will induce them to relinquish. They refuse to accept these things ready-made from the hands of rulers whom they have not chosen, and whose credentials they do not recognize. They demand justice and do not ask for charity; indeed, they know too well that justice can never be doled out from above, like alms to the poor. They have discovered that in other countries nazi and fascist autocracies reduced labor to slavish routine, but did nothing to suppress the privileges of the capitalist property owner. Even in France they can see that if the slogans with which they are bombarded were honestly translated into action, then the whole bourgeois structure would be destroyed, and they know that if it is not, it is because the inventors of the slogans are themselves bourgeois, convinced of the importance of their class and doing all they can to preserve it. The achievement of the political sovereignty of the people is therefore a concept and a task indissolubly allied to the parallel concept of social justice. The foundation of a social democracy in the full meaning of the term, which was yesterday's hope, has become tomorrow's program. . . .

The winds of history are favorable, and everywhere the workers are conscious of being carried by the tide. But this is where the real difficulty arises. Will they be worthy of their destiny? Will they be able to play the parts for which history has cast them? Will they understand, or can they be made to understand, that favorable material conditions, even if they are overwhelmingly favorable, cannot alone carry them into power, much less keep them there? Can they understand that if, to seize power, they will need both the force and the authority that come from being in harmony with the nature and the trend of economic evolution, they will have no less need of dignity, of the ascendancy, in a word, that comes from moral superiority and efficiency? For a transfer of power to be consolidated and established before history, it must be acceptable to the conscience of mankind no less than to human emotion and to human reason. It must call forth from every sincere man the spontaneous tribute, "It had to be," but not that alone. He must also say, "It is right, it is good, and it is beautiful." Like all other peoples, the French people will fulfill their mission—in other words, they will build the world of their ideals—only if they show themselves able to cultivate and cherish in themselves those virtues that must be present to justify any form of human supremacy, the virtues of courage, generosity of heart, righteousness of mind and conscience, abnegation of self in favor of the good of all. . . .

Moreover, at every stage of this collective life subordination of private interests to those of the community must be recognized as an inescapable obligation and treated as such. Social life would be impossible if the individual did not subordinate his particular and temporary interests to the more general and permanent interests of the group. The difficulty is to secure from political and social groups what is required of the individual—namely, voluntary subordination to the general and permanent interests of humanity. Obstinate partisanship, narrow-minded clannishness, and jingo nationalism are essentially the same as the selfishness of the individual. This renunciation of rivalry and of claims arising from the divergence of immediate interests, this spontaneous surrender to a higher will, this consciousness of permanent contact with and dependence on a higher order of reality extending by stages to embrace the broadest of all concepts, is what Socrates and Plato meant by wisdom and what a Christian thinker like Pascal called humility. But humility of this kind should be a source of strength, and then men should be proud to feel it. In the past men felt that it implied faith and obedience. We must see that it leads to faith and action.

Can it be a socialist who is putting forward this view? Indeed it can, and one, moreover, who flatters himself that he is being perfectly consistent. The aim of socialism is to set up a universal society founded on equal justice for all men and on equal peace for all nations. Many means must work together to this end, but no socialist worthy of the name would claim that the end could be achieved unless human personality is perfected, enriched, and deepened in the process, or unless the spirit of discipline and sacrifice is continually developed and more widely spread. Socialism has never denied either "moral" or "spiritual" values and has never repudiated either the sentiment of virtue or that of honor. All that it has done, like Christianity before it, is to interpret these concepts differently. . . .

The development of great human ideas, and even of religions, is influenced as much by the resistance they encounter as by the nature of their own initial impetus. Socialism had first to survive, then to make a niche for itself and to make its way; in order to establish its right to live, it had first to criticize its opponents, and, to protect its early achievements, it had to struggle. Capitalist society, misled by the instinct of self-preservation, treated socialism as an implacable enemy with which no compromise was possible and which must be overthrown and destroyed without mercy. Attack was held to be the best form of self-defense, and so the pulpit gave way to the battlefield, and battles inevitably call forth all man's most primitive instincts, including fear —on both sides—greed, and intolerance.

This polemical phase now belongs to the past. Socialism can move from the militant to the victorious period. The social system which it attacked and by which it was in turn attacked is now falling into ruin, and even where it still survives does so without belief in itself and in contradiction with its own laws. The men and parties who have most bitterly opposed socialist assumptions and axioms have now taken them over for their own purposes. Today, whether consciously or not, society is being reconstituted everywhere on principles laid down by the socialists. Even the Catholic Church, although it has never withdrawn its condemnation of the principles of socialism, has, in the course of the last fifty years, adopted points of view, particularly on the problems of labor and property, that take it along a road parallel with ours and perhaps even converging with ours, in a way that at least rules out all real incompatibilty. In such a situation polemics are almost pointless and conflict baseless. The task of the socialist movement is now only one of preaching and conversion. Like the Church in those periods of history when its temporal interests dangerously obscured the real purpose for which it existed, it must now rediscover the purity of its initial inspiration.

C.   THE SOCIALIST STATE

In July 1945 socialism was voted into power for the first time in Europe when the British electorate gave an overwhelming majority to the British Labour Party. The ultimate character and structure of the socialist state cannot yet be assessed, first because sufficient time for its development has not yet elapsed, and secondly because the requirements of the postwar crisis have demanded at least as much attention, in the form of emergency measures, as the execution of socialism. Consequently, even nationalization and the controls which have been instituted furnish no clear picture, and the form which the socialist state has taken must be seen through policy statements by leaders of the party in power.

1. *Socialist Foreign Policy.* As opposition parties with no responsibility for the positive formation of foreign policy, the socialists, even in the postwar period, maintained the old slogans of peace and disarmament as their line in international relations. In England, however, where an exclusively socialist government has been possible ever since the decline of the Liberal Party during the 1920's, more constructive approaches to foreign policy were suggested even before Labour came to power. In the following selection, Richard H. S. Crossman, a Labour M.P., developed as early as 1935 the new attitude which has been largely characteristic of the Labour government in this field. The prevalence of this attitude in British socialism is attested by the fact that, while the principles which he lays down are clearly being followed by the government, Crossman is currently one of the leaders of the minority within the Labour Party which opposes much of the conduct of present British foreign policy. The conflict revolves around the application of these principles, especially to the Soviet Union, which Crossman holds to be a kindred socialist state, but the principles themselves remain common to both wings of British socialism. (10)

Nothing has been more striking in the history of European socialism than the contrast between the scientific realism of its home policy and the sentimentalism of its attitude to foreign affairs. Whatever the brand of doctrine, be it communist, social democrat, or homely labor, this contrast is always to be found; and any attempt to answer the question "What should be the foreign policy of a socialist government in England?" is useless, unless we take the preliminary step of asking ourselves why socialist foreign policy in the past has assumed such multifarious and fantastic forms.

It should be remembered that English socialism —like German social democracy—grew up under the firm protection of the national state. For all its pretensions to internationalism, it was a movement of the English working classes for an amelioration of their lot. The eyes of the Labour Party and its middle-class sympathizers were naturally fixed upon England, and especially upon the industrial problems of England. Their aim was a solution of those problems which would afford security and equality of opportunity for the industrial workers. Under the protection of constitutional government the working classes were able to put their claims in Parliament, and organize their trades unions outside; and in the early years the socialist paid scant attention to the relations between the national state which he was to reconstruct from within, and other national states outside it. Speculations on foreign policy were left to those intellectuals who happened to have traveled abroad. The party hardly bothered its head about it, relying on the government and the governing classes, who monopolized the Foreign Office, to continue the traditional policy which had served us so well for three hundred years. . . .

We may put this point in another way. Up till 1918 foreign policy was admittedly in the hands of the Foreign Office, the generals, and the admirals. It was they who saw to it that this England continued to exist, and that these empire communications were maintained without which there would have been no economic system for the socialist to reconstruct. Just as the fierce revolutionary armies of the fascist and the communist can only wave their banners under the solicitous protection of the police, so the socialist plans for building Jerusalem in England's green and pleasant land all presupposed the existence of a very unsocialist army and navy and a very unsocialist foreign policy. A comparable simple fact was brought to the notice of the German Social Democrats in November 1918. Suddenly the protection of the government they had fulminated against for fifty years was removed: overnight they became the government and discovered two things: (1) that a government needs military force, and that even a socialist cannot do without generals and officers; (2) that foreign policy is an expert job, for which trained diplomats are necessary. These two things still await discovery by most English socialists.

Granted their truth, however, two conclusions of vital importance become clear: (1) a socialist foreign policy must be one which will at least not nauseate any available staff of the War Office and the Admiralty, and (2) a socialist government must either restaff the Foreign Office with its own experts or acquiesce in the traditional methods and technique of British foreign policy. Any policy which does not recognize these two principles is sentimental utopianism.

In the years immediately succeeding the war the first wave of this liberal utopianism swept over the victor countries. . . .

The 1934 conference at Southport showed a welcome return to sanity and common sense. Of course the Utopians had to have their say: the foreign policy of the party had to be directed to the formation of a world state, and the proposed defensive alliance with Russia and France had to be veiled under the high-sounding title of "pooled security." These, however, were mere sops to the liberal and pacifist vote. What was important was the shelving of the general strike and the admission (1) that the world was still a jungle in which sovereign national states fought one another for existence: and (2) that while the world remained of this sort, a socialist government would be constrained to act as beseems any rational creature who finds himself alone in a jungle. His first job is to defend himself and make sure that at least one rational being remains alive; his second job is to try to instill some sense into the remaining inhabitants, or, failing that, to build some barriers between those beast which show particular aversions from one another. The moral law that one man must die for the people does not and cannot extend to the policies of government. . . .

Nothing perhaps has done more to convince the socialist of these salutary, if depressing, conclusions than the entry of Russia into the League, and the recent Franco-Italian pact. . . . The world revolution is a weapon in the armory of Russian foreign policy, just as the war against fascism is a weapon in the armory of French foreign policy. This does not imply that the French or the Russians are hypocrites. Far from it: it merely shows that *ideals always take second place to national interests.* The French government honestly detests National Socialist methods; the Russian honestly desires world revolution, but both these preferences will always yield to national interests, if those interests are urgent enough. And a socialist government in England, whatever its ideals and aspirations may be, will find that it is compelled to bow the knee to this irrevocable necessity of community life. *If it is to give itself the opportunity of playing a part in the reconstruction of Europe or of the world, it must secure the position of its own country, and it must possess that military and naval force which is the only weapon of foreign policy.* If its ideal is pooled security, it must maintain an army and a navy to pool: and it must be prepared for the possibility that it may eventually fail to achieve that pooled security. Only that nation is, with safety, generous and high-minded which has the naval and military strength to afford it. The socialist must recognize this truism as much as the conservative, and far more than the liberal, who has the advantage of being able to preach with no fear of ever facing the responsibility of government.

If the socialist is to admit that international relations are a matter, not of sentiment, but of power, and that his first task must be to promote the interests of his nation by the skillful use of diplomatic and military weapons, in what will his conduct of foreign affairs differ from that of a nationalist, or Tory?

That it should be necessary to ask such a question indicates the distance to which the confusion in radical thought has gone. Socialist policy cannot be distinguished by its *methods*—a moment's study of M. Litvinoff or of the organization of the Russian air force would show that. What marks it off from other party programs is its notion of *what* the nation's interests are, not of how we are to achieve them. It is by its ends, not by its means, that socialism is to be known. The aim and objective of the foreign policy of any socialist government must be simply and solely to maintain and raise the standard of living of the community or communities which it rules. The difference between the policy of a socialist and a nationalist government can only be that the former considers the interests of the nation, the latter the profits of industry and finance. . . .

In brief, if the Labour Party is to gain the confidence of the British people that it really can maintain peace in Europe, it can do so only by (1) stating clearly and decisively for what it is prepared to fight, and (2) making the necessary naval and military preparations.

2. *The Position of the Socialist State in the World Today.* After the defeat of the organized forces of fascism in the late war, British socialism has had to redefine its general orientation in order to make clear its stand in a world dominated by the extremes of communism and individualism. Clement Attlee, prime minister of the British Labour government, has attempted to fulfill this function in a series of radio broadcasts. A selection from his address of January 3, 1948, follows. (11)

Mr. Walter Elliott a fortnight ago said that we wanted a restatement of the old controversy between freedom and order, liberty and authority. What is needed is not so much a restatement as a reconciliation for we need both authority and liberty.

My contention is that this reconciliation can only be achieved through the application of the principles of democratic socialism, of which the British Labour Party is the outstanding champion. I claim that here in Britain the British people through the Labour government are giving a practical lead to the world, a lead which is needed today in order to preserve our heritage of European civilization, a lead which cannot be given by a Conservative or Liberal government.

In the nineteenth century the contest between liberal and authority was fought largely on political issues. Liberalism rendered a great service to the world in fighting for freedom of democracy, but it failed to deal with the problem of economic freedom. In the name of freedom it left in the hands of the few the power which the possession of land and capital gives to its possessors over the many. Therefore when the struggle passed from the political to the economic field the Liberal Party was superseded. It had finished its task. The freedoms which it won are cherished today in this country not only by the Labour Party but also by its old opponents the Conservatives who have to a large extent accepted its political principles. That is why the Liberal Party is reduced so low today. What is true and vital in liberalism has become the common doctrine of all democratic parties. But liberalism which triumphed in western Europe was never really accepted or put into practice in eastern Europe. Today in eastern Europe the Communist Party while overthrowing an economic tyranny of landlordism and capitalism has renounced the doctrines of individual freedom and political democracy and rejected the whole spiritual heritage of western Europe.

The history of Soviet Russia provides us with a warning here—a warning that without political freedom, collectivism can quickly go astray and lead to new forms of oppression and injustice. For political freedom is not merely a noble thing in itself, essential for the full development of human personality—it is also a means of achieving economic rights and social justice, and of preserving these things when they have been won. Where there is no political freedom privilege and injustice creep back. In communist Russia "privilege for the few" is a growing phenomenon, and the gap between the highest and lowest incomes is constantly widening. Soviet communism pursues a policy which threatens with a new form of imperialism—ideological, economic, and strategic —the welfare and way of life of the other nations of Europe.

At the one end of the scale are the communist countries; at the other end the United States of America stands for individual liberty in the political sphere and for the maintenance of human rights. But its economy is based on capitalism with all the problems which it presents and with the characteristic extreme inequality of wealth in its citizens. As a new country with immense resources it has not yet had to face the acute problems which have arisen in the other capitalist countries.

Great Britain like the other countries of western Europe is placed geographically and from the point of view of economic and political theory between these two great continental states. That is not to say that our ideas are in any sense "watered-down capitalism" or "watered-down communism" or that they constitute a temporary halting-place on a journey from one creed to the other. Ours is a philosophy in its own right. Our task is to work out a system of a new and challenging kind which combines individual freedom with a planned economy, democracy with social justice. This task which faces not only ourselves but all the Western democracies requires a government inspired by a new conception of society with a dynamic policy in accord with the needs of a new situation. It could not be accomplished by any of the old parties nor by a totalitarian party whether fascist or communist.

VI

The Legacy of the Nineteenth Century— Modern Liberalism

Bᴜᴛ the dynamic force of liberty, that great motive power of progress, though a good servant, may be a bad master; and the perennial problem of society is to harmonize its aims with those of the common good.

W. T. LAYTON, 1922

CONTENTS

[133]

QUESTIONS FOR STUDY

PART I

1. What were the dominant features of the German liberals' program in 1884?

2. In what way did Friedrich Naumann reorientate German liberal doctrine in 1900? How did he justify this reorientation?

3. According to Wolff, why did the Weimar Republic fail? Can you think of any factors overlooked by Wolff?

4. Analyze the Belleville Manifesto of 1869. What were the essential points in the French radical program?

5. What is the character of Chartier's Radicalism? How does it compare with Gambetta's?

6. A French Radical in 1936 characterized the program of the Popular Front as "Worker's Restaurant, Middle-class Cooking." What does this indicate about the development of French liberalism?

7. Compare Maritain's program with the Belleville Manifesto. What is new? What is unchanged?

PART II

8. What were the main points in Chamberlain's "New Liberalism"? To what did Rosebery object?

9. How did Blease justify the measures of the Liberal ministry of 1906–14?

10. How did Blease distinguish between liberalism and socialism? Would Phillips have agreed with him?

11. How did Slesser account for the decline of the Liberal Party? What connection did he see between Liberal doctrine and the Party decline?

12. How did Laski appraise modern English liberalism? What did he think necessary if liberalism were to have "great prospects" in the future?

By the middle of the nineteenth century doctrinaire liberalism had been subjected to many vicissitudes. The high hopes of English Chartists and Continental liberals had been dashed by the disasters of 1848, and unsolved industrial problems seemed to give good reason for a cooling of the ardent liberal faith. After mid-century there were many defections from the ranks of liberalism. Bismarck proclaimed that Germany's hope lay, not in liberalism, but in armed might, and men of the stamp of Treitschke went over to his camp. French liberalism was submerged in the resurgence of Napoleonic caesarism. Italy fell back under foreign reactionary domination, while Piedmont alone, under the leadership of Cavour, clung to a faith in the efficacy of liberal principles. England continued along the path of free trade and domestic reform, but the doctrinaire liberal frowned upon multiplying factory acts, and John Stuart Mill hoped that "socialistic experiments by select individuals" might find a substitute for the liberal doctrines of his youth. The man of the 1860's might well have pondered if, after such setbacks, liberalism could survive.

Yet a resilient faith in liberalism did survive—and survived to face even severer tests. Despite the role played by violence in the unifications of Germany and Italy and in the rise of the Third Republic from the military collapse of the Napoleonic Empire, liberal forces were still strong enough to make their wishes, in the form of constitutions, components in the political structures of central and western Europe after 1870. The towering figure of the great liberal leader Gladstone dominated English politics in the last three decades of the century. Mid-century disillusion seemed to have given way to a late-century reaffirmation of faith, despite the new difficulties with which liberalism had to contend.

These difficulties were many and increased with the passage of time. Quickening industrialization posed new social problems. Protective tariff systems deleted the laissez-faire economic sections which had formed part of the liberal program from the eighteenth century. Imperialism strained liberal doctrines at every point and brought further problems in the administration of colonial peoples. Socialism grew as a powerful rival and challenged the efficacy of liberal principles in the modern world. The twentieth century saw the intensification of all these difficulties for the liberal, and to them were added still others. World War I imposed the necessity of strict national discipline, repugnant to liberal doctrine and seemingly destructive of the liberal's most cherished ideals. After the war apparently successful totalitarian dictatorships were erected upon the ruins of liberalism in Italy and Germany, and communist success in Russia trumpeted a challenge to the Western powers. The great depression of the 1930's made imperative a re-evaluation of social ideals, and World War II raised the issue of whether liberalism, if it survived, could solve the problems of the future.

In the midst of these difficulties, the professed liberal has constantly maintained that, despite the undermining of important elements of his program, *his basic principles* still provide the sole valid basis for solutions of political, social, and economic problems. But, the historian may well ask, what are liberal principles in the concrete terms of present issues? How is the liberalism of today related to the liberalism of Gladstone and Cavour? In what measure does today's liberal still hold to the writings of Bentham and Adam Smith, of Montesquieu and Locke?

This Problem provides materials in which may be found answers to these questions. Part I includes documents which indicate the development and condition of French and German liberalism from Bismarck to Hitler. The documents in Part II illustrate the evolution of British liberalism during the same period and offer an interpretation of the liberal role for the future.

Part I. THE EVOLUTION OF CONTINENTAL LIBERALISM

The complexity of liberal developments on the Continent makes it impossible to deal with them all in brief compass. France and Germany have been chosen, therefore, as significantly representative of the evolution of liberalism in Europe.

A. GERMAN LIBERALISM

Between the monarchical and aristocratic domination of the newly formed German Empire on the one hand and the rapid rise of social democracy on the other, the minority of German liberals who refused to make their peace with Bismarck felt themselves, in the period from 1867 to 1918, constrained to agitate for political and civil, rather than social, liberties. Condemned to impotence in the German political structure, these parties led an evanescent life, splitting, disappearing, and re-emerging under a variety of names, such as Progressive Party, German People's Party, Liberal (*Freisinnige*) Union, and Liberal People's Party. In the last decade of the nineteenth century, however, a new element entered the liberal movement with the appearance of a short-lived National Social Union under Friedrich Naumann (1860–1919). A Lutheran minister, Naumann moved toward liberalism from an entirely different tradition—the politically conservative social emphasis of certain nationalistic clerical circles. While Naumann had little effect upon the liberal parties before World War I, he played a predominant role in the programmatic development of the German Democratic Party, founded in 1918 to carry on their tradition in the German republic. The selections which follow show this development and its fate.

1. *The Initial Program of the German Liberal Party, 1884.* The following program, adopted by the *Deutsche Freisinnige Partei* on March 5, 1884, represents German liberal ideas in the last quarter of the nineteenth century. (1)

1. Development of a truly constitutional life in a secure cooperation between government and the popular representation and through the legal organization of a responsible Reich ministry. . . .
2. Guarantee of the rights of the people: maintenance of secret, general, equal, and direct suffrage, securing of electoral freedom . . . ; freedom of press, assembly, association; equality before the law . . . ; complete freedom of conscience and religion. . . .
3. Furthering of popular welfare on the basis of the existing social order. With full guarantee of equal rights for the activity and free association of the working classes, support of all strivings aiming at their improvement. Fight against state socialism and against measures directed toward the control and binding of manufacture and trade of economic freedom. . . .

All this for the consolidation of the national unification of Germany, in loyalty to the emperor and on the constitutional basis of the federal state.

2. *Democracy and Empire, 1900.* The greatest contributions to German liberalism made by Friedrich Naumann are to be found in his *Democracy and Empire,* published in 1900. Selections from this work follow. (2)

That bourgeois liberalism can attain to political leadership without the social democracy even its warmest supporters can no longer seriously believe. The liberal principle will not be victorious without the liberalism of the masses. The question is not whether bourgeois liberalism will reabsorb the social democracy. The question is rather whether the social democracy will so develop that it will take over the old liberal task and make it possible for the truly liberal parts of the bourgeoisie to join the movement born by the social democracy without sacrificing its convictions. . . .

Fifty years ago liberalism was the great progressive movement. Everything of protest and reforming energy in the people was gathered in its ranks. . . . And this old liberal movement has had its political result. Everything that we have in the way of electoral rights and free civil rights comes from it. Its cooperation in the creation of the German national state is unforgettable. . . . But certainly this movement has lacked one thing that the social democracy possesses: uniformity of the masses. Liberalism was and still is today diversely composed. It has prized this composition as its finest characteristic . . . but in politics it is not so much variety as uniformity that decides. . . . Certainly it is hard to be referred for the realization of political ideals to victorious rivals. But what can help it? There will be no democratic government in Germany, no new creative policy in general, if workers and bourgeoisie do not, despite all internal differences, cooperate in the main lines. . . .

Progress and personality—in these two words lies the content of old and new democracy! . . . The distinction between liberalism and socialism lies only apparently in the sphere of the ideal of personality. This is common to both tendencies. The difference emerges only when one asks how far this common ideal can and should be extended. Liberalism represents the ideal of personality vis-à-vis the state, socialism vis-à-vis every great enterprise in general. . . . What does and did liberalism want? It saw itself opposed to the first of the modern great enterprises, the absolutist state. Its aim was not to destroy the state but to protect personality in it and from it. This happened in a twofold way.

(1) The state was to be based on the cooperation of all persons included in it; principle of popular representation, electoral rights, constitution, republic, popular referendum, etc.

(2) The activity of the state is to be kept within definite limits by constitution and law; rights of man, civil rights, fundamental rights, equality before the law, freedom of religion, freedom of movement, economic freedom, etc.

On this double way liberalism has gone for a century. It ever had a double feeling vis-à-vis the state—it wanted to rule in it, and it wanted to tie its hands. Which of these two views had the upper hand depended mostly on the degree of the feeling of force that liberalism possessed at the time. Periods with strong hopes of rule have preferred the first method to the second. Both views return in social democracy in radical form, and especially in its early days did the first dominate the second. No one thought of limiting the state, since he dreamed of conquering it soon.

If, in relation to the state, there are only differences in temperature between liberalism and socialism, the relationship becomes more involved as soon as one considers the great economic enterprises which have risen during the past century. These are, on the one hand, private enterprises like every handicraft establishment, and so liberalism sees them. But they are on the other hand great capitalistic enterprises, like the state, often mightier than the "despots" which the old liberalism fought. So they appear in the eyes of socialism. The real essence of socialism in con-

tradistinction to the older liberalism is that it applies the double method of which we spoke to economic enterprises too. To wit:

(1) The great enterprise is to be based on the cooperation of all persons participating in it. . . .

(2) The great enterprise is to be bound by law to protect and maintain the physical and moral human rights of all participants. . . .

That they are old liberal principles which socialism applies vis-à-vis the modern great enterprise will not be easily disputed; the difference of opinion consists only in whether the economic enterprise may be viewed according to these principles. There are still some representatives of the old liberal principles today who deny this on fundamental grounds, but their number has become very small. The real situation is that liberalism slowly but with growing determination has found itself ready to recognize the new way of posing the question as justified, preferring certainly the second method to the first. For the most part it is a matter here too of differences in temperature which are noticeable, not differences of pure principle. . . . The problem of the new democratic Left will be whether there can be a common working on this basis. . . . Liberalism feels it a blessing, when it thinks its own old principles through to their conclusions, to be able to face the new age freely and joyously.

3. *The Weimar Republic, 1919–33.* The collapse of the German Empire in 1918 provided German liberals with an opportunity to implement their ideals. The constitution drawn up at Weimar, where Naumann took an active part, incorporated all the major principles advocated by Naumann and his group, and hopes were high that the day of liberalism had dawned in Germany. But within fifteen years Hitler's Nazis had taken over the government, and the liberal experiment had failed. Following is an analysis of its failure by Theodor Wolff (1868–1943), editor of the liberal *Berliner Tageblatt* during the period of Weimar Republic. His book *Through Two Decades,* from which this selection is taken, was written in exile in 1936. Wolff is believed to have died in the Jewish hospital in Berlin in 1943 as the result of ill treatment received in a concentration camp. (3)

Whether a republic had any chance of life on German soil, and whether under more favorable circumstances it would really have struck root, is a difficult question. In the manner of its birth, and in the form it took, it bore within it the seeds of all the evils which are fatal to any system of government. The Third Republic in

France was also the result of defeat in the field; its birth certificate bore the date of Sedan. But the defeated emperor was a "usurper," and in the eyes of all lovers of liberty worse even than that; and there was also Gambetta to raise once more the banner of resistance. The German revolution exploded blindly at the worst possible moment, and the republicans were far too ready to relieve the old regime and its paladins of the odious duty of signing the peace treaty.

The republic brought chaos into order in the country, but, for all its exertions and its services, it was congenitally crippled. For the rich bourgeoisie, the big industrialists, and the professional elite, for whom life had never been so pleasant as it was under the republic, its leaders were too plebeian, and many people regarded themselves as very gracious when they accepted official invitations. The subordinate officials, the small shopkeepers, and the cellar cafe owners were as sour as always toward the hated "proletarians"; they saw no further than their own domestic troubles, and laid the blame for them all on these "cursed times." Youngsters of "good family" felt the new competition from the clever working-class boys. It all used to be so simple: their conservative papas had gone through their examinations, joined some students' corps, and then passed steadily from one rung to the next in the state service. Now these fellows of common or unknown origin were everywhere, and not only that but getting on best and forging ahead. At a time when every profession was overcrowded, the competition for every career was enormous, and the difficulty of getting a living was steadily increasing, the thought of these rivals (whose importance was less than was imagined) contributed greatly to hardening hearts.

It must always be borne in mind that the peace treaty had greatly diminished Germany's territory. Officials, physicians, teachers, engineers, businessmen from the lost territories, had taken refuge in Germany and tried to start life afresh there, and in the narrowed environment everyone was treading on his neighbor's toes and feeling his neighbor's elbows. There was not room enough and not work enough for the new generation. The republic offered them fine ideals such as freedom and democratic self-determination. They were ideals for which eighty or a hundred years earlier the German *Burschenschaften,* the patriotic students' associations, had been full of enthusiasm, but they were not to the taste of young fellows who still received in the *gymnasien,* the secondary schools, history teaching that was an incentive to violence. Clever political jugglers can make the public believe in all sorts of lands of promise; but the republican régisseurs knew nothing of these arts. Very soon, as was to be expected, all those who had gone into hiding during the November revolution of 1918 ventured out again; and from all the scenes of war now evacuated countless men of spirit whose fighting instinct had been aroused, who were thirsting for vengeance, and who intended to stick to their congenial trade of fighting when they got home, had been streaming back into the country. They won over to their side a large part of the youth. They brought to the justified national demands the spirit of wild hatred and civil war. They knew and taught the use of hand grenades, flamethrowers, and poison gas. They were expert in the organization of a prolonged and intensive bombardment that decimates the ranks before the attack and unnerves the last defenders. . . .

But, quite apart from the line taken by one public man or another, and quite apart from the special circumstances of the time, the inflation, the economic crisis, the devastating unemployment, and all the plagues that were afflicting the nation and its governments, did the coat that had been cut out at Weimar fit this nation? We must admit that it had not been cut to the measure of the average German but to the pretty pattern devised by the political tailors, and that it did not sit very well. In spite of all that happened we may agree with Mommsen that the worst constitutional state is preferable to the best autocratic regime. The democratic republic, whatever form its leadership may take, represents to us the highest attainable form of state. But in Germany, where it was an emergency creation rather than a deliberate one, it was not built up on a solidly established foundation, and insufficient attention was paid in its architectural layout to the German political climate, which is so different from that of other countries. The need for subordination, for sharp tones of command, for marching in strict formation, in companies under rigid leadership, is part of the German character; the Germans find satisfaction not only in commanding but in obeying, and it is no mere chance that the finest military marches are German. There remain the great men, the men of intellectual importance and of strong character. They are the incalculable element. In every state system there is room and need for them; but they cannot take the place of a system. Those who summon them without fitting them into a fixed framework of guarantees, without effectively binding them to the clauses of a constitution, place themselves in their power.

German liberalism has always taken the British constitution for its model. But the British constitution has only reached its present shape after various processes of refining and adjusting. It rests on a tradition that governs popular feeling, on a remarkable acceptance of their lot by the poorer classes, which in their insular segregation know nothing of the ways of life of the Continental town worker, and on the political breadth of mind of an aristocracy which has not a vestige of community with the majority of the Prussian junkers. It rests on a special national possession which is every citizen's from birth, which makes even the "have-nots" self-respecting citizens—the assured possession of absolutely unquestioned personal freedom, the knowledge that within the limits of the law every British citizen, even the poorest and most insignificant, has his inviolate human rights. No doubt the cultural level of the ordinary Englishman is lower than that of the German; the dweller in the remotest of German villages will have learnt two or three poems of Goethe and Schiller, while among the masses in England few could quote as much of Shakespeare. But the inherited consciousness of innate rights is perhaps the first condition and the foundation of all true civilization, and acquired culture is often no more than a thin protective stucco. The great creations in imaginative literature and the arts mean no more to the ordinary citizen than a transient gleam of sunshine. Such a monumental achievement in civilization as the habeas corpus act of 1679, which guarantees to every Englishman the liberty and inviolacy of his person and protection from arbitrary arrest and imprisonment, has done more for the progress and happiness of a nation than *Faust* could do.

B.   FRENCH LIBERALISM

The uncertain manner in which the constitution of the Third Republic was developed from 1871 to 1875 made the problem of its consolidation the primary issue in French politics for more than a generation. The economic and social problems arising from industrialism became important issues only after 1905 and rose to predominance over all others between the two world wars. In view of the incessant trend of French politics to the Left until 1940, the radicals, bearers of the French democratic traditions, constitute the best single vehicle for the study of the development of the liberal outlook under the new conditions. The Radical Party, emphasizing the ideas of equality and active political rights inherited from Rousseau, was able to make some adaptation to the new conditions and the new issues.

1. *The Belleville Manifesto, 1869.* The revival of political liberalism under the "Liberal Empire" was strongly evidenced by the resurgence of the Radical Party. Its program was the work of the fiery democratic politician, Leon Gambetta (1838–82). In 1869 Gambetta ran for election to the Chamber of Deputies from Belleville, and his election platform, known as the Belleville Manifesto, so clearly represented the liberal ideals of his party that it served as the basis for most subsequent radical programs down through World War I. (4)

I. The Cahiers of the Electors

In the name of universal suffrage, basis of every political and social organization, let us instruct our deputy to reaffirm the principles of radical democracy and to demand with vigor: the most radical application of universal suffrage, both for the election of mayors and municipal councilors, with no local differentiation, and for the election of deputies; repartitioning of constituencies according to the actual number of electors entitled to vote and not according to the number of electors on the register; individual liberty to be in future protected by the law and not left at the mercy of arbitrary administrators; repeal of the law of general security; suppression of Article 75 of the constitution of the year VIII, and the direct responsibility of all *fonctionnaires;* trial by jury for every kind of political offense; complete freedom of the press unrestricted by stamp-duty and caution-money; suppression of licensing of printers and publishers; freedom of meeting without let or hindrance, with liberty to discuss all religious, philosophical, political, and social affairs; repeal of Article 29 of the penal code; full and complete freedom of association; suppression of the ecclesiastical budget and separation of church and state; free, compulsory, secular primary education with competitive examinations for children of greatest intelligence for admission to higher education, which shall likewise be free; suppression of town dues, suppression of high salaries and pluralities, and modification of our system of taxation; appointment of all public *fonctionnaires* by election; suppression of standing armies, the cause of ruin to the nation's finances and business, a source of hatred between peoples and of distrust at home; abolition of privileges and monopolies, which we define in these words: "a bonus to idleness"; economic reforms are connected with the social problem, the solution of which—although subordinate to political change—must be constantly studied and sought in the name of the principles of justice and social equality. Indeed this principle alone, put into general application, can cause social antagonism to disappear and give complete reality to our slogan: liberty, equality, fraternity!

II. *The reply of Gambetta*

Citizen electors—I accept this mandate. On these conditions I shall be especially proud to represent you because this election will have been conducted in conformity with the true principles of universal suffrage. The electors will have freely chosen their candidate. The electors will have determined the political program of their delegate. This method seems to me at once right and in line with the traditions of the early days of the French revolution. I therefore in my turn adhere freely to the declaration of principles and the rightful claims which you commission me to press at the tribune.

With you, I think that there is no other sovereign but the people, and that universal suffrage, the instrument of this sovereignty, has no value and basis and carries no obligation, unless it be radically free. The most urgent reform must therefore be to free universal suffrage from every tutelage, every shackle, every pressure, every corruption. With you, I think that universal suffrage, once made the master, would suffice to sweep away all the things which your program demands, and to establish all the freedoms, all the institutions which we are seeking to bring about. With you, I think that France, the home of indestructible democracy, will know liberty, peace, order, justice, material prosperity, and moral greatness only through the triumph of the principles of the French Revolution. With you, I think that a legal and loyal democracy is the political system par excellence which achieves most promptly and certainly the moral and material emancipation of the greatest number, and best ensures social equality in laws, actions, and customs.

But—with you also—I consider that the progressive achievement of these reforms depends absolutely on the political regime and on political reforms, and it is for me axiomatic in these matters that the form involves and determines the substance. It is, furthermore, this sequence and order of priority which our fathers have indicated and fixed in the profound and comprehensive slogan beyond which there is no safety: liberty, equality, fraternity. We are thus in mutual agreement. Our contract is completed. I am at once your delegate and your trustee. I go further than signifying agreement. I give you my vow: I swear obedience to this present contract and fidelity to the sovereign people.

2. *Elements of a Radical Doctrine, 1906–10.* After the turn of the century Radical Party doctrine was overlarded with the views of her philosophers, prominent among whom was Émile Chartier (1868–   ), who wrote under the pen name of Alain. Following are selections from three of his writings in the immediate prewar era. (5)

Radicalism Exists [May 14, 1906]

How many friends have told me before the last elections: "The Radicals should disappear, because they do not exist. What is a progressive? He is a man who has a horror of socialism. What is a Radical? He is a man who has a secret tenderness for socialism. This tenderness is avowed by the Radical Socialist; he avows it but he defies it. Can you call these opinions?"

And I said to myself and I said to them: "It seems to me that Radicalism exists, as political doctrine; it has for principle the government, as real, as direct as possible, of the people by the people. To maintain universal suffrage loyally; to assure the secrecy of the ballot; to break tyrannies, whether they employ corruption or intimidation; to assure control of the Chambers; to support the ministers against everything around them which seeks to make them believe that they are the true masters and to make them forget they are the servants of the people; to crush the bureaucrats, the intriguers, the purveyors of favors, the sellers of votes; to have no other ideal than that the law conform to the view of the greatest number; it seems to me that is a fine program."

And this does not assume at all that one has preference for collectivism or for communism; nor does it assume an obstinate attachment to the traditional forms of property. Communist institutions like the police, public works, primary education, can live very well alongside collectivist institutions like the postal system and secondary education; and it is not necessary, because private property is sometimes injurious to the general interest, to suppress all individual property. . . .

No, no Utopias. No abstract systems. Let each man vote according to his interests and his preferences; the Radical submits in advance his ideal, whatever it be, to the law, whatever it be.

That is why Radicalism and socialism are not fused nor are they opposed to each other. Radicalism has two enemies, aristocratism and anarchy; and that suffices for it to live.

Dogmatics in Action [October 23, 1906]

One can be Radical without being socialist. The republican Radical is a man of principles, who, consequently, is not always comfortable. His god, it is the law. He devotes all his energy to curbing other men and himself before the law.

Man of principles, that does not mean dogmatic man, self-complacent man, man bound up in doctrine. The Radical is naturally a philosopher; he knows that every doctrine is provisional, and that no project is proportioned to the events which supervene. . . .

If you talk to him of a better future and of the distant destinies of humanity, he will listen to you while fixing you with his clear eye. . . . But already his eye turns away and sparkles at something else. His whole being gathers itself for an energetic action. He has smelled out some enemy of liberty. And then he is dogmatic for action, sure of himself, imperturbable and unpitying.

Yes, dogmatic in action, skeptical in reflection, that is the Radical. And there are few Radicals. Many find it more comfortable to be, on the contrary, dogmatic in theory, and sceptical in action. The latter can be socialists, they are not Radicals.

The People Are on the Firing Line
[April 26, 1910]

When I think of the Radicals with confidence and friendship, when I say that they form a noble party, it is of the electors of which I think rather than of the deputies. And, among the Radical electors I should put, whatever they may say, a great part of those who vote for the socialists, and a great part also of those who vote for the moderates. For I see that they vote principally against tyranny, against injustice, and to affirm the sovereignty of the people. For the socialists it is evident enough; and there will be no doubt of it if they explain themselves more clearly on the subject of individual property; for fundamentally they wish only to assure it to all those who produce, so that this instrument of liberty may not become the weapon of a small number of tyrants. . . .

Nearly everyone agrees in desiring peace without humiliation or abasement, taxes distributed justly, useful and strictly controlled expenditures; they dispute only on the means. . . .

3. *The Popular Front, 1936.* Between the two world wars, the Radical Party found itself often in alliance with others of a Left-wing complexion, and in 1936 the Radicals joined nine other parties in promulgating the program of the Popular Front. It is interesting to observe that the communists supported it as a "minimum program" but refused to join the government based upon it. On the other hand, it was the program that Radical congresses had previously discussed but had never put into legislation. The program follows. (6)

I: Defense of Freedom

1. A general amnesty.
2. Measures against the fascist leagues: (*a*) The effective disarmament and dissolution of all semimilitary formations, in accordance with the law. (*b*) The enforcement of legal measures in cases of incitement to murder or any attempt against the safety of the state.
3. Measures for the cleansing of public life, especially by forbidding deputies to combine their parliamentary functions with certain other forms of activity.
4. The press: (*a*) The repeal of the laws and decrees restricting freedom of opinion. (*b*) Reform of the press by the following legislative measures: (*i*) measures effectively repressing libel and blackmail; (*ii*) measures which will guarantee the normal means of existence to newspapers, and compel publication of their financial resources; (*iii*) measures ending the private monopoly of commercial advertising and the scandals of financial advertising, and preventing the formation of newspaper trusts. (*c*) Organization by the state of wireless broadcasts with a view to assuring the accuracy of wireless news and the equality of political and social organizations in relation to radio.
5. Trade union liberties: (*a*) Application and observance of trade union freedom for all. (*b*) Recognition of women's labor rights.
6. Education and freedom of conscience: (*a*) Measures safeguarding the development of public education, by the necessary grants and by reforms such as the raising of the age for compulsory education to fourteen and, in secondary education, the proper selection of pupils as an essential accompaniment of grants. (*b*) Measures guaranteeing to all concerned, pupils and teachers, perfect freedom of conscience, particularly by ensuring the neutrality of education, its nonreligious character, and the civic rights of teachers.
7. Colonies: formation of a parliamentary committee of inquiry into the political, economic, and cultural situation in France's territories overseas, especially French North Africa and Indo-China.

II: Defense of Peace

1. Appeal to the people, and especially the working classes, for collaboration in the maintenance and organization of peace.
2. International collaboration within the framework of the League of Nations for collective security, by defining the aggressor and by joint application of sanctions in cases of aggression.
3. Ceaseless endeavor to pass from armed peace to disarmed peace, first by a convention of

limitation, and then by the general, simultaneous, and effectively controlled reduction of armaments.

4. Nationalization of war industries and suppression of private trade in armaments.

5. Repudiation of secret diplomacy; international action and public negotiation to bring back to Geneva the states which have left it, without weakening the essential principles of the League of Nations, which are the principles of collective security and indivisible peace.

6. Greater flexibility in the procedure provided by the League of Nations' covenant for the peaceful adjustment of treaties which have become dangerous to the peace of the world.

7. Extension of the system of pacts open to all nations, particularly in eastern Europe, on the lines of the Franco-Soviet pact.

III: Economic Demands

1. Restoration of purchasing power destroyed or reduced by the crisis. (a) Against unemployment and the crisis in industry; (i) establishment of a national unemployment fund; (ii) reduction of the working week without reduction of the weekly wage; (iii) bringing young workers into employment by establishing a system of adequate pensions for aged workers; (iv) rapid execution of a public-works program, both urban and rural, linking local investments with schemes financed by the state and local authorities. (b) Against the agricultural and commercial crisis; (i) revaluation of agricultural produce, combined with measures against speculation and high prices, in order to reduce the gap between wholesale and retail prices; (ii) establishment of a national grain board to abolish the tribute levied by speculators against both the producer and the consumer; (iii) strengthening of agricultural co-operatives, and supply of fertilizers at cost prices by the national boards for nitrogen and potash, control and certification of sales of superphosphates and other fertilizers, extension of agricultural credits, reduction of leasehold rents; (iv) suspension of distraints and regulation of debt repayments; (v) pending the complete and earliest possible removal of all unjust measures imposed by the economy decrees, immediate abolition of measures affecting those groups whose conditions of life have been most severely endangered by these decrees.

2. Against the robbery of investors and for the better organization of credit: (a) Regulation of banking business. Regulation of balance sheets issued by banks and joint-stock companies. Further regulation of the powers of directors of joint-stock companies. (b) State officials who have retired or are on the reserve list to be prohibited from joining the board of directors of a joint-stock company. (c) In order to remove credit and investment from the control of the economic oligarchy, the bank of France must cease to be a private concern, and "the Bank of France" must become "France's Bank." The council of regents of the Bank of France must be abolished: the powers of the governor of the Bank of France must be increased, under the permanent control of a council composed of representatives of Parliament, of the executive authority, and of the main organized forces of labor and of industrial, commercial, and agricultural activity. The capital of the Bank must be converted into debentures, with measures to safeguard the interests of small shareholders.

IV: Financial Purification

1. Control of the trade in armaments, in conjunction with the nationalization of armaments industries. Prevention of waste in the civil and military departments.

2. Establishment of a war pensions fund.

3. Democratic reform of the system of taxation so as to relax the fiscal burden blocking economic recovery, and raising revenue by measures against large fortunes. Rapid steepening of income tax on incomes above 75,000 francs a year; reorganization of death duties; special taxes on monopoly profits, but in such a way as to have no effects on retail prices. Measures against tax evasions, in connection with transferable ("bearer") securities.

4. Control of export of capital, and punishment of evasion by rigorous measures, including confiscation of property concealed abroad or of its equivalent value in France.

4. *The Rights of Man and Natural Law, 1942.* The collapse of the Third Republic amid military defeat in 1940 annihilated French political parties and called into question the validity of liberal doctrine. Pétain reigned at Vichy in the shadow of the German army, and totalitarianism seemed triumphant. But French liberals sought a revaluation of their ideals in the hour of defeat, and notable among their new tracts was *The Rights of Man and Natural Law* by Jacques Maritain (1882–), a Catholic liberal who sought hope for his country in a combination of liberalism with the religion of the majority of his countrymen. Selections from Maritain's work follow. (7)

Introduction

One of the causes of the debilities and weaknesses from which the democracies suffered at the beginning of the war was that they partly lost faith in themselves. In the midst of disaster they have now regained a belief in their principles. At the same time they fully realize that they must profoundly revivify their philosophy to put themselves in a position to accomplish what the world expects of them. Peace will be won and civilization reconstructed only if the free peoples are clearly aware of their principles and their aims, and only if a strong and generous hope animates the desire for their realization.

Of particular concern for France is the fact that among the French people a profound disgust for all previous political organizations is joined with a love of liberty which is stronger than ever before. Military defeat, then the armistice and capitulation, then the policy of collaboration have successfully liquidated all parties. Abandoned by their leaders and their government, the French people can rely on none but themselves; and when they have regained their liberty, they will have to construct a wholly new edifice.

The new declaration of rights will be their work. The political and social institutions of the France of tomorrow will be the result of an infinitely bitter experience. . . . If one may take it for granted that the French people will not return to the particular forms of the prewar regime, everything that we know indicates that they aspire to a regime whose new forms will realize better and more completely an ideal democracy, both in the social and political order. In an abyss of suffering, France has taken up again her true vocation, that vocation which has its source in the Gospel and in reason, that vocation which is essentially one of liberation. It is fidelity to this mission of freedom—the instinct for justice, the knowledge of the rights of the human individual, of liberty, equality, and fraternity—which has inspired the mass of the people to run every risk in resisting the yoke of foreign domination. But to succeed in their heroic task, they will need a revivified vocabulary and ideology. . . .

We have not discussed in this study the rights concerned with the international order, whose consideration belongs to a special field, and among which the most important are the right of each state, large or small, to freedom and respect for its autonomy, the right to the respecting of solemn oaths and the sanctity of treaties, the right to peaceful development (a right which, being valid for all, requires for its own development the establishment of an international community having juridical power, and the development of federative forms of organization). It may not be altogether unnecessary at this point to make a summary list of those rights of which we have spoken.

Rights of the Human Person as Such—The Right to Existence

The right to personal liberty or the right to conduct one's own life as master of oneself and of one's acts, responsible for them before God and the law of the community. The right to the pursuit of the perfection of rational and moral human life. The right to the pursuit of eternal life along the path which conscience has recognized as the path indicated by God. The right of the Church and other religious families to the free exercise of their spiritual activity. The right of pursuing a religious vocation; the freedom of religious orders and groups. The right to marry according to one's choice and to raise a family, which will in its turn be assured of the liberties due it; the right of the family society to respect for its constitution, which is based on natural law, not on the law of the state, and which fundamentally involves the morality of the human being. The right to keep one's body whole. The right to property. Finally, the right of every human being to be treated as a person, not as a thing.

Rights of the Civic Person

The right of every citizen to participate actively in political life, and in particular the right of equal suffrage for all. The right of the people to establish the constitution of the state and to determine for themselves their form of government. The right of association, limited only by the juridically recognized necessities of the common good, and in particular the right to form political parties or political schools. The right of free investigation and discussion (freedom of expression). Political equality, and the equal right of every citizen to his security and his liberties within the state. The equal right of every one to the guarantees of an independent judiciary power. Equal possibility of admission to public employment and free access to the various professions.

Rights of the Social Person, and More Particularly of the Working Person

The right freely to choose his work. The right freely to form vocational groups or trade unions. The right of the worker to be considered socially as an adult. The right of economic groups (trade unions and working communities) and other social groups to freedom and autonomy. The right to a just wage. The right to work. And wherever an associative system can be substituted for the wage system, the right to the joint ownership and joint management of the enterprise, and to the "worker's title." The right to relief, unemployment insurance, sick benefits, and social security. The right to have a part, free of charge, depending on the possibilities of the community, in the elementary goods, both material and spiritual, of civilization.

Part II. THE EVOLUTION OF ENGLISH LIBERALISM

No cataclysm of military defeat and occupation affected the course of liberalism in England, as had been the case in France and Germany. But the march of events nevertheless made its mark upon English liberal doctrine and its advocates, the Liberal Party. The documents in this Part represent the evolution of liberalism in England.

A. ENGLISH LIBERALISM, 1880–1914

The last years of the nineteenth century saw the introduction of new elements into British liberal thought, as new figures entered the Liberal Party and new situations demanded new policies. The election of 1906 gave the Party an overwhelming popular mandate to effectuate its principles. Following are excerpts from the utterances of Liberal leaders in this period.

1. *The Creed of a New Liberal, 1885.* Prominent among the younger Liberals was Joseph Chamberlain (1836–1914). After the third reform bill of 1884–85, Chamberlain promoted the publication of a Liberal platform called "The Radical Program" and supported its principles in numerous speeches throughout the country. Following are selections from the publication and speeches. (8).

The Radical Program, 1885

New conceptions of public duty, new developments of social enterprise, new estimates of the natural obligations of the members of the community to one another, have come into view, and demand consideration. . . .

Thus far the agricultural laborer has been regarded by the political economists as a mere machine—an instrument to be used for the creation of wealth, deposited in the hands of the few; not as a human being whose comfort, health, and home are to be considered, and who has a claim to such benefits as were conferred by the Factory Acts upon the laborers in towns. If his welfare cannot be sufficiently protected without the taxation of property, then property will be taxed. . . .

But it is needless now to attempt to define the measures that may be necessary for these ends. It is enough to indicate their general character. They sound the death knell of the laissez-faire system; and if the agricultural laborer is not strong enough to look after himself, to take the initiative in the social reforms prompted by a rational estimate of private interest, there is an organized body of politicians in this country who will at least do thus much for him. If it be said

that this is communism, the answer is that it is not. If it be said that it is legislation of a socialist tendency, the impeachment may readily be admitted. Between such legislation and communism there is all the difference in the world. Communism means the reduction of everything to a dead level, the destruction of private adventure, the paralysis of private industry, the atrophy of private effort. The socialistic measures now contemplated would preserve in their normal vigor and freshness all the individual activities of English citizenship, and would know nothing more spoliatory than tax—if and in what degree necessary—aggregations of wealth for the good of the country.

Chamberlain's Speeches, 1885

It is not desirable, even if it were possible, that all Liberals should think exactly alike, and that every candidate should be cut to precisely the same pattern. In the Liberal army there must be pioneers to clear the way, and there must be men who watch the rear. Some may always be in advance, others may occasionally lag behind; but the only thing we have a right to demand is, that no one shall stand still, and that all should be willing to follow the main lines of Liberal progress to which the whole Party are committed. I do not conceal from you my own opinion that the pace will be a little faster in the future than it has been in the past. Everywhere the reforms to which the resolution has made reference are casting their shadows before. Everywhere in the country I see a quickening of political life. Everywhere there is discussion, and hope, and expectation. . . .

I have been solemnly excommunicated by

some of the great authorities who claim a monopoly of the orthodox Liberal faith and doctrine. Gentlemen, I am not discouraged; I am not repentant. I am told if I pursue this course that I shall break up the Party, and that I shall altogether destroy any chance which I might otherwise have had of office. I do not believe it. But if it were true, I say that I care little for Party, and nothing at all for office, except so far as these things may be made instrumental in promoting the objects which I publicly avowed when I first entered Parliament, and which I will prosecute so long as I remain in public life. The Liberal Party has always seemed to me the great agency of progress and reform, and by the changes which have recently taken place it has secured a vantage-ground which I myself had hardly ever dared to anticipate. I had looked forward with hope to the future, but I had not supposed in my time so great a change could have been successfully effected. But now that my wildest expectations have been surpassed, I am not willing to be silent as to the uses to which I believe the people ought to put the new power and the privileges which have been conferred upon them. I had already a deep conviction that when the people came to govern themselves, and when the clamor of vested interests and class privileges was overborne by the powerful voice of the whole nation, that then the social evils which disgrace our civilization and the wrongs which have cried vainly for redress would at last find a hearing and a remedy. And if that be not so, it will be no longer statesmen or governments that you will have to blame. It will not be the fault of parties or of individuals, it will be the apathy or the ignorance, the indifference or the folly of the people themselves which alone can hinder their progress and their prosperity. . . .

I am not a communist, although some people will have it that I am. Considering the difference in the character and the capacity of men, I do not believe that there can ever be an absolute equality of conditions, and I think that nothing would be more undesirable than that we should remove the stimulus to industry and thrift and exertion which is afforded by the security given to every man in the enjoyment of the fruits of his own individual exertions. I am opposed to confiscation in every shape or form, because I believe that it would destroy that security, and lessen that stimulus. But, on the other hand, I am in favor of accompanying the protection which is afforded to property with a large and stringent interpretation of the obligations of property. . . .

The Liberal Party of the past has been the popular party. It has been reinforced from time to time by successive Reform Bills, and now, after the greatest of them all, it would be false to its trust and unworthy of its high mission if it did not strive to bring the institutions of the country into harmony with the wants and aspirations of the people; if it did not seek continuously the greatest happiness of the greatest number; if it did not serve the poor with at least as much zeal as it brings to the protection of the rich; and if it did not enforce the obligations of property as strenuously as it defends its rights. . . .

Politics is the science of human happiness, and the business of a statesman and of politicians is to find out how they can raise the general condition of the people; how they can increase the happiness of those who are less fortunate among them.

2. *The Creed of an Old Liberal, 1908.* The Earl of Rosebery (1847–1929) succeeded Gladstone as leader of the Liberal Party for a short time. He professed himself a thoroughgoing Liberal, but he strongly objected to the principles of his Party as expressed by Chamberlain. He resigned the leadership after three years, and thereafter he denounced such Acts of the Liberal ministry of 1906–14 as Workingman's Compensation, Labor Exchanges, and National Insurance. Following is a selection from a diatribe against his own party at Glasgow in 1908. (9)

But the state invites us every day to lean upon it. I seem to hear the wheedling and alluring whisper, "Sound you may be; we bid you be a cripple. Do you see? Be blind. Do you hear? Be deaf. Do you walk? Be not so venturesome. Here is a crutch for one arm; when you get accustomed to it, you will soon want another—the sooner the better." The strongest man if encouraged may soon accustom himself to the methods of an invalid; he may train himself to totter, or to be fed with a spoon.

The ancient sculptors represent Hercules leaning on his club; our modern Hercules would have his club elongated and duplicated and resting under his arms. The lesson of our . . . teaching was "level up": the cry of modern civilization is "level down": "let the government have a finger in every pie," probing, propping, disturbing. Every day the area for initiative is being narrowed, every day the standing ground for self-reliance is being undermined; every day the public infringes—with the best intentions, no doubt—on the individual; the nation is being taken into custody by the state.

Perhaps this current cannot now be stemmed; agitation or protest may be alike unavailing. The world rolls on. It may be part of its destiny, a necessary phase in its long evolution, a stage in its blind, toilsome progress to an invisible goal. I neither affirm nor deny; all in the long run is doubtless for the best. . . . I plead for our historical character, for the maintenance of those sterling national qualities which have meant so much to [us] in the past. I should like, at least, to think that in one powerful city in the world he must do for himself. I should like to think that there was here being taught [that] empire rests on the character of the nation that aspires to it; and that the British Empire, greater than the Roman, requires at least Roman character to maintain it; that if the Empire, a glorious but weighty burden, is to be worthily sustained, it must be by husbanding our resources, and equipping our people both in character and attainment for their task. It was not by leaning on state support that Drake or Raleigh or Hastings succeeded, but by relying on themselves in despite of their government. It was self-reliance that built the Empire; it is by self-reliance, and all that that implies, that it must be welded and continued.

> 3. *A Short History of Liberalism, 1913.* Liberal publicists of the official Party felt called upon to answer the objections of Liberal schismatics like Lord Rosebery. Following is a selection from *A Short History of Liberalism,* written in 1913 by W. L. Blease (1884–) as an apologia for the measures passed by the Liberal ministry that had been in power since 1906. (10)

Liberals were bound to apply themselves to the new conditions in a new way, and it savors of pedantry to accuse Liberal economists of 1906 of having departed from the principles of Liberal economists of 1846. Paradoxical as it may appear to say that a positive policy of constant interference is the same as a negative policy of constant abstention, it is true that the mental habit at the back of the one is identical with that at the back of the other. Both aim at emancipating the individual from the things which prevent him from developing his natural capacities. The Manchester School saw only the fetters which directly impeded him. The modern Liberal sees also the want of the positive aids without which he is only half free. "Of all the obstacles which obstruct men's advance toward good living, and of all the evils with which politics can help to deal, there is no obstacle more formidable and no evil more grave than poverty. . . . Our first principle leads clearly and directly to a policy of social reform. Whoever admits that the duty of the state is to secure, so far as it is able, the fullest opportunities to lead the best life, cannot refuse to accept the further proposition, that to lessen the causes of poverty and to lighten its effects are es-

sential parts of a right policy of state action." Poverty cripples the individual in many ways. . . . No one who seriously believes that it is the duty of society to secure freedom of growth to every one of its members can doubt that it is its duty to mitigate, so far as it is able, those consequences of poverty which no degree of thrift, enterprise, or fortitude can avert.

To this end the economic reforms of the new Liberalism have been directed. The Labor Exchanges Act did not furnish work for all. It provided facilities for obtaining work for all who sought for it. The workman is no longer left to scramble about for fresh employment. He goes to a public office, where he learns what posts are vacant, and is put in touch with those who may be willing to employ him. No man can now complain that because he cannot afford to travel in search of work, or to delay for more than a day or two before he finds it, he has suffered a permanent deterioration in health or character. If this Act can eliminate the evils of casual and irregular labor, it will have enormously increased individual liberty for growth. The Old Age Pensions Act removed from the shoulders of working-class families what was to many an intolerable burden. Before the Act came into force some thousands of men and women, from no cause but the lapse of time, became incapable of supporting themselves. The alternatives were the workhouse and the generosity of their children. The first meant a loss of independence for themselves, the second a fetter upon the freedom of their relations. . . . All these measures are based upon the same principle that absolute liberty of the individual meant the degradation, if not the destruction, of many individuals who were poor. There can be no equal chance of growth so long as accidents which cannot be averted, by any effort of the individual, may permanently impair his natural capacity. Social reform is justified as a national army is justified. It is a system of common organization for the purpose of common protection. . . .

This elaboration of the system of protection is not inconsistent with such competition as is necessary for the development of character, and for the production of the wealth which is so distributed among the members of society. It is not socialism. It is not a system of doles. It removes only some of the risks of failure, and only those which are beyond individual control. . . . The benefit of competition remains. The disasters inevitably attendant on it are averted. The poorer people no longer wrestle on the brink of an unfenced precipice. "I do not want to see impaired the vigor of competition, but we can do much to mitigate the consequences of failure. We want to draw a line below which we will not allow persons to live and labor, yet above which they may compete with all the strength of their manhood. We want to have free competition upwards; we decline to allow free competition to run downwards. We do not want to pull down the structures of science and civilization, but to spread a net over the abyss. . . ."

It is obvious that this new economic liberalism has borrowed largely from socialism, and it has one character in common with protection. Once we admit that it is right for the state to interfere with economic freedom, we have advanced one step on the road which leads toward the nationalization of industry and toward the regulation of production by tariffs. The difference between social reform and tariff reform is nevertheless clear. Social reform operates directly, only where it is needed, and without substantially interfering with any individual's enjoyment of life. Tariff reform, if it can destroy poverty at all, can only destroy it indirectly by giving higher profits to the employer, who may or may not share his increased gains with his work-people. . . .

The resemblance between social reform and socialism is much more real. The sympathies and the objects of the two are not dissimilar, though their practical proposals are essentially different. Socialism, so far as it is ever expressed in definite terms, makes a logical application of a general formula. Private ownership of the means of production, distribution, and exchange means a combination of the owners of capital against the wage earners to the injury of the class which is economically the weaker of the two. Therefore society as a whole must take possession of industrial capital, production for use must be substituted for production for profit, work at a good wage must be guaranteed to everyone who asks for it, and the fair distribution of wealth among the workers must be regarded as of more primary importance than the quantity which is produced. Socialists differ widely about methods and the rapidity with which the economic change is to be effected. Generally, the modern socialist of the Fabian type prefers a gradual evolution to the cruder appropriations of early thinkers, he is prepared to exempt certain industries from his scheme, and the equal distribution of rewards has gone the way of the class war and community of goods. But all agree that, sooner or later, society, as politically organized in the form of the state, shall produce and distribute or control the production and distribution of wealth according to ethical principles. The Liberal is less universal in his proposals. He does not object to the municipalization, or even nationalization, of mechanical monopolies, of industries which in fact do not admit of competition. Such industries as the supply of water, gas and electricity, tramways and railways are not in fact competitive, and efficiency is probably as well maintained by aggrieved payers of rates and taxes as by shareholders disappointed of their profits. But the Liberal is not disposed to admit that similar conditions would produce similar results in industries of a more speculative or hazardous character. Nor can he admit that private ownership of capital necessarily involves the exploitation of labor. In certain industries, notably the cotton industry of Lancashire, he sees examples of the successful combination of individual enterprise in management with minimum standards of life and wages fixed either by the factory acts or by powerful trade unions, and he is not satisfied that the enterprise would be as brilliant or the minimum standards as high if the capital engaged were owned by the state.

In particular, the Liberal distrusts the bureaucratic system of management which socialism involves. . . . Social reform requires the appointment of many officials. But the functions of such as have already been appointed are confined to inspection, to advice, and to the collection of money or information. We have had no experience of officials engaged in the manufacture of goods for export, or in the conduct of the shipping trade. Such experience as we have had of municipal enterprise has only satisfied us of the capacity of officials who are controlled and criticized by unofficial ratepayers, who have a personal and pecuniary interest in the efficiency of the official. No Liberal government has yet proposed to extend official management to those many fields where success depends upon the judicious calculation of risks. Until that proposal is made there will always be a gulf between Liberals and Socialists, and a distinction between the policy which limits the destructiveness of competition for private gain and that which abolishes such competition altogether.

B.
ENGLISH LIBERALISM, 1918-51

The Liberal Party after World War I shrank in size and influence, pressed by the Conservatives on one hand and the Labourites on the other. But a small remnant of the once great party clung to its principles, continued to fight parliamentary elections, and regularly published manifestoes of Liberalism. Following are selections from a Liberal publication of the postwar era and two liberal philosophers in the era of World War II.

1. *The Liberal Outlook, 1929.* This work was published by Hubert Phillips (1891–   ), journalist and adviser to the parliamentary Liberal Party. (11)

To begin with, the vaguely expressed enthusiasm of the Labour Party for social and economic progress has, obviously, nothing exclusively socialist about it. So far as the immediate objectives of social reform are concerned, there is no difference of opinion between good socialists and good Liberals. Upon the necessity for certain social and economic measures, all progressively minded men are agreed; these measures are the extension of, or logical development from the program of social reform which Liberal governments inaugurated during the years 1906–14, of which so much was definitely accomplished. And the "inevitability of gradualness" is a phrase which half disguises the necessity of approaching socialist objectives along the well-defined road that Liberal administrations have already charted and in part laid down. . . .

A time will come when there will be no denial, to any human being, of the opportunity of giving full expression to the powers that are latent in him. Just as we shall cease to waste (as today we do waste) the greater part of the energy which the physical world makes available, so, in time, we shall cease to waste the capacities—artistic, intellectual, spiritual—of the sons and daughters whom we bear. We shall learn that in the one field, as in the other, to waste opportunity is to destroy wealth—the wealth that in a sanely planned economy is identified with life itself. The distribution of livelihood in the community will not, as now, cut across its educational processes, but will be the crown and the consummation of them.

Then, and not until then, shall we appreciate to the full the meaning of the possibilities of liberty, with which Liberalism and Liberal policy have always been identified—liberty to serve, but not liberty to enslave; liberty to enjoy, but not liberty to monopolize; liberty to create, but not liberty to destroy.

Here, as far as can be judged in the light of our imperfect apprehension, lies the ultimate ideal.

But these things are not yet. They lie, perhaps, beyond the pale of those activities which here and now we can foresee. Experience has taught us to be sceptical both of the perfectibility of society and of the perfectibility of man. And yet— we do progress. Politicians may be poor creatures, but some of those whose memories we honor have not lived quite in vain. May we not hope, then, that the posterity we work for may have as much to say for us?

2. *Liberalism and the Liberal Party, 1944.* The Rt. Hon. Sir Henry Slesser (1883–   ), a Liberal lawyer and judge, published in 1944 *A History of the Liberal Party* as a survey of the Liberal past and an endeavor to assess the potency of liberalism in his own time. In the following selection Slesser states his conclusions. (12)

Three reasons, perhaps incompatible, have been advanced to account for the disappearance of the Liberal Party as an effective force in politics. The first, and more superficial, is to assert that the purposes for which the Whigs and their successors stood have been fully achieved: the relations of Crown and Parliament have been finally determined, the rule of law has been irrevocably established, and the Commons, under adult suffrage, have been finally accepted as the rulers of the nation, to govern according to the people's will; there is nothing more for Liberalism to do. They have perished of success; their work is done.

Another explanation for their failure to continue as a party with any reasonable prospect of power lies in the assertion that the ideal for which Liberalism contended is spent. Sociology, it is said, has exploded the notion of the free autonomous individual—man is but the creature of his race and environment; the exact influences of each may be a subject of dispute, but essentially he is but a unit in society—we are back with Plato and Hegel.

In this latter view, planning by competent authority must be the prime concern of governments and society. Irresponsible plutocrats are to be condemned as much as eccentric anarchs; both distract the community from its essential purpose, to breed, educate, and sustain functionaries to serve and fight for the nation—all else is futile and may be dangerous. Liberalism is negative, it relies upon the notion of liberty; social purpose, not freedom, is the modern ideal; from this standpoint, fascism and communism are but extreme illustrations of the good life—even a religious sanction can be found in the notion of uncritical dedication to service.

Whether, therefore, a resurrection of Liberalism is probable may depend upon the possibility of the recapture of the vision of the basic invaluable quality of personality. If the present collective outlook persists or develops, the very notion may be incomprehensible to future generations. Recurrent war has done much to destroy Liberalism. It is not an accident that Asquith, the last Liberal leader, was unable to weather the upheaval of 1914. As has been said, his prejudices against conscription and compulsory labor delayed the passing of the Military Service Acts.

As to the common law, for which the first Liberal parliamentarians contended, ever since the introduction of the National Insurance Acts, one civic function after another has been withdrawn from juridical determination. The decision of the House of Lords in a recent case, that a minister has but to state that he has reasonable grounds for the exercise of his powers under some statute or regulation to justify detentions without trial, opens up a possibility of autocracy which need not necessarily be confined to the exigencies of war.

The decay of party government may assist the progress of benevolent surveillance; in the Middle Ages, the cities of Italy won their freedom through the contending claims of Pope and emperor—when all are agreed how to organize and educate the citizen, his prospects of independence are poor.

At the same time it must be confessed that the present program of the Liberals, as exemplified in the publications of Ramsay Muir, their political philosopher, is very inconclusive. In 1920, under the title, *Liberalism and Industry,* he wrote: "Real liberty is not mere absence of restraint, it is security in doing, by a man's free choice, all or any of the things that are worth doing and that are not harmful to his neighbors—first and foremost the Liberal concern is to preserve or increase human liberty—Liberalism attaches an infinite value to human personality." . . .

This is very fine, no instructed civilized man could dissent from it. He goes on to point out how nineteenth-century Liberalism, in its limited advocacy of the mere removal of restriction in the economic sphere, meant that "the rich were left free to employ the power that their riches gave them over the unprotected poor." . . .

"Liberals, nevertheless," he declares, "believe in a man being allowed to save what he earns." . . . "Far from agreeing to the abolition of the ownership of capital, the Liberal would desire to extend it more widely. In the ideal Liberal state everybody would have the chance of creating capital by thrift.". . . This kind of capitalism, it appears, Liberals still defend. In conclusion, the author, not very convincingly, asserts that "modern Liberalism is not merely helpless and bewildered in face of the problems which surround us." Those not in the Liberal assembly may be less sure.

Yet a third suggestion which has been advanced to account for the fact that in this present age few boys and girls are "born little Liberals" (or become so) is that liberalism has so converted the other two parties that the modern Conservative and supporter of labor alike accept all Mr. Muir's assumptions. There is much to be said for this view. If it be correct, the fall of the Liberal Party is but an incident in the general acceptance of libertarian ideals; if it be false, the failure of liberalism may prove to be an unqualified disaster.

3. A Conservative Speaks to the Liberals, 1951. The answer to the questions posed by Slesser may be found in the following selections from an address made by Winston Churchill (1874—) during the election campaign of 1951. Churchill, who had commenced his political career as a member of the Liberal government formed in 1906 later became a Conservative and served as prime minister from 1940 to 1945. In 1951 he was returned to power by an election in which Liberals and Conservatives joined forces in many constituencies. Below Churchill appeals to Conservative electors in the Colne Valley of Yorkshire to vote for a Liberal candidate, the daughter of Lord Asquith, who had been prime minister of the Liberal cabinet in which Churchill had been a member. (13)

Conservatives in the Colne Valley have made a party sacrifice in not running a candidate of their own and in giving all their support to the Liberal Candidate. Considering that nearly 16,000 electors voted Conservative at the last election, and about 10,000 Liberal, this must be considered a remarkable decision. It shows how deeply anxious the Conservatives in the Colne Valley are about the state of our country and that they have come to the conclusion after much heart-searching that our safety, honor and progress as a nation depend upon the defeat of the Socialist Government. . . .

Let me mention to you some of the great issues on which Conservatives and Liberals are agreed, and which constitute the elements of the common cause vital to our national welfare. First, we proclaim that the state is the servant and not the master of the people. We reject altogether the Socialist conception of a division of society between officials and the common mass. We repudiate their policy of levelling down to a minimum uniformity, above which only politicians and their agents may rise. We stand for the increasingly higher expression of individual independence. We hold most strongly to the Declaration of Human Rights, as set forth by the United Nations at Geneva.

It is worth noting that among all these United Nations we are the only great power under Socialist rule. That is why Socialist policy has been in these past years increasingly out of step and out of harmony with, or lagging behind, the movement of thought among the free democracies of the modern world.

We then declare ourselves inveterately opposed to any further nationalization of industry, including of course, and especially, the nationalization of steel.

No doubt there are other points upon which Liberals and Conservatives do not agree. But how small they are in scale and importance compared to the great body of fundamental principles and practical schemes of application on which both anti-Socialist parties are in accord, and which are now supported by a large majority of electors all over the country. There is a wide overlap of agreement, both in doctrine and in action, between those who have hitherto been brought up to regard themselves as political opponents. But now the times are very grave, and it is the duty of every man and woman who agrees upon so large a proportion of the main principles and practical steps, to make sure that these are not overwhelmed by the ignorant and obsolete doctrine of Socialism, against which the British nation stands today in marked recoil. . . .

More than 40 years ago I sat myself in a Left-wing Government with a great majority, and I was one of their most prominent and controversial figures. . . . The Liberal Government of 1906 was built around and upon those great principles of liberalism, which have since passed into the possession of every Party except the Communists, and are still spreading with irresistible appeal throughout the world. But now our opponents are not ranged around the great truths of liberalism; they are ranged around the fallacy of Socialism, which is in principle contrary to human nature and which I believe can only be enforced upon nations in its entirety in the wholesale fashion of Communism. . . .

I find comfort in the broad harmony of thought which prevails between the modern Tory democracy and the doctrines of the famous Liberal leaders of the past. I am sure that in accord with their speeches and writings, men like Asquith, Morley and Grey whom I knew so well in my youth would have regarded the establishment of a Socialist State and the enforcement of the collectivist theory as one of the worst evils that could befall Britain and her slowly evolved, long-cherished way of life. . . .

The supreme question is, are we after our experiences of the last 6 years to take another deep plunge into Socialism or regain the high road, which all the rest of the English-speaking world are now treading, of free enterprise and opportunity for all, and of the strong helping the weak? It is better for the strong to help the weak, than for the weak to hinder the strong. Basic standards of life and labor must be secured in our society and civilization, and on this foundation everyone should be free to use his or her gifts and qualities to the full. In this way alone can our 50 millions, crowded in our island, safeguard their food, their work and their homes.

But beware! For we may be at the parting of the ways. The wisdom of our ancestors for more than 300 years has sought the division of power in the constitution. Crown, Lords and Commons have been checks and restraints upon one another. The limitation of the power of the monarchy was the cause for which, as Liberals used to say, "Hampden died in the field and Sidney on the scaffold." The concentration of all power over the daily lives of ordinary men and women in what is called "the state," exercised by what is virtually single-chamber government, is a reactionary step contrary to the whole trend of British history and to the message we have given to the world.

The British race have always abhorred arbitrary and absolute government in every form. The great men who founded the American Constitution embodied this separation of authority in the strongest and most durable form. Not only did they divide executive, legislative and judicial functions, but also by instituting a federal system they preserved immense and sovereign rights to local communities, and by all these means they have preserved—often at some inconvenience—a system of law and liberty under which they have thrived and reached the leadership of the world.

The Socialist conception of the all-powerful state entering into the smallest detail of the life and conduct of the individual and claiming to plan and shape his work and its rewards is odious and repellent to every friend of freedom. These absolute powers would make the group of politicians who obtained a majority of seats in Parliament the masters and not the servants of the people and would centralise all government in Whitehall. . . .

The worship of an all-powerful state, beneath which the ordinary mass of citizens lies prostrate, is one of the most deadly and insidious delusions by which a free people, as we still are, can cast away rights and liberties, which for their own sake and the sake of their children, they ought to hold dearer than life itself. The British nation now has to make one of the most momentous choices in its history.

That choice is between two ways of life; between individual liberty and state domination; between the concentration of ownership in the hands of the state and the extension of a property-owning democracy; between a policy of increasing control and restriction, and a policy of liberating energy and ingenuity; between a policy of levelling down and a policy of finding opportunity for all to rise upwards from a basic standard. . . .

We must not lose faith in our race and in our destiny. We are the same people, in the same island, as we were in the great days we can all remember. Our spirit is unconquerable, our ingenuity and craftsmanship unsurpassed. Our latent resources are unmeasured. Our underlying unities are enduring. We have but to cast away by an effort of will the enfeebling tendencies and mental infirmities of Socialism and free ourselves from Socialist rule to stand erect once more and take our place amongst the great powers of the world.